PASSIVE-
AGGRESSIVENESS
Theory and Practice

PASSIVE-AGGRESSIVENESS

Theory and Practice

Edited by
Richard Dean Parsons, Ph.D.,
and
Robert J. Wicks, Psy.D.

BRUNNER/MAZEL, *Publishers* • New York

Library of Congress Cataloging in Publication Data
Main entry under title:

Passive-aggressiveness, theory and practice.

Includes bibliographies and index.
1. Passive-aggressive personality. I. Parsons,
Richard D. II. Wicks, Robert J.
RC569.5.P37P37 1983   616.85'8   83-15383
ISBN 0-87630-344-0

Copyright © 1983 by Richard D. Parsons and Robert J. Wicks

Published by
BRUNNER/MAZEL, INC.
19 Union Square West, New York, N. Y. 10003

MANUFACTURED IN THE UNITED STATES OF AMERICA

For our children . . .

Since the early days of our research and publications, your warmth and spontaneity have influenced our work and lightened our days. The current text, as with those which preceded it, would not have been possible, or even desired, were it not for your loving support. You are four very special people.

Your open, free, expression of feelings has taught us not to fear genuineness. Your enthusiasm and excitement over each new life adventure have reminded us not only to do, but to enjoy. But most of all your ever present love has been a constant reminder of what it is all about.

It is with our love that we dedicate this book to you—our children—Kristian, Drew, Jonathan, and Michaele.

Contents

Contributors

FRANCES BONDS-WHITE, M.ED.
Clinical Director
Eastern Institute of TA/Gestalt,
Philadelphia

DAVID D. BURNS, M.D.
Assistant Professor of Psychiatry,
University of Pennsylvania,
Philadelphia

DAVID F. BUSH, PH.D.
Associate Professor of Psychology,
Villanova University, Villanova,
Pennsylvania

NORMAN EPSTEIN, PH.D.
Department of Family and
Community Development,
University of Maryland,
College Park, Maryland

FLORENCE W. KASLOW, PH.D.
Director, Florida Couples and Family
Institute, West Palm Beach, Florida

ALVIN R. MAHRER, PH.D.
Professor of Psychology, School of
Psychology, University of Ottawa,
Canada

HAROLD R. MUSIKER, PH.D.
Director, Psychology Behavioral
Medicine Clinic, Rhode Island
Hospital, Providence

ROBERT G. NORTON, M.H.A.
Vice President, Rhode Island
Hospital, Providence

RICHARD DEAN PARSONS, PH.D.
*Associate Professor of Psychology
and Assistant Academic Dean,
Neumann College, Aston,
Pennsylvania*

JEROME J. PLATT, PH.D.
*Professor and Director, Division of
Research, Department of Mental
Health Sciences, Hahnemann
Medical College, Philadelphia*

MAURICE F. PROUT, PH.D.
*Director of the Behavioral Therapies,
Department of Mental Health
Sciences, Hahnemann Medical
College, Philadelphia*

GEORGE STRICKER, PH.D.
*Professor of Psychology and
Assistant Dean, Institute of
Advanced Psychological Studies at
Adelphi University, Garden City,
New York*

ROBERT J. WICKS, PSY.D.
*Associate Professor of Psychology;
Director, Graduate Program in
Pastoral Counseling, Neumann
College, Aston, Pennsylvania*

Preface

Although passive-aggressiveness with its many clinical manifestations and organizational forms has been and remains a topic of concern, discussion, and research across varied human service professional arenas, it has not been broadly addressed within a single, contemporary work. Accordingly, given the need for a central source of information regarding etiology, clinical manifestations, and intervention strategies, experienced research practitioners were invited to address the topic of passive-aggressiveness from a number of essential vantage points.

A surprise came for these contributors when they did their preliminary literature search (which further supported the need for the presence of a collection of views on passive-aggressiveness). They all found a paucity of readily available material (clinical research, position papers) relating to the topic. Moreover, even when it was addressed (e.g., under-achievement in children), the intervention methodology did not have a specific body of literature on passive-aggressiveness upon which to draw.

A further surprise is left for the reader of this volume to experience—namely, the amount of consensus and difference among

the theoreticians and organizational consultants in this book with respect to their view of passive-aggressiveness.

The Diagnostic and Statistical Manual of Mental Disorders (APA, 1980) describes Passive-Aggressive Personality Disorder as that in "which there is resistance to demands for adequate performance in both occupational and social functioning; the resistance is expressed indirectly rather than directly. The consequence is pervasive and persistent social or occupational ineffectiveness, even when more self-assertive and effective behavior is possible. The name of the disorder is based on the assumption that such individuals are passively expressing covert aggression" (p. 328).

Yet, this description still does not offer proof or an answer to the basic questions about "passive-aggressiveness." Is it a trait? Is it a state? Is it truly a clinical entity as is described in the DSM-III? These questions will be addressed in the epilogue, but certainly they are reference points to be used in reviewing each of the following papers.

The book is divided into two sections. Section I—The Clinical Profile—contains presentations of the major therapeutic orientations (dynamic, behavioral, transactional analysis, cognitive, experiential, and family systems) written by principal representatives of those theoretical positions. Each presentation will address such elements as clinical profile, theorized etiological factors, suggested intervention strategies, and case examples.

Section II—The Organizational Profile—presents analyses of a number of organizations (business, education, medicine, organized religion) where passive-aggressiveness is often identified and in which the mental health consultant is often employed. Each paper notes: organizational manifestations, factors in diagnostic analysis, consultant strategies, and case examples. Both sections provide an effort to begin creative and meaningful dialogue on the topic of passive-aggressiveness as a stepping-stone to in-depth serious clinical research on the subject and as an opportunity to see that, when professionals commonly employ the terminology "passive-aggressiveness," the implications communicated often do not translate into an understanding that is universally held.

Richard D. Parsons   Robert J. Wicks

REFERENCE

American Psychiatric Association. *Diagnostic and statistical manual of mental disorders.* Third Edition, Washington, D.C., 1980.

PASSIVE-AGGRESSIVENESS
Theory and Practice

SECTION I

The Clinical Profile

1

Passive-Aggressiveness: A Condition Especially Suited to the Psychodynamic Approach

George Stricker

Passive-aggressiveness is a condition which seems to require, by definition, a psychodynamic approach to understanding, although a wider variety of therapeutic interventions may be appropriate. The concept contains the idea that overt behavior, which takes the form of passivity, is being used, without conscious awareness, to express feelings of aggression. This multilevel conception suggests that behavior is not to be taken at face value. It can express unconscious needs, and it can do so without the patient's recognizing the meaning of the behavior. It is difficult to make sense of the behavior of the passive-aggressive without invoking these concepts, which are the hallmark of a psychodynamic approach. Nevertheless, despite the pervasiveness of the pattern and the unique applicability of a psychodynamic formulation, no psychodynamic writer has addressed this problem in other than a peripheral way.

CLINICAL PROFILE: A THEORETICAL PERSPECTIVE

In this chapter, passive-aggressiveness will be considered as a pervasive character disorder, a position consistent with each of the accepted diagnostic manuals. This implies that the behavior is generalized, rather than restricted to any isolated conflictual circumstance. This is in line with the psychodynamic definition of character as a "pattern of adaptation to instinctual and environmental forces that is typical or habitual for a given person" (Meissner, Mack, & Semrad, 1975, p. 541). It rules out the consideration of the occasional passive-aggressive act which is probably an aspect of the repertoire of behavioral expression available to almost every individual. The distinction is one of quantity rather than quality, since the isolated act will have the same form and may have the same dynamic function as the pervasive pattern but will differ in frequency and extensiveness of use.

The history of the specific term, *Passive-aggressive personality*, is relatively new and has undergone a significant degree of change (Millon, 1981). It was first used in 1945 in a Technical Bulletin issued by the War Department, and later it was included in a nosological system introduced in 1949 by the United States Joint Armed Services. In 1951, it was listed in the *Standard V.A. Classification*, included as one of the "immaturity reactions," which constituted a subgroup of the character and behavior disorders. It was included along with "emotional instability," "passive dependency," and "aggressive reaction."

This Veterans Administration system was influential in the development of the first *Diagnostic and Statistical Manual of Mental Disorders* (DSM-I), which the American Psychiatric Association published in 1952. Here the term *passive-aggressive personality* was used, but three subtypes were identified. Aside from the passive-aggressive, the passive-dependent and aggressive personalities were also incorporated, presumably because of a common psychodynamic etiology. In the DSM-II, issued in 1968, the passive-aggressive type was the only form of passive-aggressive personality disorder which was listed. The specific description of this disorder was:

> This behavior pattern is characterized by both passivity and aggressiveness. The aggressiveness may be expressed passively, for example, by obstructionism, pouting, procrastination, intentional inefficiency or stubbornness. This behavior commonly reflects hostility which the individual feels he dare not express openly. Often the behavior is one expression of the patient's resentment of failing

to find gratification in a relationship with an individual or institution upon which he is overdependent (American Psychiatric Association, 1968).

Finally, the diagnosis *passive-aggressive personality disorder* has been retained in DSM-III (American Psychiatric Association, 1980). DSM-III has been developed as an attempt to increase the reliability of diagnosis, so that specific behavioral criteria are supplied for each diagnostic entity. For the passive-aggressive personality disorder, it is necessary that the patient display a resistance to demands for adequate performance in both occupational and social functioning, expressed indirectly through at least two acts such as procrastination, dawdling, stubbornness, intentional inefficiency, and forgetfulness. As a consequence of this, there is pervasive and long-standing social and occupational ineffectiveness, and the behavior persists even when more self-assertive and effective behavior is possible. Interestingly, the text accompanying the diagnostic criteria adds that "the name of this disorder is based on the assumption that such individuals are passively expressing covert aggression" (American Psychiatric Association, 1980, p. 328). This assumption embodies the psychodynamic formulation, is decidedly non-behavioral and, perhaps, contributes to the fact that this classification produces the poorest diagnostic agreement of any personality disorder included in DSM-III (Millon, 1981).

Two central aspects of this clinical profile are worthy of note. First, there is widespread agreement in the descriptive symptomatology which suggests that behavior which appears to be passive is being utilized to express underlying aggressive feelings. The conscious intention of the patient is typically benign, but the impact of the behavior in an interpersonal setting makes clear the effectiveness of the passive-aggressive acts in expressing the underlying hostility. Second, since the behavioral-dynamic link is an unconscious one, the diagnosis can only be arrived at by inferring motivation, a task which contributes to the murkiness of the category and the unreliability of the diagnosis. The empirical literature is sparse and each of the studies suffers from the problem of diagnostic unreliability.

The first empirical approach to defining the passive-aggressive personality was by Whitman, Trosman, and Koenig (1954), whose study was based on the DSM-I classification which incorporated the three subdivisions of a generic diagnostic category. During the year 1952-1953, 400 patients were seen in an outpatient psychiatric clinic in Chicago which utilized a brief psychodynamic model of psychotherapy. In a

manner which strikingly anticipated DSM-III, each patient was given a clinical diagnosis (Axis I) and a basic personality diagnosis (Axis II). The passive-aggressive subtype was the fourth most frequently used basic personality diagnosis, and occurred in 15.5% of the patients. Among these patients, the presenting clinical diagnoses which were most prevalent were anxiety (41%) and depression (25%), with no patients presenting schizophrenic or organic pathology. The modal age for this group was in the 31-40 decade and 70% were male. The use of a dual diagnostic system is of particular usefulness with the passive-aggressive personality because the pervasive personality dysfunction, which is of concern in this chapter, is rarely the reason that the patient is brought to our attention. More frequently, it is either a clinical symptom, such as anxiety or depression, or some environmental failure, such as at work, in school, or in a relationship, which will lead the patient to seek treatment, often at the encouragement or insistence of a significant other.

Small, Small, Alig, and Moore (1970) conducted a follow-up study of 100 patients hospitalized with a diagnosis of passive-aggressive personality disorder. The patients had been admitted to a hospital in Indiana between 1952 and 1962, and the follow-up efforts were conducted between 1966 and 1968, so that the follow-up period ranged from seven to 15 years. The subjects represented about 3% of the hospital admissions during that period, and a comparison with Whitman et al. (1954) appropriately shows that passive-aggressiveness is at least three times more likely to be treated in an outpatient context. In contrast to Whitman et al., these patients were younger (mean age 26.7) and more likely to be female (63%), but this may be due to the use of the more heterogeneous DSM-I category. Small et al. identified three distinct subgroups, including patients with no other diagnosis (N = 52), those who were alcoholic (N = 18), and those who were also depressed (N = 30). They did not separate the passive-aggressive subtype from the passive-dependent or aggressive, so that the value of the data for our purposes is compromised. In any case, 73 of the patients were able to be traced, and 58 of these were considered to have persisting psychiatric difficulties. The primary area of disturbance was interpersonal, and the greatest improvement was in those patients who received continued supportive psychotherapy. Interestingly, the authors comment on how difficult it was to achieve cooperation from these patients and how many obstructions they imposed, in contrast to a control group—an observation which seems to confirm the diagnosis. Aside from the problem of the use of a generic diagnosis, this study also addressed an atypical group of passive-aggressives, since treatment usually occurs outside of a hospital

setting. Nevertheless, the long-standing lack of remission is consistent with the picture of a pervasive problem, and the interpersonal problems of these patients are highlighted. While DSM-III would lead us to look for occupational problems, which were not prominent, these usually consist of underachieving rather than total failure, and often are a further result of the impact that the passive-aggressive style of relating has on others.

The two studies cited above were the only ones which could be located which directly addressed the clinical picture presented by the passive-aggressive personality. As a transition to the next section, which will deal with etiology, two other studies will be noted which dealt with widely different groups of subjects, but which made prominent use of the concept of passive-aggressiveness. Castelnuovo-Tedesco and Schiebel (1975) studied the characteristics of superobese patients, who were hospitalized in California. This group might ordinarily be considered as oral characters, although the authors feel that such a description is insufficient. Of the 12 patients studied, none were considered to be seriously disturbed. Five were considered to be primarily passive-aggressive, and all but one had prominent passive-aggressive traits. The patients were initially superficially friendly and cooperative, but became increasingly labile and irritable, displaying resentment, stubbornness, and defiance. This pattern of superficial cordiality which gives way to obstructionism is quite common among passive-aggressives. The viewing of the trait within the context of an apparently unrelated symptom (in this case superobesity) is also common, as the behavior pattern itself is rarely the reason why patients seek treatment.

Fischer and Juni (1982) studied the anal personality, a psychodynamic construct which shares some characteristics with the passive-aggressive personality, such as the prominence of negativism and withholding behaviors. The subjects were college students in the Buffalo area who had been selected on the basis of extreme scores on an anality scale. High anal subjects were much more likely than low anal subjects to refuse to participate in the study but, having once agreed, were no less likely to participate. This is consistent with the inclination of passive-aggressive subjects to be defiant where it is safe to do so, since refusal of the telephone solicitation was impersonal and sanction free. On the other hand, having once agreed, the subjects maintained a cooperative stance and followed through with the agreement. This contrast between the façade of compliant behavior and the harboring of defiant inclinations, which can only be expressed indirectly, is the hallmark of the passive-aggressive personality. Interestingly, the limited empirical studies that

have been done have shown this characteristic to be stable over 30 years in differing geographic areas and in groups as contrasting as essentially normal college students and hospitalized psychiatric patients.

ETIOLOGY

A thorough explication of the psychodynamic approach to etiology is well beyond the scope of this paper. The term *psychodynamic* embraces classical psychoanalysis, as represented by the works of Freud and his disciples, major neo-Freudian positions such as ego psychology, object relations and self theory, and the work of a large number of revisionists such as Sullivan, Jung, Adler, and Horney. Any of these individual positions, taken by itself, would require extensive coverage to do it justice, and a summary of each would be difficult to accomplish in an entire volume.

There are, however, a number of principles which seem to be common to all of these approaches. Foremost among these principles is the belief in the existence of unconscious processes, which implies that significant cognitive and motivational activity can exist outside of the awareness of the individual. This leads to a belief in psychic determinism, a principle which holds that all behavior is the result of the current situation and prior mental events, often of an unconscious nature, so that the understanding of any contemporary act requires an appreciation of a range of preceding experiences. This principle is particularly useful when a passive-aggressive patient will disclaim intention or responsibility for behavior which is annoying or hurtful to others. Finally, the recognition of the importance of prior events extends back to the earliest events, so that the psychodynamic approach is developmental in nature and emphasizes the crucial role of early experience as the foundation upon which later development is built.

The role of passive-aggressiveness within psychodynamic theory is unclear, and it has rarely been addressed directly. While Meissner et al. (1975) refer to passive-aggressive behavior as an immature defense, and define it as "aggression toward an object expressed indirectly and ineffectively through passivity, masochism and turning against the self" (p. 535), Anna Freud (1946), in her thorough explication of the defense mechanisms, does not refer to passive-aggressive behavior, although she does deal with the more general mechanism of turning against the self. It is more typical to think of passive-aggression as a syndrome rather than an isolated defense, but neither Reich (1949), who talks about character pathology, nor Fenichel (1945), who discusses neurotic con-

ditions, considers it as an independent entity. While it is not unusual to read psychodynamic theorists who refer to passive-aggressive behavior in a manner that assumes it is a familiar term, which indeed it is, no writer has written extensively about it taken by itself. Its inclusion by Castelnuovo-Tedesco and Schiebel (1975) in a discussion of a primarily oral syndrome and by Fischer and Juni (1982) in their research on anality further suggests the lack of a single conception and the pervasiveness of this behavioral expression.

There does seem to be wide agreement on the basic dynamic configuration of passive-aggressive behavior, whether it is in the form of a syndrome or an isolated experience. By definition, passive overt behavior, which takes the form of some oppositional or obstructionist act, is used to express hostility which the patient does not feel comfortable expressing in a more direct manner. The two questions which any approach to this problem must address are why the patient is so angry and why he or she cannot express the anger more directly.

The anger is typically related to early problems with dependency, and the failure of the patient to have dependency needs gratified (for example, Pasternack, 1974). It is this relationship of the passive-aggressive pattern to dependency and anger that undoubtedly contributed to the original linking in DSM-I of passive-aggressive, passive-dependent, and aggressive patterns within the same syndrome. In any case, every child is utterly dependent at birth and remains dependent for an extended period of time. The very existence of the neonate requires the nurturance of others, so that the frustration of dependency needs can be fatal if extreme, and the assurance that these needs will be met is vital to the survival and well-being of the organism. A child who receives good-enough nurturance will be relatively secure about being cared for, while feelings of dependency are likely to arouse great anxiety in a child who is not certain that those needs will be addressed. Where there is a history of failure to satisfy dependency needs, there also is likely to be a great deal of frustration and anger, as well as much insecurity.

The frustration of dependency needs is basic to a wide variety of pathological developments. In some cases, it is so extreme that the resulting insecurity is thoroughly disorganizing and a psychotic adjustment can eventuate. In other cases, the frustration can lead to a resentful rage which is expressed directly in a variety of antisocial ways. In a passive-aggressive personality, the frustration of dependency is accompanied by parenting which is so threatening that the child does not dare to express feelings directly. The threat may be due to harsh, demanding parental attitudes or it may be due to tenuous parenting, so that the

child does not dare risk losing whatever little support he or she has been able to gather. In either case, the direct expression of the anger would lead to consequences so noxious that the expression is inhibited, but the feeling remains sufficiently compelling that its expression is sought through alternate channels. The child is unlikely to be able to tell a parent to stop being overly restrictive and demanding, but he or she may be able to wet the bed or stutter or eat poorly without drawing an excessively punitive response. The child is, thus, likely to get a good deal more attention, negative though it may be, and will also cause the parents to suffer without having to take individual responsibility for doing so. Unfortunately, the choice of such an approach is likely to provide the child with a history of failure experiences and serve to exaggerate the deficit in self-esteem which has already been initiated by the early failures of the infant to have its needs met.

To recapitulate in a somewhat oversimplified fashion, the sequence seems to be initiated by a failure of the parenting object to meet the dependency needs of the child, resulting in frustration, insecurity, and anger. This occurs in a context often marked by harsh or demanding parenting, where the child does not feel safe in showing the anger and inhibits its direct expression. Instead, indirect methods are chosen, which have the advantage of causing frustration and irritation to the source of the child's anger without the child having to address the consequences of the act. Unfortunately, they also have the disadvantage of creating a series of failures undermining self-esteem and contributing to the child's inability to develop the sense of competence that comes with assuming responsibility for one's actions.

In the adult, we can expect to see a relatively agreeable façade, for the person has learned long ago not to express anger directly. Any demand placed on the person, however, is likely to recall earlier demands and lead to similar responses, namely, oppositional and negativistic resistance while maintaining an aura of compliance. The clearer the demands or the more frustrated the dependency needs, the more we can expect to see the person becoming angry, inhibiting the anger, becoming resistant, and feeling anxious lest the anger be discovered. This anxiety, as Whitman et al. (1954) showed, is the primary symptom that will bring the passive-aggressive person into treatment. Second to anxiety as a presenting problem is depression, which is the result of the lowered self-esteem that accompanies the developmental difficulties that have been traced. Finally, we also see patients because of underachievement, which is a consequence of some of the self-destructive expressions of anger, or because of interpersonal difficulties, which are a direct result of the trouble others have in relating to passive-aggressive people.

One further concept related to dynamics must be developed before dealing with treatment issues. Typically, the behavior pattern of the passive-aggressive person is one with which he is comfortable, since he is not aware of the underlying meaning, denies any hostile intent, and has the self-concept of a rather sweet, if unfortunate, person. The behaviors thus are called ego-syntonic, since they are acceptable to the person. On the other hand, the presenting symptoms, whether they be anxiety, depression, underachievement, or interpersonal failures, are a source of great discomfort. They are referred to as ego-dystonic and provide the primary motivation for seeking treatment.

THERAPEUTIC STRATEGY AND PROCESS

The key decision that must be made by the therapist follows from the distinction which has been made between the ego-syntonic and the ego-dystonic. This division implies that there are two levels of problem brought to therapy by the passive-aggressive patient. The first of these is the ego-dystonic symptom which creates discomfort and brings the patient to treatment, while the second is the ego-syntonic character structure which underlies the symptom, may well have produced it, but is not viewed as problematic by the patient. The therapist must decide whether to restrict interventions to the presenting problem, in which case treatment will be short-term, focused, goal-oriented, and likely to be successful, or to attempt to deal with the character problem, which will lead to long-term intensive treatment. This latter approach is difficult and does not have a promising prognosis.

Ordinarily, a therapeutic decision of this sort should be made along with the patient for whom the very act of participation in self-determination is therapeutic. Not only is the passive-aggressive patient likely to resist, as many of those with character disorders will, the prospect of an expensive long-term commitment to the remediation of a problem which, being ego-syntonic, is not viewed as troublesome, but there is an additional difficulty. In a characteristic way, the passive-aggressive patient may well show surface compliance, agree to the approach, and then produce the type of defiant behavior which will undermine the treatment, despite the appearance of cooperativeness.

It is the hallmark of the psychodynamic approach, and perhaps a unique feature, that attention to the underlying problem is seen as critical. A question may be raised as to why it is of value to deal with a personality style which the patient does not recognize as a source of difficulty and will resist changing. The answer to the question lies in the impact the patient has on others, whose response is likely to be

counteraggressive and assures that the patient will not get the satisfaction he or she seeks. The self-defeating nature of the style is the main justification for altering it, but this is difficult for the patient to grasp. First, the patient does not have conscious awareness of the hostility and will deny it. If the hostile impact can be fathomed without attributing intention, there may be a conscious expression of regret, but there will be a failure to acknowledge that the hurt and anger experienced by the other is exactly the response desired. Even if this can be acknowledged and there is a recognition that the behavior will make the presumed wishes of the patient difficult to achieve, any change will require a further acknowledgment of dependent wishes, which is the final obstacle to successful treatment.

The essence of the approach to intervention is described well by Leaff (1974). Leaff indicates that

> . . . interpretation, defense analysis, or conflict resolution cannot be expected to be successful unless the opportunity for ego growth (maturation, support, education, stable identification, repair of the defect) is also provided. Conversion of long-standing syntonic personality patterns into dystonic, alien modes is accomplished by repeated confrontations with the pathological nature, rigidity, and maladaptiveness of these patterns. At the same time, alternative coping mechanisms and stable figures for identification must be provided (p. 4).

While confrontation with the maladaptive aspects of ego-syntonic behavior is absolutely crucial, and they can only be altered if they become ego-dystonic, the process is fraught with risk to the treatment. In their seminal survey, Whitman et al. (1954) found that 39% of the passive-aggressive patients either did not return for treatment after intake or terminated treatment without advice after one visit. Both of these categories had significantly higher rates than the proportion in a control group. In further support of this finding, Castelnuovo-Tedesco and Schiebel (1975) in their work with the superobese note that missing of appointments among their patients was very common. They added that the patients were casual about taking their prescribed vitamins and minerals. Clearly, passive-aggressive patients will fight to cling to their style, using the familiar passive-aggressive weapons that are at their disposal.

If the patient can be engaged in a therapeutic alliance, we can expect that the work will be inconsistent and much vacillation will be displayed.

For each step forward, meaning that the patient comes closer to recognizing his/her anger and dependency, there will be a corresponding fear of recognition, resulting in anxiety and the interposition of characteristic passive-aggressive defenses. If the alliance is sufficiently well developed and the steps are small enough to be tolerable, the defensive efforts will fall short of terminating treatment and will take the form of some blocking mechanism which also can be subject to examination.

One of the most characteristic therapeutic stances for the passive-aggressive patient is a bewildered failure to understand, taking the form of responses such as, "What should I do?" "How do I feel?" or "Why do I do that?" In part, these responses convey the dependency of the patient and ask for assistance, although they do so in a form that places upon the therapist the entire burden for the success of psychotherapy, along with the responsibility for subsequent failure. Thus, while they are passive, compliant responses, they also contain the seeds of an angry defiance of the therapist to do anything about the situation. In part, however, these responses are also an honest portrayal of a lack of insight and a bafflement about internal processes which must be respected if the therapist is to rectify them.

The first order of response by the therapist should consist of interventions which return the responsibility to the patient, such as, "What do you think?" "Why do you ask?" and "What are your options?" In each case, the passivity of the patient is not accepted, but a sense of respect for the patient's ability to contribute to the solution is conveyed. There is also a development of an attitude of self-examination which will be useful in promoting the patient's future examination of extra-therapeutic behaviors.

As therapy progresses, and the patient begins to assume, on an occasional basis, more willingness to examine his or her behavior, a more searching therapeutic response can be made. If the therapist reflects, "You would like me to make decisions for you," the patient can begin to appreciate the experience of passive reliance on others. If the patient is willing to accept the wish for assistance, the therapist can then inquire about who in the past did make such decisions for him or her and, after some development of this theme, how it felt to be in that dependent position. It is important to clarify both the anger and the good feeling that accompany the dependent stance.

Some of this information can be uncovered within the transference by inquiring, "How does it feel to ask?" This, in turn, can be related to earlier dependent experiences, as well as to the anger that accompanies its frustration and the inability to express it directly. The key is in dealing

effectively with the sequence of dependency which is frustrated, leading to anger which is inhibited and then expressed in a passive-aggressive form. The relating of these early feelings to current experiences and to aspects of the transferential relationship with the therapist can lead to the interruption of the pathological sequence.

It is clear that the deeply ingrained character pattern is resistant to change and, as long as it remains ego-syntonic, there will be many difficulties created by the patient. It should also be clear that the patient is not the only source of obstacles to successful treatment. Working with a passive-aggressive patient can be a very frustrating experience for the therapist, as encouraging movement is followed in swift succession by defiant resistance, and overt compliance dimly hides subtle expressions of anger and contempt. Asked for the hundredth time, "What should I do?", a therapist may be tempted to snap back, "How would I know?" To do so would confirm the patient's view that his/her dependency needs are doomed to frustration, authority cannot be trusted, and it is too dangerous to risk giving up the old familiar ways of functioning. A more productive way of handling the countertransference would be to use it to illustrate to the patient how he undermines himself by creating a self-fulfilling prophecy, daring others to get close to him and defying them to supply what he desperately wants. To do this, however, requires a solid foundation in the therapeutic alliance or the message is certain to fall on deaf ears.

Thus far, various strategies for intervention within the framework of individual psychodynamic psychotherapy have been developed. A note should be added about two alternative modalities to be considered. Teicher (1975) has discussed the treatment of passive-aggressive children, exhibiting oppositional disorders, according to the DSM-III classification. He feels that the key to the treatment of these children is helping them to recognize and express their hostility, so they need not develop a more subtle means of rebelling against excessive parental demands. As an adjunct to this treatment, it is also recommended that the parents be seen and helped to alter their suppressive attitudes and actions.

Finally, Sadock (1975) recommends the use of group therapy as particularly suited to passive-aggressive patients. The multiple relationships provided by the group offer the patient a wide variety of substitute dependency-gratifying objects, which diminishes the anxiety attached to any single one and allows for a reduction in the use of maladaptive passive-aggressive devices. It is also more likely that the impact of the patient's style on others will be graphically portrayed and confronted

repetitively. Yet, since this will be done by the therapist and patients, the negative impact of each confrontation will be reduced, since it will be in a wider context of support. Therefore, it will be less likely to be viewed as criticism and a message to abandon any hope of gratifying dependency needs. It might also be added that, in a well led group, the impact of the therapist's countertransference will be less profound, since some of the feelings will be expressed by other group members, and other members can support the patient and point out where counter-transference is being expressed. On the other hand, in a less positive situation, other group members can identify with the countertransfer-ence, express it for the therapist, and scapegoat the patient, which even-tually leads to his leaving the group. While this will complete a self-fulfilling prophecy for the patient, it is a destructive therapeutic ap-proach.

CASE ILLUSTRATION

Evelyn, a 23-year-old only child, lived at home with her mother and stepfather. Although every indication was that she was quite bright, she had a poor high school record, dropped out of college in her first year, and was working at a menial customer relations job with the telephone company, which she aggrandized by saying she was "in communica-tions." This description was particularly interesting since she showed no interest or talent for communicating with anyone of any significance in her life. Evelyn indicated that she came to treatment at her mother's urging and, when pressed, added that her stepfather also wished her to go. She did not have any recognition of what either of them had in mind and certainly none of what she herself might wish to see accom-plished. She was seen on a weekly basis in psychodynamic psychoth-erapy for about a year. During that year there were also a number of joint sessions with her mother on approximately a bimonthly basis, usually at her mother's initiative, which Evelyn always gave permission for but probably resented. The primary areas reviewed in treatment were her social life, work experiences, and relationship with her mother.

Evelyn's social life was strikingly unsatisfying and was the one area of functioning she experienced as ego-dystonic. She described herself as essentially shy and insecure, although this was covered by a façade of rather immature charm. She had had only one relationship of any degree of closeness with a male, and that had ended a number of years prior to treatment, largely because Evelyn was unable to sustain the intimacy that her partner had wished. Her relationships with females

were superficial and pleasant, but here, too, none was marked by any real closeness or sharing. Much of her time was spent in solitude, with her occasional social forays of the sort in which she acted in a "life of the party" way. She was always surprised when nobody took her seriously or wished to pursue a relationship with her. She was clear that her style did not encourage closeness, came to recognize that it served to protect her from showing her shyness and sense of inadequacy, but never was able to take any positive steps to change. She probably would have been more able to be responsive if an assertive man took command of a relationship with her, but none did and she was not able to be more assertive herself. This potential solution to her problem was consistent with her general wish to be changed rather than to change. Further, while she clearly added to her discomfort with her lack of social success, she also enjoyed the role of the charming center of attention and was reluctant to give it up, regardless of how self-defeating it proved to be. When asked about her feeling in the role, she had difficulty responding, acknowledging that she never really paid much attention to her feelings. Any further pressure resulted in her feeling tense and either withdrawing from the topic or attempting to divert the therapist by discussing it in a humorous way.

The other side of her social situation was the clear contempt she felt for the people in her social circle, viewing them as shallow and beneath her. Nevertheless, she was not able to talk about why she had chosen these people or how she might find new friends who would provide more fulfilling relationships. The situation was compounded by the fact that most of her high school friends were now moving to other places in their lives (having gone to college and, in some cases, married), leaving her behind. She could neither find new friends nor ask old ones for help, since she was not able to risk rejection or to let others know of her desperation. As a result, she was content to function as a source of entertainment and an outsider within a social gathering.

During the course of treatment, Evelyn made a few tentative attempts to expand her social activities. On one occasion, when she did behave assertively but was rejected, she reported feeling depressed and angry. She quickly added that her anger was certainly not at the man who rejected her, and this helped to clarify how unaware she was of the depth or direction of her anger, and how it tended to be diverted into depression. She also expressed a continuing sense of wonder and outrage that people seemed not to trust her, but had difficulty in relating that to her constant flaunting of rules and her attempt to govern her behavior by what she felt she could get away with. In retrospect, it

might have been a better therapeutic strategy to focus more on social problems, since that was the one area that was painful and ego-dystonic. This was not done as much as it could have been because of a series of distracting crises at home and work, and because Evelyn was reluctant to pursue matters beyond a surface acknowledgment. Nevertheless, progress in this area might have solidified a therapeutic alliance and allowed greater progress to be made in the more compelling areas.

When Evelyn began treatment she was working, although in a position that was well beneath her level of ability. This was acceptable to her, since she felt she was lazy and preferred coasting on her natural ability to working hard towards a goal that might not be attained. When she was confronted with a difficult task, she tended to become anxious and withdrew. She enjoyed the job and did work harder than she did at home or school, areas which were dominated by her mother's demands on her. Although at work she had independence from her mother and a sense of responsibility and power, she also tended to abuse the power by being harsh with customers. Early in treatment, she was reprimanded at work for engaging in some petty thievery and felt badly about it, more because she was caught than because she did it. There was some recognition that her inept cover-up contributed to her discovery. This was related to her inclination to break rules, a way she saw she had of getting back at authority without directly expressing her anger. She pointed out that "boss" spelled backwards is "double s.o.b.," a cute saying embodying her use of an engaging manner to express intolerance of authority.

Shortly after the reprimand, she impulsively left the job she had held for about two years and always enjoyed for a position she was unsuited for on the basis of temperament, training and education. Within a month she was fired, tried unsuccessfully to return to the first job, and found it difficult to understand why she was not rehired. She then found a haven in unemployment insurance, a means of getting something for nothing, while aggravating her mother and pleading innocence of any complicity. Her insistence on a job in communications, the only field she knew, assured that she would remain unemployed, and she recognized the pleasure she got from that status.

When she finally tired of doing nothing, perhaps because her unemployment insurance was almost exhausted, she plaintively asked what she should do. Trial and error were frightening to her because she couldn't tolerate failure. She longed for dispassionate advice, but suspected the motives of anyone, usually her mother, who offered it. This led to a recognition of how difficult it was to separate advice from crit-

icism, making it particularly difficult to take good advice. Since her mother, a woman of good judgment, advised her to do most of the appropriate activities, thereby preempting all of her constructive options, she experienced anything she did for herself as giving in to her mother. While she insisted that she wanted to be left alone, she also recognized that she really wanted to be taken care of, with no strings attached. She clearly saw the gap between what she did and what she felt she ought to do, but had little understanding of why she did not act in her best interests. Just before the end of treatment, she obtained a job with new hours at a different location, providing her with a partial rationalization for a termination of treatment.

Evelyn's relationship with her mother was a central theme throughout therapy and, indeed, throughout her life. Evelyn's parents had been divorced when she was five and her mother remarried during her early adolescence. Her relationship with her stepfather was perfunctory and with her father distant, although she did use it, upon occasion, to annoy her mother, who was certain that Evelyn was fated to be the same type of talented, charming underachiever that he was. Evelyn came to recognize that both parents saw her as being like the other one, but had difficulty seeing that it was the disliked part of the other one, and she may well have served as the displaced object of the anger of both parents. Being identified with the father, she also felt compelled to inhibit her anger and conform in a way he had not done, for his fate was to be thrown out of the house.

The crux of the relationship between Evelyn and her mother was characterized by her inability to act without having someone tell her what to do, and her subsequent resentment at being told what to do. Her passivity and procrastination often provoked advice from her mother, which she resented, but relied on to get anything done. She was comfortable in her role as a well-cared-for child, resented any attempt to make her do anything in return, and did not want to make any change that would jeopardize her areas of perceived entitlement. Communication between them was superficial and limited, as both were private and secretive people; however, Evelyn felt a continuous sense of being left out, even though she never made any independent overtures. One interesting prototype of their relationship occurred when Evelyn's parents were planning a vacation and she wanted to have a party in their absence. She did not intend to tell her mother about this plan, only did so when she saw that she was inviting reproach and probably couldn't get away with keeping it a secret, and then felt very disappointed that her mother did not seem very interested in her plans

for the party. She was also disappointed when she wasn't complimented after the party for her sense of responsibility in cleaning the house, and had trouble seeing how large a role mutual disappointment had played in her relationship with her mother. During the course of treatment, the two major areas of conflict between Evelyn and her mother concerned her room, which was filthy beyond her mother's tolerance and provided a continuing arena for a power struggle between them, and her fruitless attempts to find a job.

The occasional joint sessions with Evelyn and her mother displayed their relationship in a way that was crystal clear to the therapist, but beyond the grasp of either patient. The first session came after Evelyn's mother told her to clean the room or move out of the house, with the room seeming to represent, to her, a symbol of her failure, and to Evelyn, a stubborn declaration of independence. Evelyn, after much deliberation, agreed to be present at the therapist's meeting with her mother, who came across as a caring woman who had been protective of her only child, treated her as fragile, and was ambivalent about having her grow up. She wanted an achieving young woman of whom she could be proud, but also wanted to retain her little girl. In a parallel way, Evelyn wanted the freedom of adulthood while retaining the privileged, protected status of childhood. During the session, Evelyn was quietly angry and unusually defensive, but in the next session she claimed not to know how she felt during the session, and probably did not. At this point, Evelyn's mother was refusing to do her laundry until the room was clean and would not take Evelyn's word that it would be, which produced a good deal of resentment. Nevertheless, Evelyn began slowly and tediously to clean her room so as to restore the order that had existed, although she was angry over having to do so. She seemed to prefer being treated as fragile and saw little advantage to becoming independent, much as she said she wanted to. At the next joint session, Evelyn's mother expressed both her love for her daughter and her exasperation with her. Evelyn, in turn, was openly angry and defensive when it appeared that more rules might be in the offing.

In the following session, she could not remember either the feeling or the content of the previous session, but did talk about a social situation in which she got a good deal of attention by acting in a foolish way. The only joint session that Evelyn remembered and enjoyed was one in which her mother was very expressive of her love, but Evelyn also took this as a reason for allowing her room to revert to its original filthy state and, thereby, precipitated a real crisis in their relationship. At the next joint session she was given a month to have the room cleaned, which

she felt was an irrational demand. This led to a question of why they seemed to save their bombshells for the joint session, underlining their lack of communication and the use of therapy as an island of safety from each other. However, despite this interpretation, the same pattern continued. Evelyn felt the demand about the room meant submission and wanted to know what she would get in return. Her mother was adamant and had the power in the relationship. Evelyn was resistant and powerless, since she was afraid to leave the house. Interestingly, she blamed her current inability to act on her mother's long-term overprotectiveness, and wondered why she should have to pay for her mother's mistakes—an indication of how little responsibility she felt for her own actions. As her mother's will became more clear, the frustration mounted and Evelyn finally ran from the therapist's office saying she would walk home. Her mother was not concerned, felt Evelyn would be waiting by the car, and indeed she was.

At the next session, Evelyn was still angry, said she would clean her room, but very slowly, and did not want her mother to come to any more sessions. This resolved the room situation, which finally was cleaned just well enough and just quickly enough to satisfy Evelyn's mother, but not one bit more, despite Evelyn's own expressed disgust with its filth. It also ended joint sessions until the next crisis, which occurred in the midst of Evelyn's reluctance to find a job. Her mother came in with an ultimatum to find a job or leave the house, and also made it clear that other demands would probably follow. Some of her anger was due to Evelyn's failure to share any of her limited efforts at seeking employment, so that she provocatively appeared to be doing even less than she was. The ultimatum was effective in that Evelyn did find a job, but she also terminated treatment, which remained the one area where she could strike back at her mother.

In retrospect, the joint sessions may not have been a wise modality, although Evelyn was consulted and agreed to them. Her inclination toward compliance was such that she hardly had the courage to refuse. By identifying with her mother's wishes to hold the session, I made it more difficult for Evelyn to separate us, and her final act was to hurt her mother by disavowing me. On the other hand, had the sessions been refused, Evelyn probably would have been pleased to see someone standing up to her mother, but the realistic crisis between them would have been ignored, and the therapy may well have been terminated even earlier by her mother's refusal to pay.

This leads to the issue of transference and countertransference in the relationship. Evelyn clearly viewed me as an authority and treated me

in a stereotyped way. Initially, she was charming and deferential, but wanted me to bear sole responsibility for the direction of the sessions. While she wanted me to push her, she denied any of the anger she usually felt when pushed. She was capable of being very complimentary to me, but not either angry or resentful. Despite her expressions of gratitude and denial of anger, she made little movement in treatment, so that her praise was patently hollow, that she acknowledged that she censored what she told me so that I would not be critical of her. Her final act, to leave treatment, was a clear signal that she had not gotten what she wanted from therapy, but it was presented in a very regretful manner, with no expression of her anger. In response to Evelyn's continued attempts to get as much from me as she could, without producing the progress that was all I wanted from her, I felt continually frustrated and occasionally angry. Often I was manipulated into feeling and being like her mother, an idea confirming Evelyn's view of all authorities and not helpful to her in dealing with her feelings. Evelyn's adeptness in reproducing anger in others, despite her show of cooperativeness, served to perpetuate the self-defeating behavior, and could only have been resolved if I could have avoided the trap more frequently and successfully than I did.

Evelyn provides a very clear view of the behavior, dynamics, and treatment of the passive-aggressive patient. She displayed inadequate social and occupational performance, largely because of her stubbornness, procrastination, and inefficiency. Her pattern was initially related to deep needs for dependency which were frustrated by her parents' marital problems, followed by the divorce which led to her mother's absence from the home so that she could support the two of them. Evelyn did not risk expressing her anger over this frustration lest she also be punished, as her father had been, by being thrown out of the house—a fear which was embodied in the final pre-termination ultimatum. Instead, she disappointed her mother at every turn, dropping out of school, underachieving at work, and having a social and personal life which was a continual source of embarrassment. In treatment, she replicated this relationship in the transference, inducing a countertransference which completed her self-fulfilling prophecy. While Evelyn will continue to make small gains in response to large demands, it is not likely that she will make significant changes until her style becomes so dysfunctional that it becomes ego-dystonic, and she will then be motivated to use her considerable personal resources to alter her self-destructive, lifelong pattern.

REFERENCES

American Psychiatric Association. *Diagnostic and statistical manual of mental disorders* Second Edition. Washington, D.C., 1968.

American Psychiatric Association. *Diagnostic and statistical manual of mental disorders* Third Edition. Washington, D.C., 1980.

Castelnuovo-Tedesco, P., & Schiebel, D. Studies of superobesity: I. Psychological characteristics of superobese patients. *International Journal of Psychiatry in Medicine*, 1975, 6, 465-480.

Fenichel, O. *The psychoanalytic theory of neurosis*. New York: Norton, 1945.

Fischer, R. E., & Juni, S. The anal personality: Self-disclosure, negativism, self-esteem, and superego severity. *Journal of Personality Assessment*, 1982, 46, 50-58.

Freud, A. *The ego and the mechanisms of defense*. New York: International Universities Press, 1946.

Leaff, L. A. Psychodynamic aspects of personality disturbances. In J. R. Lion (Ed.), *Personality disorders: Dynamics and management*. Baltimore: Williams & Wilkins, 1974.

Meissner, W. W., Mack, J. E., & Semrad, E. V. Classical psychoanalysis. In A. M. Freedman, H. I. Kaplan, & B. J. Sadock (Eds.), *Comprehensive textbook of psychiatry II*. Baltimore: Williams & Wilkins, 1975.

Millon, T. *Disorders of personality*. New York: Wiley, 1981.

Pasternack, S. A. The explosive, antisocial, and passive-aggressive personalities. In J. R. Lion (Ed.), *Personality disorders: Dynamics and management*. Baltimore: Williams & Wilkins, 1974.

Reich, W. *Character analysis*. New York: Orgone Institute Press, 1949.

Sadock, B. J. Group psychotherapy. In A. M. Freedman, H. I. Kaplan, & B. J. Sadock (Eds.) *Comprehensive textbook of psychiatry II*. Baltimore: Williams & Wilkins, 1975.

Small, I. F., Small, J. G., Alig, V. B., & Moore, D. F. Passive-aggressive personality disorder: A search for a syndrome. *American Journal of Psychiatry*, 1970, 126, 973-981.

Teicher, J. D. Personality disorders. In A. M. Freedman, H. I. Kaplan, & B. J. Sadock (Eds.), *Comprehensive textbook of psychiatry II*. Baltimore: Williams & Wilkins, 1975.

Whitman, R. M., Trosman, H., & Koenig, R. Clinical assessment of passive-aggressive personality. *Archives of Neurology and Psychiatry*, 1954, 72, 540-549.

2

The Development and Maintenance
of Passive-Aggressiveness:
The Behavioral Approach

Maurice F. Prout
and Jerome J. Platt

CLINICAL PROFILE: A THEORETICAL PERSPECTIVE

An extensive review of the behavioral therapy literature indicates a booming silence with regard to the passive-aggressive personality. Since behavior therapists are actively involved in the clinical treatment of many affective, behavioral, and characterological disorders, a brief historical explanation as to the lack of interest in passive-aggressiveness may be helpful.

Behavior therapy as a clinical and scientific discipline was born out of a radical dissatisfaction with the traditional psychodynamic classifications of and implicit etiological speculations about specific disorders. In addition, there was a lack of enthusiasm with regard to the treatment methods employed by traditional practitioners in alleviating the patient's distress. As a result, the field of behavior therapy and its followers invested substantial energy in not utilizing traditional nomenclature in

describing a disorder. Rather, they focused upon specific behaviors which the patient exhibited—behaviors which could be seen and quantifiably measured. The emphasis upon measurement of behavior stemmed from a distaste for the more ephemeral descriptions of behavior offered by traditional classification procedures.

Hence, personality concepts such as passive-aggressive, borderline, narcissistic, histronic, schizoid, etc., are hardly ever cited, as such, in the behavior therapy literature. However, this does not mean that behavior therapists do not treat patients who suffer from characterological disorders. Indeed, most behaviorally oriented therapists will recognize the condition described below as passive-aggressiveness as a type of unassertive behavior.

Stanton (1978, p. 87) defines this personality:

> The passive-aggressive personality, though poorly demarcated, is primarily characterized by the use of submissive or passive intrapersonal techniques as ways of attacking others, usually those on whom the patient is dependent. Withdrawal, disinterest, obstructionism, negativism, procrastination, inefficiency, direct or indirect sabotage, often by errors of omission, mark his actions; in more direct contacts, hurt feelings and lack of initiative are typical. Usually passive techniques are the only significant way of expressing aggression, although brief temper outbursts may occur.

Davison and Neale (1982, p. 275) offer another definition:

> . . . the passive-aggressive personality indirectly resists the demands of others, either socially or at work. The resistance, which is thought to be aggression in disguise, takes the form of thoroughgoing stubbornness and ineffectuality. They are habitually late for appointments, do not return phone calls, procrastinate, and forget. This persistent behavior pattern usually provokes further problems, such as marital discord and not being offered promotions. The dawdling of passive-aggressive personalities can be considered a hostile way of controlling others without assuming responsibility for their own anger. . . .

These authors also note that "the personality disorders make up what many workers regard as an unreliable, cluttered grab bag of a category" (p. 275).

Finally, Klein, Gittelman, Quitkin, and Rifkin (1980, pp. 510-511) offer this view:

> The passive-aggressive personality is also controversial. The central theme seems to be a sneaky covert resistance to authority or the demand to perform effectively. Often, this takes the form of procrastination, dawdling, forgetfulness, etc. We wonder whether this is not the final common pathway of many conflicted states in which the person wishes to behave aggressively and is blocked from doing so either by external circumstances or by internal inhibition. . . .

There are two common themes in all of the above descriptions of the passive-aggressive personality: 1) The condition, as a distinct personality type, is not well defined as to specifics; and 2) the overt behaviors which allow for some level of identification of the condition are seen as covert expressions of anger or dissatisfaction. To further elaborate on this theme, the patient is seen as not acting in an assertive and direct manner in expressing his or her feelings. Rather, he/she must always remain hidden or "shadow" his reactions. No direct representation can be allowed, for it either is not known in terms of expression or cannot be afforded with regard to consequences.

With respect to unassertive behavior, as characterized most frequently in the behavior therapy literature and as related to the passive-aggressive personality, the following would apply:

1) Unassertive behavior is mainly interpersonal in nature and involves the dishonest and/or indirect expression of thoughts and feelings.
2) Unassertive behavior is, for the most part, socially inappropriate,—
3) When a person is behaving unassertively, he is mainly concerned about himself, not the feelings or welfare of others.
4) Unassertive behavior may be expressed verbally and also includes the following nonverbal parameters:
   a) loudness and tone of voice;
   b) fluency of spoken words;
   c) eye contact;
   d) facial expression;
   e) body expression (general posture); and
   f) lean of body (toward or away from other person).

In summary, then, most behaviorally oriented clinicians do not refer

to the diagnostic entity of passive-aggressive personality as such. Rather, clinicians of the behavioral persuasion would view what is typically referred to as the passive-aggressive personality as a type of unassertive behavior. This behavior is viewed primarily as interpersonal in nature and includes behaviors related to procrastination, lateness, forgetfulness, etc. Behavior therapists also emphasize *how* the message is delivered, i.e., the verbal and nonverbal components of unassertiveness.

ETIOLOGICAL FACTORS

The etiology of various psychological conditions may be explained by any number of concepts, such as genetic vulnerability, developmental events, psychosocial stressors, physiological stressors, reinforcement theory, etc. While behavior therapy has an appreciation for the contribution of other factors as they impinge on behavior, the area most often emphasizes relates to learning theory, specifically operant reinforcement and social learning concepts.

Operant Conditioning

Contrary to popular opinion, operant conditioning is not "anti-human" or "black box" oriented. Primarily, it provides a model for examining and understanding behavior. The major writer identified with operant conditioning is B. F. Skinner (1950, 1953, 1969, 1971, 1974, 1978).

Operant conditioning theory views behavior as significantly influenced by its consequences. The four major areas related to consequences and behavior are: 1) positive reinforcement; 2) negative reinforcement; 3) extinction; and 4) punishment.

Positive reinforcement suggests that if a behavior is followed by something pleasant or valued, the behavior is likely to occur again. If direct, assertive behavior is met by most important people in the individual's environment in a positive manner, the behavior is reinforced and is likely to be maintained or developed into a "style," i.e. a generalized way of interacting with the world. In essence, behavior is increased as a result of the consequences which follow the behavior.

Negative reinforcement also refers to an increase in behavior, but for reasons other than receiving pleasant consequences. In negative reinforcement the person perceives the stimulus (s) as painful; he then performs a behavior and as a result the pain diminishes or terminates. The behavior then reduces or takes away the hurt (s). In doing so, the behavior is quite successful, in that it allows the person to negotiate suc-

cessfully an event which he perceives to be painful or fraught with anxiety.

If an interpersonal situation is seen as potentially anxiety-provoking (painful) to the person, he may behave in an unassertive, covert, passive-aggressive manner. Following his passivity, the anxiety may diminish or "pass him by." Thus, his unassertiveness is felt to be successful and therefore has a high probability of repetition in that or a similar situation. In essence, the unassertive position "works."

An example of the above would be someone who receives an invitation to the annual company party. Social gatherings, especially when authority figures are present, arouse a significant amount of anxiety in this person. However, the patient feels inhibited about declining the invitation in a direct manner, for fear of criticism or reprisal by others. As a result, he handles the anxiety situation by avoiding it—forgetting, becoming ill at the last minute, making up an excuse, getting the dates confused, etc. All the above strategies allow for the reduction of anxiety; therefore, the unassertive or passive-aggressive behaviors are reinforced. Our patient manages the anxiety by becoming hidden or shadowlike. Unfortunately, our patient is caught in a paradox; i.e., the strategies work for the moment, but are likely to backfire in the long run. However, he feels the anxiety in the present and behaves in response to the short-term consequences of behavior. His unassertive or passive behavior works, at least for a while.

Extinction refers to a process whereby a behavior which was previously maintained by specific consequences is no longer reinforced. In essence, the behavior no longer works. It is assumed that, after repeated failures to obtain the desired consequence, the behavior will disappear, i.e., extinguish, as a result of non-nourishment.

An example of the above might be as follows: Person A has always been assertive in her environment. This style of interacting with the world had, for the most part, allowed her to be successful in her academic, business, and personal life. She has been reinforced by others for being straightforward, responsible, self-initiating, and open in her communication. However, she has recently been hired by another company and has assumed a new position. Her new colleagues respond to her self-assertion, directness, and openness by ignoring her. One colleague even tells her that while self-assertive behavior may have been OK for company X, she won't remain long with company Y if she continues in like manner. After a few such encounters, Person A's assertive behavior may well begin to wane in her new setting as a result of non-reinforcement.

The critical element to be appreciated with extinction is that the behavior which is no longer reinforced is changed *gradually*, over time and experience. Also, the behavior may be reinforced at any moment and, if it is, paradoxically it may be more difficult to extinguish in the future.

Punishment refers to a process where a behavior is followed by a painful consequence. The consequence is phenomenologically aversive to the person. The pain in this case may be a social shunning, loss of job or status, insult to self-concept or ideal, rejection by another, anxiety, etc.

One does not have to wait in this instance for behavior to change. The effects of punishment can be immediate and dramatic:

1) As a result of pain, behavior is reduced in a dramatic manner. If extinction is analogous to atrophy, punishment would be viewed as immediate death. The behavior drops out rather quickly.
2) The punisher is reinforced for administering the punishment, since the undesired behavior is eliminated or suppressed rather quickly. The punisher has discovered a method, albeit painful, with which to control the behavior of others. There is always a danger that if one's learning environment is not rich and varied enough, an individual may experience punishment as the preferred and perhaps only way of getting what one desires.
3) Finally, if punishment is employed as the primary means of influencing behavior, people experiencing the pain tend to become affectively disturbed. Usually agitation will be followed by a demoralization and clinical depression. There is no joy in life, only a series of aversive events.

Consider Person A in our previous example. Let us say that, instead of being warned and gradually "shaped" to become less assertive, she is, as a result of her appropriate directness, fired or demoted. Since work constitutes a source of economic and social gratification, she has learned that to be assertive may be associated with considerable pain and assertive behavior may be decreased or suppressed rapidly.

Social Learning Theory

Another major approach to understanding the development of the passive-aggressive personality lies in the area referred to as social learning theory. This area, best represented by the work of Albert Bandura (1969, 1977; Bandura, Jeffrey, & Bachicha, 1974; Bandura & Rosenthal,

1966; Bandura & Walters, 1963), will be only briefly summarized here since, as a cognitively oriented theory, it will be elaborated upon in Chapter 4. Briefly, characterological development is viewed as the interactive result of principles of operant conditioning and observational learning. Most behavior is probably acquired not through tedious trial and error, but rather from observing the behavior of others around us, how they act, and what happens as a result of their actions. The two basic assumptions of social learning theory are: 1) Learning can take place without the person emitting a response and receiving positive or negative reinforcement and, 2) the critical element in this type of learning is cognitive, which is an internal state and thus not directly observable.

According to Bandura, it is possible for a person to observe the way another behaves in response to a stimulus or event, and then, when he himself is in that situation, respond in a similar manner. An example of the above might be a son who both passively and actively attends to how his parents interact when having a disagreement. It may be that the father, feeling slighted for whatever reason, withdraws verbally and physically from the family. The wife feels the loss and attempts to open communication between them by asking, "Is there anything wrong?" To this he replies a quick and sullen, "No," and walks away. Father is aware that he can usually hold out longer than mother, and it will only be a matter of time before she queries further, attempting to discover what is wrong and how she can make amends. It works every time—or nearly!

As a result of his observations, the child learns a method of handling disagreements which is passive-aggressive in nature, and which is externally reinforced. The child may eventually assess this interpersonal strategy as the only or preferred way of interacting when feeling slighted or hurt. He now has a modeled method of interacting with his world which probably is reinforced at least some of the time, thereby ensuring its maintenance.

THERAPEUTIC STRATEGY AND PROCESS

As we have seen from the section on etiological considerations, a passive-aggressive personality or unassertive character may develop, according to the behavioral focus, via two methods: 1) through direct experience and interpersonal reinforcement; or 2) by observing the behaviors of others and eventually modeling the same behaviors in similar situations.

Behavioral Assessment

To treat this condition behaviorally we must proceed with a behavioral assessment, a method which allows us to zero in on the triggers of the disorder. To his lasting credit, Wolpe (1958, 1961, 1964, 1973, 1976, 1977) emphasized that behavior therapy is not a grab bag of techniques that can be applied indiscriminately; rather, a careful assessment of the individual is required prior to selecting the treatment techniques. The five general areas which require careful assessment are: 1) antecedent stimulus variables; 2) the overt maladaptive behavior; 3) the environmental consequences; 4) misconceptions or cognitive distortion; and 5) emotional factors.

The area of *antecedent stimulus variables* refers to an assessment of what triggers the behavior. This requires a rather exhaustive asking of when, how, what, with whom, etc. types of questions. It is highly desirable to have the patient begin a therapeutic journal, in which he enters this type of data at least once per day. By doing so the patient, as well as the therapist, becomes more sensitive to and aware of the situations which trigger his behavior.

Overt maladaptive behavior refers to a detailed description by the patient and perhaps others, e.g., spouse, friend, etc., of exact behaviors the patient exhibits to be labeled passive-aggressive or unassertive. Specifically, we would be interested in which strategies and variations of the passive-aggressive theme are employed. We are more concerned here with gathering a listing of behaviors he actually performs than with assigning a diagnostic label.

Environmental consequences include supports for this characterological style. In essence, the therapist is attempting to identify the "payoffs" for the behavior. These may include reduction of anxiety, sadistic gratification, nurture from a spouse, etc. Reinforcers may be internal as well as external. Notations in the patient's journal about consequences can be quite helpful in planning therapeutic strategy.

Cognitive misconceptions refer to our assumptions, attitudes, beliefs, expectations, and interpretations about specific events and the world in general. Since our behavior and emotions are somewhat dependent upon how we view things, it is important to have an assessment of how people think and perceive their world.

An assessment of *emotional factors* requires that careful identification and sequencing of affects be obtained. For example, the patient may be initially anxious and, as a result of his passive-aggressive behaviors, becomes less anxious. Or, as a result of his behavior, he not only becomes less anxious, but experiences sadistic gratification as well. Once the sequencing and timing can be identified, intervention strategies can then be developed.

Treatment Techniques

Generally, treatment techniques will include, but are not limited to, the following: 1) relaxation training; 2) role-playing; 3) cognitive restructuring; and 4) use of the therapeutic relationship.

Relaxation training was initially developed by Jacobson (1938) and later modified by Wolpe (1958) and Schultz and Luthe (1959). It is assumed that relaxation is able to counteract the negative and inhibitory effects of anxiety. As inhibition is reduced, the patient is better able to utilize previously "damned-up" resources. In addition, he may avail himself of new learning opportunities, explore new options for himself, become more an observer of himself in relation to the world, as opposed to solely reacting to it, etc. While this may appear at first glance to be a rather grandiose list, anyone who has experienced crippling anxiety and/or seen it in his patients knows that a reduction of anxiety allows for further opportunities and assessments.

Usually relaxation is conducted initially by employing the progressive muscular relaxation (PMR) method. PMR consists of a series of tensing and relaxing specific muscle groups, with a careful prior assessment as to previous injuries, muscle pulls, vulnerable areas, etc. After the patient becomes comfortable with PMR, variations on the relaxation theme can be developed. Usually these take the form of deep, slow, rhythmic breathing; construction of relaxation scenes or memories which are calming and soothing; or specific sounds or music which provide a similar effect. It should be emphasized that the relaxation response is not viewed here as a cure-all. Rather, it is introduced as only one, albeit important, method of coping for the anxiety-prone patient.

Role-playing or behavioral rehearsal represents a critical intervention for many passive-aggressive patients. Remember, the passive-aggressive or unassertive personality is trapped by his behavior. He may be likened to a man who fits his auto with square wheels. While the ride is bumpy,

he still manages to get there. To attempt something new causes anxiety due to the newness of the situation, a perception that it won't work and disaster will follow, or a recollection of past trials and failures. In response to his perceptions, he maintains the familiar, which, if truth be told, does not feel so bad to him. Our patient is comfortably uncomfortable.

Patients will not change characterologic styles unless they have appropriate models available and can have some appreciation that changing style will allow for fuller interpersonal experience that need not be threatening nor engulfing.

Role-playing situations will typically be provided by the patient's everyday experience, as recorded in the therapeutic journal. If the ice is thick and must be broken, the therapist should initiate with suggestions. However, the therapist must be aware that continued initiation and offering may reinforce the very personality style he is attempting to change. It is also helpful to ask the patient to rate each situation with regard to degree of difficulty, anxiety, or personal/social risk. Remember, a patient may continue in a passive-aggressive manner not only because it is externally reinforced, but because the strategy reduces anxiety or muddies the waters of accountability.

Finally, a patient may exhibit extensive passive-aggressiveness simply because he knows no other way of behaving. He is caught in the early modeling/current reinforcement trap. This type of situation requires an extensively active approach on the part of the therapist. The patient literally knows no other way of behaving. Hence, the therapist must intensively teach the patient how to be different.

To engage in the above requires some appreciation of communication theory, with special emphasis upon nonverbal components. The mode of interpersonal communication, when viewed by the general public and many therapists as well, is mainly thought to be through one channel, i.e., verbal communication. While peripheral note may be taken of the nonverbal characteristics which accompany the message, they are not immediately viewed as communicating the potency of the message as well as the verbal components.

The nonverbal style with which a message is delivered can either contaminate or enhance the message. Consider the effect upon the receiver of hearing the verbal message, "I'm really excited about the possibilities," while experiencing the sender's flat vocal tone, sighs, deadpan look, lack of hand movements, and the like. The message would probably be interpreted as illegitimate or conflicting. However, if the same verbalization were accompanied by eye contact, emphasis upon certain words, and an overall expression of body excitement, the

two channels of the message would parallel one another in a congruent fashion.

Haley (1963, p. 91), in his observations of schizophrenic communication, notes that the diagnosis is based on ". . . the most obvious manifestation of schizophrenia, an incongruity between what the patient communicates and the messages which qualify that communication. His movements negate or deny what he says, and his words negate or deny the context in which he speaks."

Various laboratory studies support the notion discussed above concerning message transfer through nonverbal behavior. Mehrabian and Weiner (1967) and Mehrabian and Ferris (1967) studied the effects of positive-negative interpersonal attitudes communicated by verbal, vocal, and facial cues. Both studies employed actors to facially express a positive or negative attitude and to express the same attitude using their tone of voice (positive, negative, or neutral) while saying experimental test words. College students were asked to determine which attitude the actor was expressing and their own method for determining same. The results of the first study indicate that the raters perceived the actors' attitude as better expressed by tone of voice than by the content of the spoken words. The results of the second study suggest the raters judged the model's attitude reliably more often by his facial expression. This was accomplished when a photograph was associated with a voice recording which conveyed a positive, negative, or neutral attitude. The conclusion drawn by Mehrabian and Ferris was that raters interpreted the model's attitude primarily through facial cues, next by vocal cues, and lastly by the verbal content.

In describing her work with disturbed families, Satir (1972) found all her cases to exhibit double messages, i.e., the verbal inconsistent with the nonverbal. The sender of the double message, according to her, has one or more of the following characteristics:

1) He has low self-esteem and feels that he is bad because he feels that way.
2) He feels fearful about hurting the other's feelings.
3) He worries about retaliation from the other.
4) He fears rupture of the relationship.
5) He does not want to impose.
6) He does not attach any significance to the person or the interaction itself (p. 61).

Components 2, 3, and 5 essentially describe the unassertive person and the whys of his behavior. The work of both Haley and Satir demonstrates

the extreme effects inconsistent, two-channel communications can have upon people.

Given the complexities of communication, one of the best means of therapeutically teaching patients the effect of their behavior upon others is through videotape role-play. Not only are the verbal components of a message captured, but the more subtle nonverbal aspects are also obtained. Once a scene is videotaped, it can be replayed, freeze-framed, advanced framed, played without audio, etc.

Once the data are obtained on tape, replay should be instituted; after two or three reviews critique begins. Emphasis is upon both the patient and therapist *therapeutically* reviewing the role-play and suggesting alternative ways of behaving in the situation. Alternatives in the verbal and nonverbal spheres should be offered, rehearsed, and videotaped. This process is conceptualized as a gradual approximation of a healthier style of interacting. Coping with and mastering one component builds a base for the next, more complex role-play. The role-plays are always graded as to level of difficulty, as well as level of anxiety that may be elicited. Also, it is usually helpful to assess a few different situations during each therapy session, e.g., work, marital, social, etc.

Finally, a brief mention regarding the ethics of videotaping for therapeutic purposes is in order. It is imperative that a signed consent be obtained. Since videotaping role-plays captures the patients' behavior, the procedure by definition creates an arena of anxiety. As a means of smoothing the edges of vulnerability, it often is helpful to mention in the written consent that the tape will only be seen by the therapist and patient. As a matter of adherence to this stated policy, as well as practical economics, it is wise to erase tapes when therapy is terminated. If tapes are to be saved during the therapy process, it is appropriate to maintain "live" tapes under lock and key.

Cognitive restructuring is especially helpful when the behavioral analysis indicates that a prime generator of passive-aggressiveness is based upon internal appraisal. In other words, the patient may possess a series of irrational beliefs concerning how he and the world should interact. Examples of these beliefs or internal demands are outlined by Ellis (1962) include:

1) I need to be approved and loved by everyone.
2) It would be horrible if I "hurt" the feelings of someone else.
3) It is easier to passively avoid life's difficulties than to face them directly.

4) You always need to depend upon someone else to solve your problems.
5) The world should be fair and just.
6) One should get "even" if things don't go the way you want.

If one is to be successful in modifying behavior based on misconceptions, it is imperative that the inappropriate philosophical sets be identified, challenged, and eventually altered.

For further elaboration in this area, the reader is referred to Chapter 4, as well as to the works of Beck (1970, 1976; Beck, Rush, Shaw, & Emergy, 1979) and Ellis (1974; Ellis & Grieger, 1977).

The therapeutic relationship, while not viewed as the primary vehicle for change in behavioral therapy, is nonetheless quite necessary in facilitating that change. The very behavior demonstrated by the patient in the therapy hour can be viewed as a sample of what takes place on a more global scale. The therapist's reactions to the patient's maneuvers may indeed replicate how others respond to his various passive-aggressive strategies. Fortunately, the therapist can share his own reactions to the patient in a non-hostile environment. Through the process of sharing, reflection, and gentle confrontation, the patient may be willing to look at himself, his behavior, and its effect on others. As a result of this continuing process, other interventions can be employed as a means of reducing passive-aggressive behaviors and moving toward more appropriate styles of interaction.

In addition to serving as a non-distorted feedback resource to the patient, the therapeutic relationship can serve as a support for the patient during what, at times, may seem like a rather harrowing journey. After all, changing a square wheel to a round one cannot be accomplished without some strain, fear, risk, and, at times, disappointment. During this process, a bond with a warm, concerned and not overly involved other can attentuate the hardships of the patient's journey. The patient's typical fears, anxiety, and vulnerability can be behaviorally and cognitively managed within the context of the relationship. Also, as the patient experiences disappointments and resultant demoralization rears its head, the therapist can offer an objective appraisal of the patient's resources in light of the situation. This can be quite beneficial in obviating a downward spiral toward a return to passive-aggressive behaviors.

Finally, aside from providing an appropriate model for other styles of "being" via role rehearsal, the therapist may, on occasion, choose to self-disclose. This can be helpful to the patient in that he learns that

even the therapist encounters difficulty in his own life and that threat and perhaps defeat can be reacted to in ways other than demoralization and/or passive-aggressiveness.

In summary, then, prior to establishing which interventions are to be employed, a credible behavioral analysis must be conducted. The analysis includes assessment of antecedent stimuli variables, overt maladaptive behavior, environmental consequences, cognitive misconceptions, and finally, a scanning of emotional factors. Specific treatment methods are then employed, including but not limited to: relaxation training, role-playing, cognitive restructuring, and perceptive use of the therapeutic relationship.

CASE ILLUSTRATION

Background

The patient, P, 38 years old is an engineer by profession, following in his father's footsteps. His father is a managing partner of a prestigious engineering consulting firm. Father was remembered and presently perceived as a benevolent tyrant. Mother, who died when P was age 30, is remembered as a kindly although at times distant figure. P does not recall that his parents ever expressed harsh words during periods of disagreements. However, mother is recollected to have placated father almost always as a means of resolving most disputes. P is an only child. Mother's death was reacted to with appropriate mourning. When P was 34, father remarried to a woman P describes as being like his mother in most respects.

P himself married at the age of 35 to a woman, 30, who was divorced with no children. Their son was born approximately one year after the marriage. The pregnancy was highly desired by both. P and his wife have recently divorced as a result of the wife's dissatisfaction with P's behavior in the marriage. She expressed constantly being criticized by P and that she felt he was a failure as a marital partner and at his work. Their sex life was reported by both as being excellent. P did not contest the divorce; indeed, he wondered whether he ever really loved his wife. He admitted to verbally abusing her and said that, while he knew it was wrong, he could not help himself.

During the divorce proceedings, P apparently was quite dissatisfied with the manner in which his lawyer was handling his side. Despite this lack of confidence he never complained, although it eventually cost him custody of his child, half his assets, and child support payments. Af-

terwards he was outraged by the "utter injustice" and wrote the local bar association, bitterly denouncing his lawyer's incompetence, along with the judicial system in general.

Despite attending private elementary and secondary schools, graduating from an Ivy League college, and completing a Master's degree in engineering, P has managed to be fired by two engineering firms. These dismissals were based on his lack of attention to detail, late work, missing critical subtle components of a project, over- or underestimating financial costs of projects, etc.

In addition to his difficulty with work, P experienced a tremendous inferiority in social situations. He was uncomfortable with both clients and colleagues. He could not interact socially without considerable amounts of anxiety. This was described by him as "not knowing how to act" or "people will think me a fool." When invited to business luncheons he usually had excuses, e.g., doctor's appointment, prior engagements, or simply "forgot." This type of behavior carried over to his social life as well, much to the irritation of his wife.

Currently P is employed in his third job. While his performance is rated by his superiors as mediocre, he feels secure there for the time being. However, the firm is seen by himself and his father as substantially below his talents and education. His current boss is younger, less educated, and in P's view, considerably less talented than he is.

P initially entered therapy after his first dismissal. He says that he was devastated by this experience and spent approximately three and a half years in psychoanalysis, meeting three times a week with his psychiatrist. He says he learned much about himself; indeed, he speaks the jargon as well as any professional. P left analysis when both he and the therapist felt he had come as far as possible. Concomitant with terminating therapy, P married.

A call to P's former therapist was initiated with his permission, to elicit information about the previous therapy. P was stated diagnostically to be a passive-aggressive personality who also suffered from neurotic anxiety. P was viewed as making tremendous strides in resolving many of his unconscious conflicts. In addition, he was able to secure a second position (which he had since lost), enter a marriage (now dissolved), and begin his own family.

Therapy

P was referred to therapy by a former patient who was acquainted with him. P entered therapy in a distraught, demoralized state. He

complained of early morning awakening, some appetite disturbance, agitation, and a sense that he wanted to cry. A decision was made not to refer him for antidepressant medication, since the biological signs were thought to be amenable to behavior therapy.

Diary. P was requested to maintain a journal during the entire therapy. He was instructed in how to record his experiences, i.e., antecedents, behaviors, consequences, cognitions, and emotions. After our second session he agreed to both the diary and recording in it once a day. However, during our next three sessions, he "forgot" to make daily entries and to bring in the diary to therapy. He was gently confronted on the fifth session with his undoing of therapy and his sabatoging technique. He was asked to carefully assess whether this type of therapy was truly for him, since it did require his active participation. If he did not think he could adhere to the diary, an appropriate referral would be made at our next meeting. On the sixth session P brought his diary, complete with meticulous notes containing a surprising number of sensitive insights. P continued to bring his diary faithfully thereafter.

The diary revealed that P felt anxious in a number of settings, often expecting to be criticized by others. As a result he became quite skillful at developing excuses which would let him off the hook, at least for the time being. In addition, the cognitive and emotional sections of the diary revealed that P experienced a tremendous amount of hostility toward others. This was especially true regarding those who were perceived as potentially criticizing him. While he was fearful of disapproval, his very behavior guaranteed it.

It also became clear that P felt it "beneath" him to express his dissatisfaction or resentment to others. Later a therapy session revealed the following concern: "If I were direct with my resentment, I could be held accountable." Despite this connection, his covert behavior continued, presumably due to the anxiety reduction.

Relaxation training was instituted during the eighth session with PMR P readily took to the exercises and as a result an audio cassette tape was made of an actual session. This was done so that he could practice at home as well as in the office. While PMR was successful with the therapist, the diary indicated a dismal failure in vivo. P attempted to use the tape during times when he was almost guaranteed to be interrupted at home or office. When this was pointed out, P admitted to being less than vigilant regarding the settings and times. He was then requested, in the therapist's office, to develop other situations and times less likely

to be met with interruptions. In addition, he was asked to list five things that might interrupt his PMR and how he could circumvent the disturbances. While he was only able to identify three potential hazards, he was quite successful in determining how to problem-solve around them. Thereafter his use of PMR went quite well and generalized to his facility with relaxation imagery.

Despite his skill with relaxation, his diary indicated his passive-aggressive behaviors did not alter substantially, although his sleep and appetite improved markedly. It was then determined that he probably did not possess the skill necessary for direct interaction.

With this assessment in mind, *role-playing* was instituted. A considerable amount of time was spent over numerous sessions, concentrating on both the verbal and nonverbal components of an assertive request or reply. In order to do this each scene was videotaped, replayed, critiqued, coached, and retaped. The coaching component emphasized how to improve the qualities of assertiveness. In addition to the above, P was asked at each scene: 1) to identify the price he might be expected to pay for his assertive behavior; 2) to rank order his "payments" in terms of a) degree of stress and b) probability of occurrence; 3) to determine whether he could live with the stress if it did befall him; and 4) if he assessed the stress as being overwhelming to decide how he could better buffer himself rather than returning to passive/aggressive behavior.

After approximately 20 sessions of videotaping and role-playing, P's behavior began to change markedly at work and in social situations. This was verified by his diary, his talk in therapy, and his ex-wife, who now desired a reconciliation. P began to spend more time at his work, volunteered for more projects, and was able to become visible in positive ways. One of the senior partners offered P a consulting opportunity on a rather large project. This was successfully completed with a minimum of wheel spinning on P's part. As a result, the senior partner has taken him under his wing; so far P has not felt a need to "undo" this relationship. Although he chose not to reconcile with his former wife, he did institute a rescheduling of visiting privileges with his child. This initiative was legally successful and personally satisfying.

While P does not demonstrate assertiveness in every situation, and indeed has been advised not to be compulsive about it, he has changed his behavior and outlook considerably. The one area which remains impervious to change is his passive-aggressive behavior with his father. It might be noted that this relationship remained unmovable during his

formal analysis and, because of its protracted course, improvement in this relationship has ceased to be a goal of behavior therapy.

In summary, the significant treatment intervention in this case included: 1) the use of a diary to obtain a thorough behavioral analysis; 2) relaxation to actively reduce anticipatory anxiety; 3) role-playing with extensive use of videotaping over a number of sessions; and 4) problem-solving his passive-aggressiveness with particular interventions.

REFERENCES

Bandura, A. *Principles of behavior modification.* New York: Holt, Rinehart and Winston, 1969.

Bandura, A. Self efficacy: Toward a unifying theory of behavioral change. *Psychological Review,* 1977, *84,* 191-215.

Bandura, A., Jeffrey, R. W., & Bachicha, D. L. Analysis of memory codes and cumulative rehearsal in observational learning. *Journal of Research in Personality,* 1974, *7,* 295-305.

Bandura, A., & Rosenthal, T. L. Vicarious classical conditioning as a function of arousal level. *Journal of Personality and Social Psychology,* 1966, *3,* 54-62.

Bandura, A., & Walters, R. H. *Social learning and personality development.* New York: Holt, Rinehart and Winston, 1963.

Beck, A. T. The case problem in depression: The cognitive triad. In J. Masserman (Ed.), *Depression: Theories and therapies.* New York: Grune and Stratton, 1970.

Beck, A. T. *Cognitive therapy and the emotional disorders.* New York: International Universities Press, 1976.

Beck, A. T., Rush, A. J., Shaw, B. F., & Emery, G. *Cognitive therapy of depression.* New York: Guilford Press, 1979.

Davison, G. C., and Neale, J. M. *Abnormal psychology, an experimental clinical approach,* New York: John Wiley & Sons, Inc., 1982.

Ellis, A. *Reason and emotion in psychotherapy.* New York: Lyle Stuart, 1962.

Ellis, A. Rational emotive therapy. In A. Burton (Ed.), *Operational theories of personality.* New York: Brunner/Mazel, 1974.

Ellis, A., & Grieger, R. *Handbook of rational emotive therapy.* New York: Springer Verlag, 1977.

Haley, J. *Strategies of psychotherapy.* New York: Grune & Stratton, 1963.

Jacobson, E. *Progressive relaxation.* Chicago: University of Chicago Press, 1938.

Klein, D. F., Gittelman, R., Quitkin, F., & Rifkin, A. *Diagnosis and drug treatment of psychiatric disorders: Adults and children* (2nd ed.). Baltimore: Williams & Wilkins, 1980.

Mehrabian, A., & Ferris, S. R. Inference of attitudes from non-verbal communication in two channels. *Journal of Consulting Psychology,* 1967, *31,* 248-252.

Mehrabian, A., & Weiner, M. Non-immediacy between communicator and object of communication in verbal message: Application to the inference of attitudes. *Journal of Consulting Psychology,* 1967, *30,* 420-425.

Satir, V. *Peoplemaking.* Palo Alto: Science and Behavior Books, Inc., 1972.

Schultz, J. H., and Luthe, W. *Autogenic training.* New York: Grune & Stratton, 1959.

Skinner, B. F. Are theories of learning necessary? *Psychological Review,* 1950, *57,* 193-216.

Skinner, B. F. *Science and human behavior.* New York: Macmillan, 1953.

Skinner, B. F. *Contingencies of reinforcement: A theoretical analysis.* New York: Appleton, 1969.

Skinner, B. F. *Beyond freedom and dignity.* New York: Knopf, 1971.

Skinner, B. F. *About behaviorism.* New York: Knopf, 1974.

Skinner, B. F. *Reflections on behaviorism and society.* Englewood Cliffs, NJ: Prentice-Hall, 1978.

Stanton, A. H. Personality disorders. In A. M. Nicholi (Ed.), *The Harvard guide to modern psychiatry.* Cambridge: Harvard University Press, 1978.

Wolpe, J. *Psychotherapy by reciprocal inhibition.* Stanford: Stanford University Press, 1958.

Wolpe, J. The systematic desensitization treatment of neurosis. *Journal of Nervous and Mental Disease,* 1961, *132,* 189-203.

Wolpe, J. Behavior therapy in complex neurotic states. *British Journal of Psychiatry,* 1964, *110,* 18-34.

Wolpe, J. *The practice of behavior therapy* (2nd ed.). Oxford: Pergamon, 1973.

Wolpe, J. *Theme and variations: A behavior therapy case book.* Elmsford, NY: Pergamon, 1976.

Wolpe, J. Inadequate behavior analysis: The Achilles heel of outcome research in behavior therapy. *Journal of Behavior Therapy and Experimental Psychiatry,* 1977, *8*(1), 1-3.

3

A Transactional Analysis Perspective on Passive-Aggressiveness

Frances Bonds-White

TRANSACTIONAL ANALYSIS: DEFINITIONS

A first step in the understanding of TA treatment of the passive-aggressive personality is the definition of some terminology which will be used throughout this chapter.

Ego States: "An ego state is a coherent system of thought and feeling manifested by corresponding patterns of behavior" (Berne, 1973, p. 11). There are three types of ego states that can be observed in human beings. The *Parent* ego state feels, thinks, acts, talks, and responds just as one or both of the person's parents did when he or she was small. The "parental influence" serves the function of a conscience. The *Adult* ego state appraises the environment (human and other) objectively and calculates possibilities and probabilities on the basis of past experience. The *Child* ego state feels, thinks, and acts just as she or he did as a little girl or boy (Berne, 1973).

The study or diagnosis of thoughts and feelings of ego states is known as *structural analysis* and is the initial stage of transactional analysis treatment. These thoughts and feelings may be understood through the

44

"corresponding patterns of behavior" (Berne, 1973, p. 11) that the therapist observes. These behavior patterns are usually described in functional terms as the Nurturing or Controlling (critical) Parent and the Natural, Adapted, or Rebellious Child (see Figure 1).

Transactions: A transaction consists of a single stimulus and a single response, verbal or nonverbal, and is the unit of social action (Berne, 1973). The analysis of transactions or *transactional analysis proper* is the second step in treatment after structural analysis. *Transactional analysis proper* is the technique which enables one to understand the functioning of the ego states.

There are three types of transactions. Complementary and crossed

Figure 1. Functional Aspects of Ego States

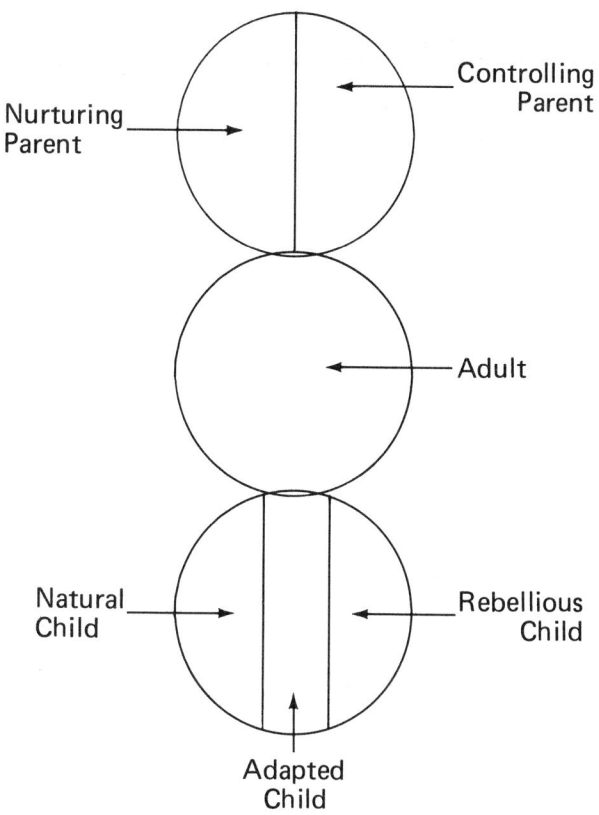

transactions are direct, single-level transactions. Conversation will either continue or cease depending upon the number of each in a given exchange. Ulterior transactions take place on both an overt or social level and a covert or psychological level. Ulterior transactions are typically the opening moves of a "game."

Game Analysis: A game is an ongoing series of complementary ulterior transactions progressing to a well defined predictable outcome (Berne, 1964, p. 48). The moves in a game are predictable and can be outlined in seven steps:

1) Ostensible Adult stimulus.
2) Psychological level stimulus.
3) Response to psychological stimulus.
4) One to hundreds of complementary trasactions.
5) Internal switch in ego states by player.
6) Crossed transactions or zap by player.
7) Payoff (feelings which both use to advance their script and justify their life position).

Games are imitative in nature and are learned in the family situation as a way to get needs met. Because games involve an exchange of strokes (recognition) that are familiar to the players, they serve a stabilizing (homeostatic) function for the player (Berne, 1964). Every game is seen to have three roles—Victim, Rescuer, and Persecutor—even if there are only two players (Karpman, 1968). Moves in the game occur as players change roles.

Script Analysis: A script is an ongoing life plan formed in early childhood under parental pressure. It is usually based on childhood illusions which are maintained throughout life (Berne, 1973). Scripts are essentially the outline or blueprint for a life course. The Child ego states of the parents of a person are the chief factors in the formation of a script. *Injunctions* (prohibitions or inhibitions of the free behavior of the child) and *attributions* (how to do things) are the primary manifestations of the Child ego state in the parent figures. The person will make a *decision* as to how to adapt to and handle the pressures of the family situations (Steiner, 1974).

The *counterscript* is transmitted by the Parent ego states of the biological parents and contains all of the cultural and familial instructions for get-

Figure 2. Script Matrix

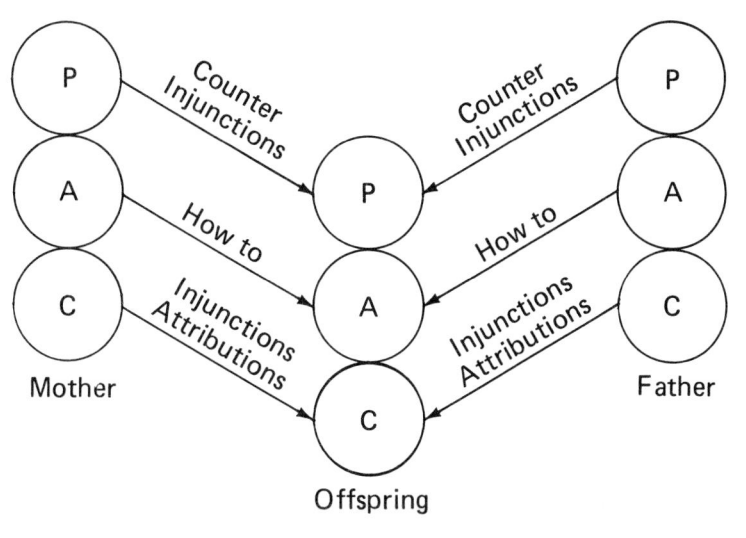

ting along in the world. The Adult ego state models how to follow (put into action) the injunctions and counterscript.

The script matrix (Steiner, 1966) illustrates how these messages are passed on and utilized (Figure 2).

CLINICAL PROFILE: A THEORETICAL PERSPECTIVE

Passivity

The most solid contribution to the understanding of the passive-aggressive personality in transactional analysis literature has been made by Schiff and Schiff in their 1971 article on "Passivity." They describe the passivity syndrome as resulting from unresolved symbiotic relationships. Normal symbiosis, the sharing of needs by both the mother and child, is necessary for healthy survival. Disruptions occur when 1) the child is not allowed to differentiate from the mother; 2) the child is separated too early; or 3) there is inadequate parenting.

The *grandiosity* of the passivity syndrome exaggerates some aspect of the self or environment in such a way as to prevent the establishment of realistic goals. Grandiosity always compensates for some sense of inadequacy.

The passive person has been reinforced for one or more of the four passive behaviors:
1) Doing nothing relevant to solving a problem.
2) Overadaptation.
3) Agitation.
4) Incapacitation or violence.

The goal of the passive behaviors is to make others so uncomfortable that they will take care of the passive person.

Passive-aggressives are seen to have "Don't be a child" and "Don't feel (especially anger)" injunctions and "Please me" counterinjunctions or drivers (Ware, 1976). Early parenting has demanded that the child give up his or her own dependent needs in order to take care of the parent and that the child suppress feelings of rage and frustration about having to do so.

Etiology—Family Structure and Early Development

In surveying the growth and development of those persons who appear in the therapist's office with a passive-aggressive personality structure two striking features emerge. First is the extreme distance that they experienced from one (usually the father) parenting figure. The distant father may be experienced as benign, but more frequently he is seen as tyrannical and emotionally cold and unfeeling. The second feature is the extent to which passive-aggressives view themselves as a special object.

Specialness: The earliest messages that passive-aggressives are aware of concern their specialness. The cause of the specialness may vary, but it is always present in their upbringing. Bill was special because of family position and wealth; Donald because he was the first son and grandson in an upper-middle-class Jewish family. Betsy was the only child of a second marriage between an older man and young woman. Jane's mother had several miscarriages before her birth. Both Ronda and Ruth were the last children their mothers were able to bear because of physical disease. John recalls being reminded many times that his mother had aborted a second child in order to devote her time to him because he was so important to her. Thus, the child becomes a prized object to the mother.

The mother and father of the passive-aggressive personality are usually involved in a symbiotic relationship. Father's Parent and Adult ego states do all of the rule-giving and thinking for the family. Mother's

Figure 3. Ego State Symbiosis

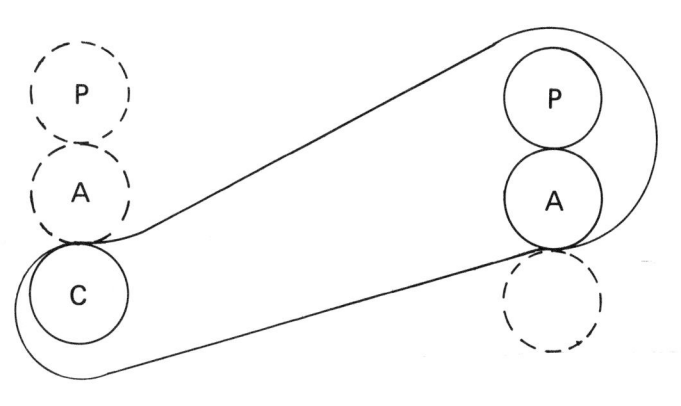

Child ego state displays feelings and interprets and carries out the messages from on high. Thus, they make one complete person (see Figure 3).

The mothering of the infant may best be described as "over"—overanxious, overdoting, overattentive, especially during the first six to eight months of normal autism and symbiosis. The mother or nurse maid is totally involved with the infant to the exclusion of everything else. The problem is that the caretaker is operating out of a Child ego state and does not use Adult reality-testing to determine the needs of the infant. It is almost as though the infant is a doll to be dressed, caressed and walked by the caretaker as the mood dictates. Photographs of clients as infants display them as elaborately overdressed and, when in the arms of the caretaker, rather stiffly held on display. When asked if father welcomed their birth, passive-aggressive clients usually respond, "Yes, so that I could keep my mother company."

Since the young child's perception of the world is primarily situational, his/her ability to comprehend the relationships of the grownups in the environment on an intentional or feeling level is severely limited (Flapan, 1968). Thus, his/her place in the family structure is perceived on the simplistic level illustrated in Figure 4. The "You are mine" message from the primary caretaker implies possession or objectness—"itness" rather than humanness. "Be with Mom" is usually evidenced by the lack of interest that the fathers of passive-aggressive personalities display toward the infant.

Mahler (1979) sees a sense of identity as maintained by comparison and contrast. This sense of identity begins to form through sensorimotor

Figure 4. Early Script Messages

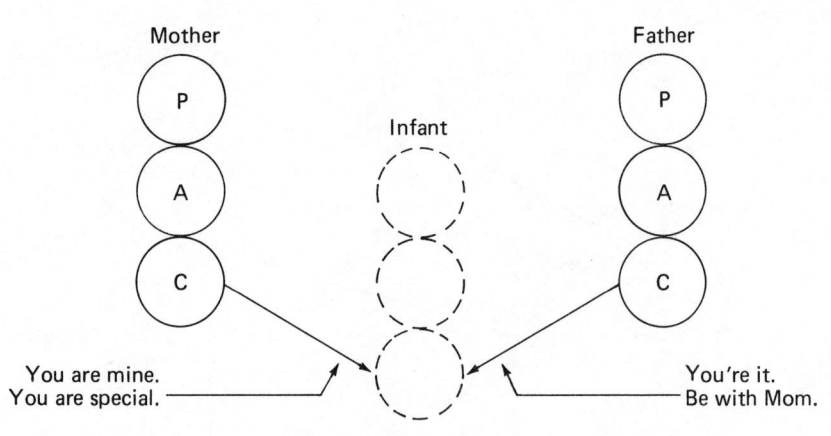

Mother   Father

P   Infant   P

A   A

C   C

You are mine.   You're it.
You are special. ——————————   —————— Be with Mom.

activity in the symbiotic phase. Self-identity is heightened when the child enters the stage of locomotion (about 6-15 months) and begins differentiating himself or herself from the mother. In normal development the junior toddler receives praise and enthusiasm from the caretaker at this point. In passive-aggressive development the "over" mother follows the baby about or even attempts to restrict mobility.

Mother's anxiety and displeasure about the separation that is beginning to take place conveys the message that the world is a dangerous place. Mother's intrusiveness also interferes with the development of a clear self-image and a sense of security in physical mastery. Many passive-aggressive clients are physically unsure of themselves and their ability to manipulate physical materials is usually stiff and clumsy. They are seldom physically active, although if given the opportunity they will criticize themselves constantly about weight, body image, looks, etc.

The internal conflict that is produced in the Child ego state between the sense of omnipotence and the sense conveyed by mother that the world is a dangerous place leads to the "stuck" feelings frequently experienced by passive-aggressives. This conflict also produces internal confusion as to how to identify oneself in the world: "I am helpless"; "I am wonderful"; "I am an object to be moved about."

Mother's rejection of independent functioning and insistence upon the child's clinging to her leads to the "hostile dependency" (Mahler, 1979, p. 69), which is one of the earmarks of the passive-aggressive personality. In an effort to keep mother available, the two-year-old alternates between wooing and temper tantrum behaviors. The extreme

egocentricity of the mothers of passive-aggressive clients leads to the constant misreading of the cues the child emanates. Therefore, the child learns to read mother's cues and adapt to mother's needs and feelings. When this does not succeed in keeping mother close, the child switches to tantrums.

It is at this stage of development that father enters the picture. When the young child's wooing of mother fails to produce the desired care-taking or support, great rage is expressed. The temper tantrums motivate father to tell mother to "take care of that child."

Three to Seven Years: During the three-to-seven-years age period the young child chooses an existential position, integrates and decides how to cope with the injunctions, and writes the basic script which will prescribe her games and rackets. A child in a healthy family will normally have completed her individuation and separation from mother at this phase and be ready to reach out to father, siblings, and playmates for emotional interaction. The passive-aggressive arrives at this age level with severe handicaps.

1) He believes he must feel what mother feels to get his needs met (*overadaptation*).
2) Mother likes him best when he is infantile (*doing nothing*).
3) Mother is overadapted to father.
4) Screaming and yelling will make father make mother take care of his needs (*agitation*).
5) Mother enjoys his getting father upset.

Mother and youngster are linked (in TA terms) in a Child-Child union of feelings and needs. They are also linked into a Child-Child competitive struggle for father's strokes, which mother usually wins. However, occasionally, Dad (when his peace and quiet are sufficiently disturbed) will support the youngster.

During the preschool and early school years (ages three to seven), one of the primary activities of the youngster is play, which is the procedure through which reality is constructed and tested (Butler, 1971). Passive-aggressive clients have little recollection of active social play. They remember drawing, playing with their dolls, walks with grownups, and making up games on their own. For the most part their play with other children was minimal. Most remember long hours of solitary play with occasional suggestions from mother about what to do. The usual orienting to the boundaries of what is imaginable, possible, effective, and

permissible (Erikson, 1972), which most children learn through their socio-dramatic play, was lacking. Thus, they are restricted in those interpersonal skills which one learns in the complex social negotiations required in play. The play is passive rather than active and restricts the youngster's ability to test strengths and increase competencies. Frequently, play seems oriented to entertaining mother.

In reviewing case histories of ten passive-aggressive clients, I found that few remembered playing with other children prior to school and few remembered family friends. Not needing others and looking down on others was a strong family theme. This superiority was usually enunciated by Father and supported by Mother in her attempts to keep the youngster close to her.

A high degree of secretiveness is fostered by the parents vis-à-vis other people and latched onto by the youngster as one protection from mother's intrusiveness. An existential position of I'm OK←→You're not OK is reached during these years.

Latency Age: When the child is between the ages of seven and 13, father starts to take an interest in his upbringing. Father is held up by mother's Parent as a guide to be listened to, while her Child snipes at his instructions or actively works to undermine them.

Mom also begins to "rip off" strokes from the child's achievements. Many clients report being in school plays or giving recitals where Mom's arrival was timed to make her the center of attention. Afterward, as people were stroking the performers, Mom would stand right next to the youngster and take the strokes and be excessively and noisily "proud of my child," drawing the attention to herself. Mothers are also seen as being envious of their children's accomplishments.

Figure 5. Functional Diagram with Decisions

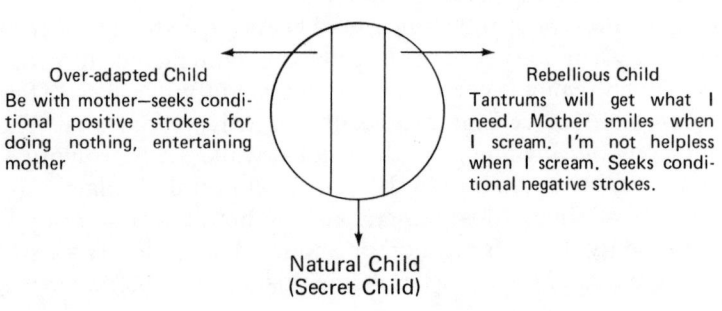

Over-adapted Child
Be with mother—seeks conditional positive strokes for doing nothing, entertaining mother

Rebellious Child
Tantrums will get what I need. Mother smiles when I scream. I'm not helpless when I scream. Seeks conditional negative strokes.

Natural Child
(Secret Child)

As a result of these conflicting messages, the passive-aggressive develops counterscript messages of "Work hard," "Be perfect," "Your father knows the world," and "Please me" on a Parent level. His earlier childhood feelings of helplessness are reinforced by the lack of adequate instruction and stimulation of thinking skills and he develops a "Don't think" injunction. A major script decision is "Why bother to do; Mom gets the strokes anyway." Although the father's Parent instructions sound solid and contrary to the early script messages, in actuality they reinforce them. Mother's Parent clearly supports the earlier messages and is usually viewed by the child as useless and ineffectual in dealing with the world. The Adult modeling of how to follow the script messages is seen as particularly strong for supporting ineffectual, nonthinking behavior and particularly useless for coping with external realities, such as school work and social relationships.

Adolescence: The basic patterns of behavior laid down in early childhood and latency become more pronounced during the teen years. If a passive-aggressive functions from the overadapted part of his Child, he will perform well in school while complaining bitterly about injustices, unfairnesses, etc. Most report few friends during high school. A few report friendships, but closer examination reveals that they are very competitive. The counterscript has held for some clients all the way through graduate and professional schools. These clients experience feelings of uncertainty about their ability and have great difficulty managing their studies. They will delay and delay starting assignments and then rush into them with a great show of work. However, the work is not thought out or planned with any sense of priorities. This delay/rush tactic carries over into their work life as grownups.

If a teenager (supported by Mom) has been involved in a power struggle with Dad during the latency years, he will function from his Rebellious Child. These are the ones who become more resistive when pressured to perform, who play "Late Paper" games with teachers and go into temper tantrums when their justifications don't work, and who "become expert at thwarting . . . their parents' plans, good intentions and actions" (Long, 1975).

During adolescence the typical games (such as Blemish, Uproar, Look How Hard I'm Trying, Schlemiel, and Why Don't You, Yes But) of the passive-aggressive family emerge full force. Games substitute for intimacy in the family circle and provide a structure for exchanging strokes and filling social time. They also help each member maintain internal psychological equilibrium (Berne, 1964).

Passive-Aggressive Games

Blemish is played as follows: Mom finds fault with the neighbors, the kid's friends, Dad, and the teachers at school. In addition to warding off her own depression and avoiding friendships, which might reveal her own deficiencies, her game binds the child to her by making him discount and look down on others. This reinforces the I'm OK↔You're not OK (I'm good↔they're bad) position. The dynamic behind the Blemish game is sexual insecurity (Berne, 1964).

Uproar games are played in families to avoid feelings of sexual intimacy. Initially played by Mom and Dad, the game is picked up by the passive-aggressive in adolescence to avoid sexual feelings toward a parent. It can also be initiated by the parent to avoid sexual feelings toward an adolescent. Following angry Parental accusations of each other, the final move in an Uproar game is played when the two players march out of the room in opposite directions, slamming doors behind them. Each then goes off to sulk alone.

The passive-aggressive learns to reestablish contact with Mother through *Look How Hard I'm Trying* and *Schlemiel* games. The dynamics of *Look How Hard I'm Trying* are anal passivity. *Look How Hard I'm Trying* provides the player the internal psychological freedom from guilt for his/her aggression and the "legitimate" reason for evading responsibilities. It also reinforces the Child feelings of helplessness.

In *Schlemiel*, the dynamics are anal aggression. The player gets the psychological pleasure of making messes and avoiding punishment for them. Existentially the player's sense of specialness at getting away with things blamelessly is reinforced.

The passive-aggressive person learns to play *Why Don't You, Yes But* and *Now I've Got You, You Son of a Bitch* with Dad. *Why Don't You, Yes But* enables the player to get reassurance of Parental interest and frustrate the Parent at the same time. Since Dad is the person who has issued the *Don't Be Close* injunctions, *Why Don't You, Yes But* enables the player to make some contact under the guise of discussions about hobbies, work, school. At the same time, the player gets justification for her belief that everyone wants to dominate her. This belief fuels her resentment at Dad for leaving her to mother's whims.

Now I've Got You, You Son of a Bitch provides another opportunity for recognition from Dad through belligerent exchanges while furthering the belief that people can't be trusted. *Now I've Got You, You Son of a Bitch* provides a justification for the feelings of rage the kid feels because Dad can walk in and get Mother's attention at any time.

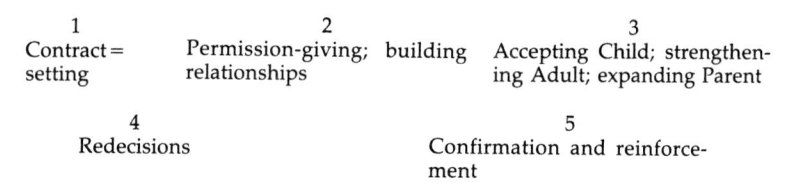

Figure 6. Stages of Treatment with Passive-Aggressives

Eric Berne (1964) defined game players as two types of people: sulks (men angry with mother or females angry at father) and jerks (people overly sensitive to parental influence). One problem with passive-aggressive clients is that they are both. Sulk and jerk are other names for the Rebellious and Overadapted Child, respectively.

A high proportion of passive-aggressive persons' time is spent in game playing. Their Adult data-processing and Child spontaneity are so disturbed by their basic script beliefs that it is difficult to respond to non-gamey transactions.

A racket is a substitute feeling that replaces a more genuine feeling which was prohibited in the past (English, 1971). The basic racket feelings of passive-aggressive clients are anger and helplessness. These are learned from their parents and substituted for almost all other feelings. The racket feelings expressed and the games played are derivatives of the existential position and the early script messages. The unconscious script motto is, "I'm pretending I'm a prince/princess, but I don't really believe it." Thus, every small setback produces feelings of helplessness and rage.

THERAPEUTIC STRATEGY AND PROCESS

The first stage of treatment is the establishment of a workable therapeutic contract. This may take several individual sessions, since the contract must be both specific and possible. This is a general rule of thumb in TA treatment and is absolutely essential with passive-aggressives.

The first step in this stage is to insist that the client decide what she wishes to change about her life. Therapists who get seduced into setting goals for the client immediately move into a Rescuer role, thus permitting the client to be a Victim.

Refusing to think and set goals for the patient gives a clear message that you see him as a grown person who is capable of being in charge

of his own life and starts defusing possibilities of *Look How Hard I'm Trying* and *Why Don't You, Yes But.*

Next, ask how the client will find a way to find fault (Blemish) with the therapist and be justified in quitting treatment. Confronting the possibilities of *Blemish* puts the client on notice that, although you will consider it a shame for him to quit treatment, you, the therapist, plan to stay OK. It also gives the opportunity for an agreement that the client will deliver complaints in an Adult manner and not from a Persecutor role.

Last, check suicide, homicide, and going crazy fantasies. If such fantasies are active, no suicide, no homicide and no psychosis contracts (Goulding, 1979) must be established before proceeding with treatment.

Therapist: Do you ever think about going crazy?
Harold: Yeah, I imagine I'm catatonic.
Therapist: How would you go catatonic?
Harold: I don't know, I just wouldn't move.
Therapist: Show me how you wouldn't move.
Harold (curling up in a fetal position on sofa): Like this.
Therapist: Then what would happen?
Harold: My mother would have to take care of me and stop being a martyr.
Therapist: If you collapse and go home, she'll have even more of an excuse to be a martyr.
Harold (suddenly sitting up): Then, I'll kill myself and she'll be sorry (said in a very angry tone).
Therapist: No, she'll have more of an excuse to be a martyr.
Harold: Then you'll be sorry.
Therapist: I haven't known you long enough.
Harold: Then what can I do?
Therapist: Make a contract to stay sane and solve problems.

The severity of the pathology can be assessed by the willingness or unwillingness of the client to deal with no suicide, homicide or psychosis contracts. Too ready and nonthoughtful agreement should be confronted as an overadaptation, which is highly likely to be followed after years of work by vengeful breaking of the overadapted Child promise. Frequently, the patient is told to go home and give some serious thought to his commitment to staying alive, well, and out of jail. This neatly and nonpejoratively puts the responsibility back on the client's shoulders.

It further serves notice that this particular therapist is not interested or impressed by easy acquiescence. Finally, should a client refuse to make any one or all of these contracts, he should firmly and politely be asked to seek treatment elsewhere. He should be reminded that throwing away a life is extremely wasteful and that you as a therapist do not want to see your time, energy, and caring go to waste.

These initial stages of treatment allow the therapist to evaluate the level of confusion of the client and allow the client an opportunity to appraise the therapist (Berne, 1966). Additionally, they convey the message to the client that the therapist is:

1) concerned about the client's well-being;
2) respectful of the client's boundaries;
3) does not need anything emotionally from the client.

These are important messages to convey to all clients and imperative with passive-aggressive clients, whose emotional needs have always been secondary to those of their parents.

Many clients will quit at this point and go in search of a therapist who is willing to think for them. Arthur called the therapist to make an appointment after reading one of the TA books. In the process of the initial interview, he revealed that he had been therapy with his previous therapist for ten years.

Therapist: What do you want from therapy now?
Arthur: Whatever you say.
Therapist: I am not willing to tell you what you want. I want you to think about what you need in your life.

Arthur canceled his second appointment, announcing that he was returning to his previous therapist.

In the first few weeks of group attendance, doing nothing or overadaptive passive behaviors may emerge. It is best to observe these behaviors for two or three sessions. This gives the client a chance to observe the therapist in action and settle into the group. Observing without comment allows the therapist to become aware of the nonverbal reactions of the client to her and other group members. It also gives a sense of how long the client will persist in doing nothing or overadapting before escalating into agitated behavior, usually in the form of temper tantrums or attacks on the therapist or other group members.

The passive-aggressive client who initiates contact by overadaptation will attempt to hook the therapist or other group members into telling her what to do. The treatment intervention with overadapted clients is to ask them to agree to do everything you instruct them to do in the group session. After this agreement is reached the therapist gives two or three pointless instructions each session until the patient refuses to comply. This is the first step out of the overadaptation and the client should be stroked for thinking for herself:

Therapist: Ronda will you go in the bathroom and get a cup of water?
(Ronda complies and returns with the water.)
Therapist: Thank you. Take the water back to the bathroom and pour it out.
(Ronda does so and returns.)
Therapist: How do you feel?
Ronda: A little silly, I don't understand why you made me do that.
Therapist: I didn't make you, you agreed to do so. You think about why you agreed and let me know what you think in 15 minutes.
Therapist (after 20 minutes have passed without Ronda speaking up): Ronda will you go to the typewriter in the secretary's office and type out the Star Spangled Banner?
Ronda: You're crazy. That's the dumbest thing I ever heard of. What kind of therapist are you?
(Shift of ego states from overadapted Child to Critical Parent.)
Therapist: You may not call me names. If you do not want to do what I ask tell me straight.
Ronda (after a long pause): I will not type out that silly song.
Therapist: Congratulations on thinking and deciding for yourself. Will you continue to think for yourself in this group and begin by deciding what you want from therapy?

Do nothing clients (passive-aggressives who are looking for an excuse to unleash their anger) will sit in the treatment group like lumps. With a look of pained resignation, they will silently wait for the therapist to get busy reading their mind. This silence is the first move in a Now I've Got You game which will justify their leaving therapy. If the therapist gets hooked by the silent *Con* and (like mother) starts trying to figure out what the client wants, he is trapped. The therapist can now feel unappreciated and be angry with the client and move into an Uproar game with him. The client is justified in walking out of treatment because the therapist is silly and ineffective.

Instead of attempting to draw the client into the group, the therapist

needs to cross the silent challenge from an Adult ego state. This will sometimes be sufficient to engage the client's Adult.

Some clients will escalate their passive behaviors from doing nothing to agitation. Agitation must be stopped by a firm Parent ego state or it will escalate into violence or incapacitation. For example, consider Mike in Figure 7. The firm Parent to Child transaction at the end of this

Figure 7. Stopping Agitation

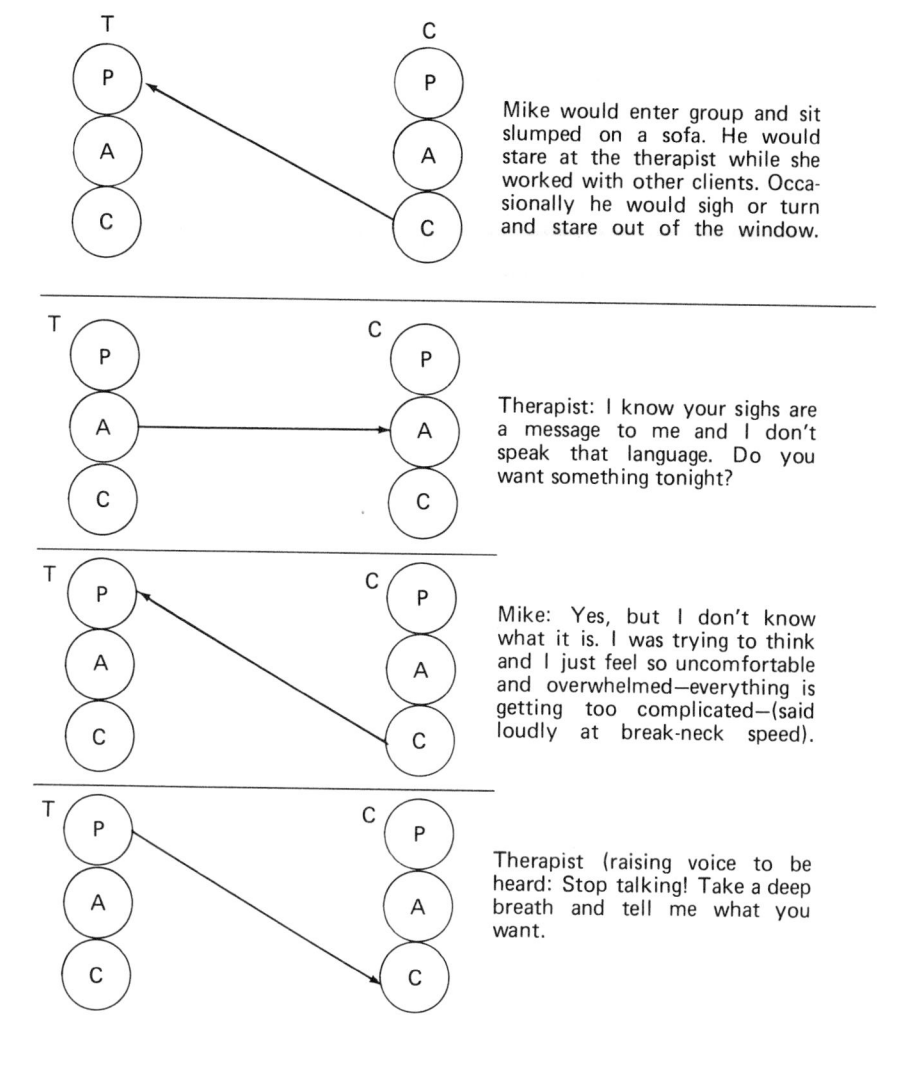

Mike would enter group and sit slumped on a sofa. He would stare at the therapist while she worked with other clients. Occasionally he would sigh or turn and stare out of the window.

Therapist: I know your sighs are a message to me and I don't speak that language. Do you want something tonight?

Mike: Yes, but I don't know what it is. I was trying to think and I just feel so uncomfortable and overwhelmed—everything is getting too complicated—(said loudly at break-neck speed).

Therapist (raising voice to be heard: Stop talking! Take a deep breath and tell me what you want.

transaction provides the structure that Mike needs without making him dependent, because *this* Parent demands thinking and feeling.

Although spoken of as occurring in the early weeks of therapy, it is important to be aware that these same sequences will occur repeatedly during the first year or so. For this reason, a therapist working with passive-aggressive personalities must be prepared for the client to fold his tent and walk away at any point that the therapist confronts non-thinking. Indeed, many will not return after the first two or three sessions when they get the first hint that they will be expected to think for themselves. The therapist's expectation of thinking confronts both the "Don't Think" injunction from father and "Don't Grow Up" injunction from mother. The more severe the pathology, the stronger the injunctions and the greater the fear of being abandoned by the internal Parent if the Child disobeys.

Permission-giving

During the first year of treatment the therapist must combine contracts to think and be aware of feelings with strong permissions aimed at the Child ego state of the client. These permissions need to begin with the later injunctions and work back to the earliest ones. They must be delivered from all three ego states of the therapist to be effective (Boyce, 1978). The sequence of permissions is as follows:

1) You can think and solve problems.
2) You can succeed.
3) You can enjoy your successes.
4) You can be aware of your own feelings.
5) You can like other people.
6) You can let other people like you.
7) You can maintain your own boundaries.
8) You can express your needs many ways.
9) You can grow up and take care of yourself.
10) You belong to yourself.
11) You are a feeling human being.

This permission-giving aimed at freeing up the feeling and thinking of the Child and Adult ego states of the client will also model a benign Parent ego state. This prepares the way for the client to update his Parent by disrupting the old messages (Kahler & Capers, 1974).

Strengthening the Adult

Getting the passive-aggressive client to give up whining, complaining, and attacking as a way of transacting with the therapist and the group members is the first task in helping him build a more effective Adult ego state. This begins to disrupt the typical roles, Victim and Persecutor, he plays in his games and will begin to disrupt the games. Each time game-playing begins, the therapist must stop it. Asking what kind of response the client wants from the therapist and other group members is usually effective. Alternatively, the therapist can ask what the presented complaints or people have to do with the client's meeting her therapy contract. This forces the client to stop agitating and formulate problems clearly.

Donald: My boss is so stupid. He never knows what's going on. He acts like I'm a total child. His feedback is less than useless. I might as well be working for a cretin.
Therapist: What do you want from me right now?
Donald: I don't know.
Therapist: What is the problem between you and your boss?
Donald: He's threatening to dock my pay if I'm late again.

Next the client needs to get social control over the behaviors that she uses to sabotage herself in work, school, and other reality situations. Ordinarily, social control would be the first stage of treatment. However, when working with passive-aggressive personalities it is more important for the therapist to establish a relationship with the client first. Attempting to establish a relationship with the therapist and to establish social control over her behaviors at the same time will throw the client into a state of confusion.

To begin with social control contracts when the passive-aggressive client first enters treatment sets up too many opportunities for Look How Hard I'm Trying and Schlemiel games. These games will replay the childhood stroke patterns (conditional negative strokes for messing up and conditional positive strokes for trying hard to keep contracts), reinforce the script injunctions, and push the therapist into reinforcing the Try Hard and Please Me messages.

As the client starts establishing social control in outside situations, she will resume some of the earlier passive behaviors with the therapist. There will be a period of missed appointments, late arrivals for group

and individual appointments, late payments, and long silences in group. This is a time for the therapist to be extremely scrupulous about ending appointments exactly on time, billing promptly, and ignoring silences.

Ruth did not work in group from 8:00 p.m. until 9:55 p.m. (the group ended at 10:00 p.m.). She had made comments and been involved when a few others worked. Then she announced that she wanted to work.

Therapist: We have five minutes.
Ruth: What difference does it make?
Therapist: This group ends in five minutes.
Ruth: You should have let me know time was running out.
Therapist: It is your responsibility to keep track of time.
Ruth: This is a serious problem that I've got to solve tonight.
Therapist: Ruth, I am not a mind reader. Since you have been here for
     two hours, interacting with others and not asking for anything,
     there is no way I could know you wanted time tonight.
Ruth: Well, I'm asking now.
Therapist: You are too late. The group ends at 10:00.

It is vital for the therapist to set firm Parent limits and give precise Adult reminders about contract terms. If Ruth had sensed one moment's hesitation or justification from the Child ego state of the therapist, she would have escalated into an immediate temper tantrum and begun loudly to attack the therapist. The therapist must not permit attacks from a vengeful, rebellious Child. Instead, the transactions must be crossed until the client expresses the feelings in a straight and direct manner.

Expressing feelings directly is very frightening to the Child of the passive-aggressive, who fears immediate reprisals for not overadapting and feeling what mother feels. So, the therapist must follow up the client's expression of feeling with a confirmation of the okayness of differing.

The following week, Ruth was the first person to work in the group:
Ruth: I've been thinking all weekend and I think you were very un-
     professional and irresponsible last week.
Therapist: I will not let you call me names. If you have a complaint, I'm
     willing to hear it.
Ruth: You're supposed to make sure we all work and tell us about the
     time.
Therapist: I will listen to you tell me your feelings.
Ruth: You . . .
Therapist: Stop. Begin your sentence with I feel.

(For about ten minutes Ruth kept beginning sentences with "you should," "you don't like me," "you are supposed to," etc. Each time the therapist would stop her, repeating the instructions.)

Therapist: I am willing to listen to your feelings.

Ruth: I feel angry that you wouldn't let me work last week.

Therapist: I hear you and I understand your feelings. I like for you to tell me straight how you feel.

Ruth (beginning to cry): Well, next time it'll be all right. (Like most passive-aggressives, she believes that she is so special that someone knowing what she wants will produce it.)

Therapist: No, you are still responsible to make sure you have time to work. You are angry that I would not do what you wanted last week. I hear that feeling and I will say no again if you want to work at 9:55 this week.

Ruth: Oh!

Therapist: Do you believe that we can feel differently about something and both be OK?

Ruth: No. I think you're mad at me for being angry with you.

Therapist: No. If I had let you attack me or force me into working last week, I would probably feel resentful. Since I didn't, I feel fine about you.

Ruth: Even though I'm mad at you?

Therapist: Yes. Do you believe that we can feel differently? Agree to disagree and be OK with each other?

Ruth: That's hard. I'm not sure.

Therapist: I am sure that I feel OK about you even when we disagree.

Because of the slogan-ridden parenting experienced in latency age, most passive-aggressives have poor planning and management skills. A part of strengthening the Adult is helping them to evaluate what skills they do and don't have. Once the evaluation is complete, they can begin to systematically acquire skills they need for living effectively in the world. Time management and realistic goal-setting are usually the weakest areas. Being able to set a goal, thinking through the steps for attaining it, setting aside the time for accomplishing each step, and then taking each step in turn until the goal is accomplished are essential for a sense of accomplishment and productivity. The therapist must now do what the parents did not do in latency age—give the permission and teach the skills for productivity through systematic instruction, while allowing and accepting feelings.

As the client gains social control of her games and functions more

successfully in work and social situations, the amount of positive stroking she receives will increase. The first reaction is typically to see the stroking as plastic or to pass it on to the therapist. "They only want me to come in on time, they don't really care about me," or "I couldn't have done it without you" are frequently heard at this juncture in treatment.

It is important to confront the rejection of the strokes and help the client to accept the strokes as being due to her efforts. Another increase in stroking comes about with increased competence in dealing with basic life situations.

This increase in stroking drives the first wedge in the enmeshed family structure the client carries in her head. The internal Parents begin to object to all of the changes and the Child becomes frightened. The grown-up fear is exactly the same fear experienced in early childhood when threatened with parental abandonment and produces a crisis in therapy.

Harold: I don't know what you've done to me. I feel worse this week than I did before I started therapy last year.

Therapist: What are you feeling?

Harold: I don't know. I can't sleep. It's hard to think. My stomach hurts. I'm going around in circles.

Therapist: What are you feeling?

Harold: I'm just upset.

Therapist: What does upset feel like? Describe your feelings.

(Note that Harold has great difficulty verbalizing feelings. Remember that the racket feelings are anger and helplessness.)

Harold: I am anxious all of the time?

Therapist: What are you afraid of?

Harold: I don't know. I'm just afraid something terrible is going to happen and I don't know what to do.

Therapist: Harold, put the part of you that wants to change in this chair and have him talk to the Harold who is afraid to change.

Moving to Gestalt work enables Harold to integrate the fear as his feeling and enables the therapist to make an alliance with the Natural Child who wants to grow up. At this juncture in therapy, Harold will work hard to make himself and the therapist not OK. The therapist must refuse all invitations to either attack Harold or collapse with him. Using her own Parental ego state, she continues to give the message, "I know you are an OK human being whether you know it or not." Since this is the first time Harold has heard this message, he will resist it by

protesting that he is not perfect, that he doesn't know how to figure out what people want, etc. The therapist must resist all such invitations and firmly stroke Harold for growth, change, and health.

Harold: I'm terrible. I can't do anything right. Every time I try to figure out what my girlfriend wants, I can't.

Therapist: You are not terrible. You can figure things out.

(Harold goes on protesting about how bad he is.)

Therapist: I am not going to waste time arguing. Every time I say you are OK as a human being, you say you're not. There's no point arguing when I know I'm right.

Harold: Actually, I want you to win the fight.

Therapist: I've already won it. You are an OK human being. If you tell your father to bug off and stop making static you will know you're OK also.

The permission to experience and accept feelings must now become stronger. The experience of group therapy, where one hears a variety of feelings being expressed and accepted, is very useful in helping the passive-aggressive client expand his limited awareness and expression of feelings. It also helps the client understand the difference between being aware of a feeling and how he chooses to express the feeling. A feeling is a personal reaction to something said or done by the client or another. By understanding this, a client breaks up the Child fantasy that feelings are mysterious things that sweep through one from the outside and learns that it is important to be aware of all feelings.

The insistence upon acceptance and expression of feelings in a straight way moves the client out of the Victim and Persecutor roles. This enables the client to make a more real human contact with himself, the therapist, and other group members. Since things ("its") do not have feelings, we also begin to break up the view of the Child as an "it," which the passive-aggressive has carried all of his life.

Expanding the Parent

In order for the Child of a person to maintain feelings of humanness and well-being and for his Adult to function without internal interference, he must update his Parent. This updating makes the changes he has made syntonic in all three ego states. A redistribution of energy from the Critical to the Nurturing Parent (Dusay, 1972) must take place. Three steps are useful in this process:

1) Report in group everytime nurturing support (both in and out of group) is experienced by describing what the nurturing person did.
2) Give nurturing support to people in group each week; get feedback from group members on how he sounds and restate the support until he is heard as nurturing.
3) Learn how to nurture oneself by getting care-taking, setting aside time to check out feelings, asking directly in group and at home for support.

When they enter therapy, passive-aggressive clients tend to see their mothers as helpless and ineffectual and their fathers as cold and distant. It is important to begin a reevaluation of Mom and Dad so that whatever was OK about them can be affirmed (James, 1974). In this way whatever skills and competencies the parents did have become more internally available. The stage is also set for forgiving the parents and accepting their humanness (Erskine, 1973). Next, the client can observe other people's parenting and decide which of these behaviors he wants to add to his Parent and begin to practice them. Developing alternative internal Parent responses to his own Child enables him to feel safer and more secure in the world.

Redecisions

Since each person made decisions in childhood about how he would constrict himself in order to get his needs met in his family, he can reevaluate that decision at any point and redecide to do things differently. Doing so means that a client assumes responsibility for who she is and how she will get her needs met in the world. "The client experiences the child part of self, enjoys his childlike qualities and creates fantasy scenes in which he can safely give up the constricting decisions he made in childhood" (Goulding & Goulding, 1979). Each *redecision* made moves the client closer to the autonomy for which he has been receiving permission and preparation throughout therapy.

As Mike worked in therapy and became more aware of his internal dialogues, he realized that every time he did a model (he was a model maker for an architectural firm) he would hear his father's voice finding fault with it. No matter how much outside information Mike received about the quality of his work, he still felt dissatisfied. He remembered that every time he brought home his report card his father would glance at the list of grades, which were always A's and a few B's and say, "It

could be better." He was invited to be that little boy and tell his father how he felt.

Mike: I worked hard and those are good grades. I don't have to be perfect.
Mike (as Father switching to Father's chair): You do as I say. I know you need to make good grades if you're going to grow up and be successful in the world.
Mike: I am successful. My work is good and I know how to judge when it's good. You don't know anything about what I do. I do not have to be perfect.

After the redecision is made an Adult list of standards for judging a model's completion and quality and began to use it in his work. The conflict he experienced between his Parent and Child is a *first degree impasse* (Goulding & Goulding, 1979) and is based on counterinjunctions.

An impasse occurs when two or more opposing forces meet within the person and he gets stuck. A *second degree impasse* occurs when a person hits a stuck point within his Child ego state. An early decision was made in response to an injunction rather than a counterinjunction. The resolution must take place within the Child ego state.

Mike had decided that, rather than think, he would rush about looking busy. He was asked to close his eyes and be the busy person.

Mike: I'm a busy person. I'm so busy there are 20 things to do and I have to rush around all over town. I keep busy all the time.
Therapist: So that Mike will . . .
Mike: So that Mike . . . so that Mike won't think . . .
Therapist: So that you won't think about . . .
Mike: So that I won't think about how my Dad drinks and acts really stupid and tries to pretend that nothing is wrong.

Mike went on to decide that he could and would think about his family and his feelings. After the redecision, he set up an autonomy (script change) contract. The contract was stated as, "I will stop rushing around and start thinking through what I need to do."

A *third degree impasse* occurs when a person experiences herself as always having been whatever it is she experiences. A person has accepted an injunction or attribution at such an early age that she simply experiences herself as being that way. With passive-aggressive clients

their *itness* and *specialness* are experienced that way. To work through the impasse, Mike had to take both sides of the me/not-me dialogue. "I'm a nothing—I'm a human being." Once the decision to be a human being was made, a lot of the bottled-up Natural Child feelings begin to emerge.

Impasses occur in therapy as clients begin to accept the permissions they are receiving from the therapist. The old decisions and the new freedoms produce the internal stuckness of an impasse. Most impasse and redecision work is done through Gestalt techniques in which the person enacts both of the polarities represented in the impasse.

The third degree impasses for passive-aggressives follow:

I'm an it	—	I'm a human being
I'm helpless	—	I have power
I'm special	—	I'm an average person

These represent the core beliefs about the self and influence every feeling and action of the passive-aggressive client. Their resolution is essential if he is to attain autonomy.

Mike had been in therapy for about two years. He left after making a redecision to think and figure out what he wanted. Many other issues were unresolved. He returned to therapy when his wife threatened to leave him. His fear brought all of the underlying beliefs to the surface. He would enter each treatment session and sit in the most distant seat from the therapist. After sitting and staring at the therapist for two or three minutes, he would angrily begin.

Mike: I'm awful. I'm a terrible thing. I wreck everything. I don't work right. Everything turns to dust. No matter what I do I can't get it right. I tried so hard to make this relationship work.

Therapist: Where did you get the notion you were a thing?

Mike: I don't know, but I've always thought that all my life.

Therapist: Be the part of you that thinks you're a thing and describe yourself.

Mike: I'm a thing. I have no shape. I get moved around wherever anybody wants. I have no feelings. I'm like a machine . . . (after a few moment's silence he begins to tear up).

Therapist: Things don't cry. Sit in this chair and be the person who cries and talk to the thing.

Mike: I have feelings. I hurt. I'm a person. I'm alive. I feel all kinds of

things. (His body becomes very rigid, his jaw tightens and he sits very woodenly.)

Therapist: Now you're being a thing again. Move back to the other chair and respond.

(After several moves back and forth between thingness and humanness, Mike sits in the human chair.)

Therapist: You can decide how to be a human being and have all of your feelings, good and bad.

Mike: I want to be a human being. But I don't feel safe. I need the thing to feel safe. If I'm an it I don't hurt.

Therapist: Your feelings can make you safe. Tell the it in the other chair that you don't need to be an it anymore and thank it for the protection.

Mike: Thank you. I don't need you anymore to be safe. I'm a person not a thing. I have feelings . . . I have feelings.

Therapist: Say all of that all over again.

Mike: I'm a person. I have feelings. I'm a human being. I have feelings. I have feelings (sits quietly with tears in his eyes).

Therapist: How are you feeling right now?

Mike: Relieved and scared.

Much confirmation and support for his newfound humanness was needed as Mike moved on in therapy. He got this from the therapist and his group and successfully completed therapy three years later.

Confirmation and Reinforcement

Each client in therapy needs confirmation of his or her newfound wellness and reinforcement of new patterns of behavior. This is especially so with passive-aggressive clients, who see changing as breaking up their unity with mother, thus losing the only human closeness they have experienced. Since they have seldom experienced the give and take of friendship, they have great difficulty maintaining clear boundaries while getting their emotional needs met as a human being. Every encounter becomes an opportunity to revert to old beliefs and actions.

One of the most difficult psychological tasks is to learn the difference between being special and being an ordinary mortal. This distinction is most important for moving from an I'm OK$\longleftrightarrow$You're not OK view of the world to an I'm OK$\longleftrightarrow$You're OK view. Being an ordinary human being does not mean sacrificing uniqueness or individuality. Rather, it

means accepting that I, like all human beings, have a wide range of strengths and weaknesses, good and bad feelings, and up and down times in my life—just like everybody else.

During the final phase of treatment passive-aggressive clients need the following:

1) Strokes for succeeding and thinking.
2) Support as they reach out to build friendships and intimate relationships.
3) Acceptance of feelings.
4) Reinforcement of humanness.
5) Insistence upon okayness of self and others.
6) Permission to be well and leave therapy.

The consolidation of their skills and changes will take at least a year and perhaps longer.

In a transactional analysis framework, cure is defined as an attainment of autonomy. Personal autonomy is manifested by the use of three capacities: awareness, spontaneity, and intimacy. Awareness requires living in the here-and-now, with alertness to both internal and external signals. Spontaneity means the freedom to chose options and express feelings. Intimacy is the spontaneous, game-free candidness of an aware person. It is a function of the Natural Child (Berne, 1964). The central therapeutic question for passive-aggressive clients during the final stages of treatment is, "How are you building a joyous, feeling, thinking life for yourself?" When they know how to do this and have developed the confidence to weather the setbacks and adversities which are met from day to day, treatment is over.

REFERENCES

Berne, E. *Games people play.* New York: Grove Press, 1964.
Berne, E. *Principles of group treatment.* New York: Grove Press, 1966.
Berne, E. *What do you say after you say hello? The psychology of human destiny.* New York: Bantam Books, 1973.
Boyce, M. Twelve permissions. *Transactional Analysis Journal*, 1978, *8*, (1), 30-33.
Butler, A. Areas of recent research in early childhood education. *Childhood Education*, 1971, *48*, 143-147.
Dusay, J. Egograms and the constancy hypothesis. *Transactional Analysis Journal*, 1972, 2 (3), 37-41.
English, F. The substitution factor: Rackets and real feelings. *Transactional Analysis Journal*, 1971, *1* (4), 27-32.
Erikson, E. Play and actuality. In M. W. Piers (Ed.), *Play and development: A symposium.* New York: Norton, 1972.

Erskine, R. Six stages of treatment. *Transactional Analysis Journal*, 1973, 3 (3), 17-18.

Flapan, D. *Children's understanding of social interaction.* New York: Teacher's College Press, 1968.

Goulding, M., & Goulding, R. *Changing lives through redecision therapy.* New York: Brunner/Mazel, 1979.

James, M. Self-reparenting: Theory and process. *Transactional Analysis Journal*, 1974, 4 (3), 32-39.

Kahler, T., & Capers, H. The miniscript. *Transactional Analysis Journal*, 1974, 4 (1), 26-42.

Karpman, S. Fairy tales and script drama analysis. *Transactional Analysis Journal*, 1968, 7 (26), 39-43.

Long, W. Adolescent maturation: A clinical overview. *Postgraduate Medicine*, March 1975, 54-56.

Mahler, M. *Selected papers of Margaret Mahler, M.D., Vol. II.* New York: Jason Aronson, 1979.

Schiff, A. & Schiff, J. Passivity. *Transactional Analysis Journal*, 1971, 1 (1), 71-78.

Steiner, C. Script and counterscript. *Transactional Analysis Bulletin*, 1966, 5 (18), 133-35.

Steiner, C. *Scripts people live: Transactional analysis of life scripts.* New York: Grove Press, 1974.

Ware, P. Analysis of personality types. Conference Presentation, International Transactional Analysis Association, August, 1976.

4

Passive-Aggressiveness: A Cognitive-Behavioral Approach

David D. Burns
and Norman Epstein

Cognitive approaches to the assessment and treatment of psychological disorders emphasize the roles that distorted thinking plays in mediating dysfunctional emotional and behavioral responses to life events. Understanding a syndrome such as passive-aggressiveness involves attention to both the obstructional, resistant behaviors that characterize it and the thought processes that guide these responses. A cognitive model of passive-aggressiveness suggests that responses such as resistance to other people's requests and needs are mediated by the meanings the individual attaches to those external demands. Distortions in these meanings that lead a person to be oppositional can include systematic errors in logic or information processing, unrealistic beliefs and standards about one's own behavior and those of others, and a view of oneself as ineffective in achieving one's goals in interpersonal relationships.

This chapter outlines the basic principles of cognitive therapy, presents a conceptualization of passive-aggressiveness within a cognitive framework, and describes the nature of the passive-aggressive person's relationships with significant others and in therapy. We have provided clinical examples as well as specific suggestions for working with pas-

sive-aggressive patients. In addition, recent research on cognitive and behavioral factors in passive-aggression are described, and directions for future research to clarify the nature of this problematic way of relating to other people are proposed.

At a behavioral level, passive-aggressiveness is characterized by resistance to the performance of work and social roles. The DSM-III description of passive-aggressiveness as a personality disorder emphasizes how such resistance results in the individual being ineffective in these roles because his or her procrastination, stubbornness, and intentional inefficiency alienate others and impede the achievement of his or her own goals. Millon (1969, 1981) attributes the low interrater reliability of this DSM diagnosis to the restriction of the definition to oppositional behavior; he extends it to include impulsiveness, inconsistent behavior, irritable moodiness, and the frequent expression of discontent and fault-finding.

Phenomenologically, passive-aggressive individuals are characterized as pessimistic, low in self-esteem, disappointed in their lives, envious of others' good fortune, and resentful at what they perceive to be their victimization by other people. Millon (1981) describes them as "actively ambivalent," unable to gauge what strategy (e.g., obedient dependence versus assertive independence) will best achieve the rewards they seek from their environment. It has been suggested by writers such as Millon (1981) that the passive-aggressive individual's inconsistency has its etiology in exposure to contradictory parental attitudes and inconsistent childrearing practices. Inconsistent parental responses produce conflicting attitudes toward self (e.g., view of the self as competent versus incompetent) and vacillating behavior based on indecisiveness about the appropriateness of each strategy. In terms of cognitive theory, this developmental process can be conceptualized as the formation of basic underlying assumptions that the world is an unfair, unpredictable place in which one is likely to be disappointed and in which one must be prepared to shift one's approach to people at the first sign that they will fail to meet one's needs. The passive-aggressive individual's inhibition of assertive behavior may be due to guilt-inducing schemata such as "It is not acceptable to express my desires and my anger directly," helplessness-inducing schemata such as "Nothing I do will get me what I want from other people," and anxiety-inducing schemata such as "If I express my desires or my anger, other people will retaliate against

me." Passive-aggressiveness thus serves as one means of minimizing one's expected losses from direct expressiveness while still communicating one's resentment through negativistic, oppositional behavior. Unfortunately, the person's assumption that others do not appreciate him or her can be reinforced in a self-fulfilling prophecy as he or she alienates people with such behavior (see Figure 1).

Cognitive theory (e.g., Beck, 1976; Beck, Rush, Shaw, & Emery, 1979; Burns, 1980) postulates that when an environmental event (e.g., the

Figure 1. The Self-Defeating Cognitive-Behavioral Cycle of Passive-Aggression

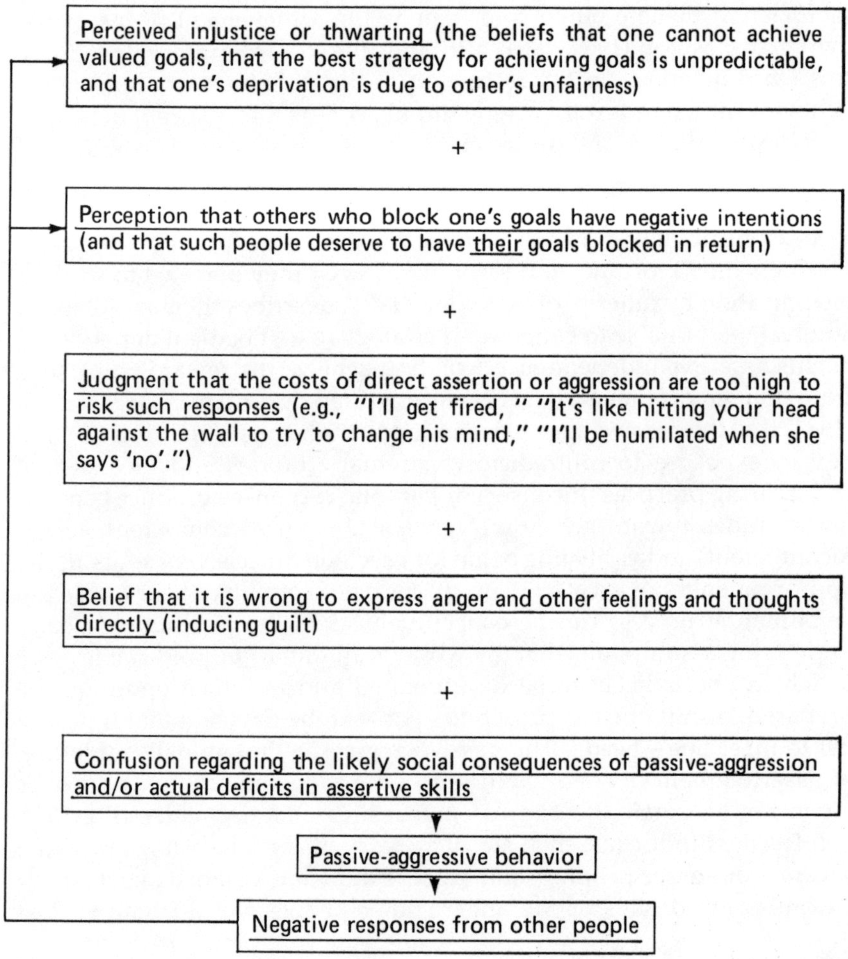

Perceived injustice or thwarting (the beliefs that one cannot achieve valued goals, that the best strategy for achieving goals is unpredictable, and that one's deprivation is due to other's unfairness)

+

Perception that others who block one's goals have negative intentions (and that such people deserve to have their goals blocked in return)

+

Judgment that the costs of direct assertion or aggression are too high to risk such responses (e.g., "I'll get fired, " "It's like hitting your head against the wall to try to change his mind," "I'll be humiliated when she says 'no'.")

+

Belief that it is wrong to express anger and other feelings and thoughts directly (inducing guilt)

+

Confusion regarding the likely social consequences of passive-aggression and/or actual deficits in assertive skills

Passive-aggressive behavior

Negative responses from other people

boss promotes one's colleague rather than oneself to a higher ranking job) activates a stable underlying assumption (e.g., "The world is unfair and I don't get the appreciation I deserve"), the results are negative cognitions or automatic thoughts (e.g., "He had no right to promote Fred after all I've done for him"), negative emotions (e.g., anger), and counterproductive behaviors (e.g., arriving late for work). In cases of passive-aggressiveness, the problematic expression of anger can thus involve confusion about the appropriateness of feeling the anger (influenced by schemata and distortions of thinking), and difficulty expressing appropriate anger in constructive rather than destructive ways.

Individuals who have difficulty with the expression of anger may be confused about whether their anger is valid and justified or whether it is irrational and should be modified. This issue can be confusing to therapists and researchers as well, unless a careful assessment is made of the situational factors and possible cognitive distortions eliciting the anger. Patients who are quite ashamed of their negative feelings conceivably might even utilize cognitive therapy techniques in a maladaptive manner to become less open and spontaneous. Such an individual might reason that, since much or all of his or her anger is caused by distorted cognitions, it is unhealthy. In contrast, other patients go to the opposite extreme and insist that all of their anger is valid, healthy, and justified.

Rather than trying to resolve this issue in a general way, it is usually more productive to focus on specific problems or situations that are upsetting the patient. As s/he learns how to deal with each of them more effectively, healthier attitudes will evolve.

Assessment of the appropriateness of feeling anger in a particular situation and the appropriateness of expressing anger in a particular manner can be facilitated when the therapist helps the patient explore several key questions.

Questions Regarding Cognitive Factors Influencing the Experience and Expression of Anger

1) "To what extent does my anger result from irrational, self-defeating attitudes and rigid, unrealistic expectations rather than from the reality of the situation?" Several self-defeating beliefs are commonly observed in people with excessive anger. These include:

* *Entitlement*—The idea that other people should meet one's expectations. When people do not do what the patient wants, s/he tends to feel unloved or betrayed and feels that he or she is being treated unfairly.

- *Reciprocity*—This is similar to entitlement except that the individual believes that he or she has *earned* good responses from others through good behavior. One may reason: "If I am a good, loving, hardworking person, then my husband (or wife, or children, or friends, or patients) should treat me in a considerate and caring way in return."
- *Conflict phobia*—Paradoxically, many people who are excessively angry have the belief that anger is wrong. They may reason that "People who care about each other shouldn't fight." This prohibition against anger leads to an escalation of conflict because the person makes the interpretation that conflicts have dangerous implications for a relationship.

2) "Do the thoughts that are making me angry contain cognitive distortions?" Several distortions are characteristic of unhealthy (dysfunctional) anger. These include:

- *Overgeneralization*—seeing someone's negative behavior as a never-ending pattern of neglect or abuse. Example: "S/he's *always* late."
- *Should statements*—use of coercive words such as "should," "ought" and "must" when thinking about something that someone did. Example: "He *shouldn't* have done that."
- *Mind-reading*—attributing negative motives to another person and assuming these interpretations are facts rather than assumptions. Example: "He's acting unfair and he knows it." Or, "If he really loved me he'd be on time."
- *Emotional reasoning*—taking one's feelings as evidence for the way things are in reality. Example: "I feel angry. This means I'm being taken advantage of." Or, "I feel guilty. This means I've done something bad."
- *Labeling*—attaching a pejorative global label to someone instead of focusing on what he or she did that was upsetting. Example: "He's *a jerk.*" Angry people can be quite rigid in their insistence on labeling people they dislike. They frequently develop the conviction that the person with whom they are angry *really is* the monster they have created mentally. Labeling provides few useful guidelines for the other person to use in modifying his or her upsetting behavior.
- *Personalization (self-blame) and blame*—finding fault and attributing blame in a judgmental, demeaning manner rather than focusing on the problem to be solved. Example: The patient's second marriage is deteriorating and she tells herself, "It's all my fault." Later, she begins to feel better about herself and she switches to the opposite extreme: "It's not my fault after all. *He's* to blame!"

• *Disqualifying the positive*—The patient becomes so convinced of another person's badness that s/he disqualifies any good behavior and maintains a uniformly negative picture of the person. Example: A woman complained bitterly during a marital therapy session that she and her husband did very little together. He acknowledged this and suggested they go out on a dinner date Saturday night. She snapped: "Oh no you don't! You've got to really *mean* it! You're just saying that so you can look good."

3) "Am I willing to be flexible, curious and open-minded with regard to the motives I attribute to the person I'm angry with? Has she or he knowingly and intentionally broken a moral code and acted unfairly in order to take advantage of me, or does it simply *appear* this way from my vantage point? To what extent do I have the capacity for accurate, non-judgmental empathy and the flexibility to modify my initial impressions as I interact with the other person?" People who are involved in unhealthy anger are so intent on being judgmental and blaming that they tend to be excessively defensive and closed to information which in any way contradicts their own perceptions.

4) "Is the intensity and duration of my anger appropriate to the situation?" Some people nurse hurt feelings far beyond what would be helpful or reasonable.

Questions Regarding the Appropriate Mode of Anger Expression

1) "What are the advantages and disadvantages of feeling and expressing anger in this situation? How will it help me and how will it hurt me? How will it help or hurt the person I feel angry with?" The cost-benefit analysis can help the patient decide whether the anger is healthy or self-defeating. For example, if one's child runs into the street chasing after a ball, one may feel angry and shout at him that what he is doing is dangerous and unacceptable. Using the first criterion above, one might decide that shouting at him in an angry voice would have a more immediate and meaningful impact than calmly and rationally discussing the dangers of getting killed by traffic. In contrast, if stopped by a police officer for speeding, one might feel furious but decide to relate to him in a friendly and courteous fashion. Some patients use a double-column technique in making this type of evaluation, listing the various advantages and disadvantages of feeling angry in a particular situation. Listing them on paper helps the patient develop a more objective perspective. It also encourages the patient to make his or her own value judgments about anger without being unduly influenced by

the therapist's personal philosophy, which is bound to be highly subjective.

2) "If I decide that my anger is appropriate, am I expressing it in a reasonably tactful, objective manner or am I using a great deal of distorted, coercive, blaming, hostile language?" Just as the thoughts that lead to anger can often contain distortions, the language that expresses this anger can contain similar distortions. This typically leads to a counterproductive pattern of arguing and bickering. Example: A woman feels hurt because her husband comes home late. She tells him: "You're so self-centered! You're always doing this." Her statement involves mindreading and overgeneralization. From his perspective, he is not "always late" and the reason for the lateness is not his self-centeredness but an emergency at work. When he snaps back, "That's a darn lie!" the argument quickly escalates. It is important for patients (and therapists) to clearly differentiate aggressive from assertive ways of expressing anger (DeGiovanni & Epstein, 1978) and for patients to practice using nonaggressive behaviors that will have positive rather than destructive consequences for their personal relationships (Epstein, 1980).

3) "Am I interested in sharing feelings and negotiating real problems, or am I interested in getting revenge or coercing the other person?" Healthy (constructive) expression of anger is more likely to involve "I" statements such as "This is how I feel" vs. "You're to blame for upsetting me." Assertive requests are likely to be expressed with statements such as "I would like you to do this" in contrast to aggressive, coercive demands: "You *should* do this" (with an implicit or explicit threat). Destructive expression of anger involves the pursuit of one's own wants and needs without taking the other person's feelings into account, whereas constructive expression of anger takes into account the interests of both parties.

The differentiation of assertion and aggression has been addressed by a number of writers (Alberti & Emmons, 1974; DeGiovanni & Epstein, 1978; Epstein, 1981; Hollandsworth, 1977; Lange & Jakubowski, 1976), and studies of the differential consequences of assertion and aggression (Epstein, 1980; Heisler & McCormack, 1982; Hollandsworth & Cooley, 1978) have indicated that both direct and passive forms of aggression elicit more negative responses from other people than does assertion. Treatments designed to increase patients' assertiveness and decrease unassertive forms of behavior such as passive-aggression (Alberti & Emmons, 1974; Epstein, 1981; Lange & Jakubowski, 1976) focus on both distorted cognitive phenomena and skill deficits.

4) "Am I involved in a nonrejecting context that permits and encourages open communication—even if it is distorted—with the person I feel angry toward?" A husband and wife might have a trusting relationship in which the statement, "Get off my blankety-blank back," implies "We love each other enough that we can fly off the handle and not feel threatened. We will sometimes be tactless and hostile, and that's perfectly acceptable. In fact, that's part of what makes our relationship special—that we can expose our childish and demanding sides to each other without the threat of rejection." In contrast, telling one's boss to "get off my blankety-blank back" might have severe consequences, because the context and the rules of the relationship are quite different.

If, according to these criteria, the patient decides that the anger is healthy and appropriate, the therapist can help him or her *accept* the anger, communicate it effectively, and modify any irrational attitudes which may lead to guilt or inhibitions about expressing it. If, in contrast, the anger appears to be excessive or inappropriate, the therapist can help the patient modify it using cognitive techniques.

THERAPEUTIC STRATEGY AND PROCESS

Cognitive therapy is a systematic approach to the treatment of mood disorders involving depression, anxiety, and anger. The basic premise of this form of treatment dates back to the Greek stoic philosopher, Epictetus, who wrote, "Men are disturbed not by things, but by the views they take of them." Since that time, many philosophers have recognized the important role of thought patterns in mediating our emotional responses, but it is only in the past two decades that this concept has captured the attention of the scientific community (Childress & Burns, 1981). Much of the increased interest in cognitively-oriented treatment stems from a number of published reports that cognitive therapy compares favorably with antidepressant agents and other specific forms of psychotherapy in the treatment of depression (Rush, Beck, Kovacs, et al., 1977; Blackburn, Bishop, Glen, et al., 1981). Basic and clinical research has expanded appreciably in the past several years, such that one investigator has described the current wave of interest in this method as the "cognitive revolution" (Dember, 1974). Initially, treatments designed to alter maladaptive cognitive phenomena such as negative expectations, irrational beliefs, hopelessness, and negative self-concepts were applied with individuals suffering from depression (Beck, 1976; Beck, Rush, Shaw, & Emery, 1979; Burns, 1980).

Clinicians are now beginning to apply this model to a wider range of disorders, including marital and sexual problems (e.g., Epstein, 1982;

Burns, in press a), anxiety and phobias (Beck, 1970), and anger problems
(Ellis, 1977; Burns, 1980).

Basic Principles

A first principle of cognitive therapy is that an individual's painful
feelings and self-defeating behavior patterns result in part from the way
he or she is thinking about experiences in the here-and-now. The cognitions associated with the emotional responses are called "automatic
thoughts," because they flow through the person's mind involuntarily
and almost instantaneously. For example, a man's fiancé told him that
she wanted to talk instead of make love one evening. He immediately
felt sad and angry. His sadness resulted from the thought "I must not
turn her on very much. I'm not very attractive." His anger resulted from
his thought, "For all I've done for her, you'd think she'd be more responsive. I helped her with editing her thesis for three hours today.
She's so self-centered." Then, instead of expressing these feelings, he
walked out and spent the night in his own apartment. This behavior,
which he later described as "passive-aggressive," resulted from the
thoughts, "I don't have the right to feel this way" and "There's no use
trying to deal with her."

A second principle of cognitive therapy is that the thoughts that lead
to painful feelings are often quite negative and distorted. However, the
individual accepts these thoughts at face value and does not think of
challenging them or questioning their validity. In the above example,
the man's telling himself that he doesn't "turn her on" involves an
arbitrary inference. By "mind-reading" he automatically interprets his
fiancé's reluctance to make love in terms of his own inadequacy, without
considering other possible explanations or inquiring about her actual
thoughts and feelings. She might, for example, simply want to discuss
some personal problems and might consider the sharing of feelings a
healthy aspect of intimacy and sensuality. The man also is engaged in
a form of cognitive distortion labeled "emotional reasoning," in which
he assumes that his feelings necessarily reflect reality. He reasons "I feel
angry; therefore I'm being taken advantage of. I feel rejected; therefore
I'm being rejected." This process illustrates the reciprocal relationship
between cognition and affect. His negative thoughts lead to bad feelings
which in turn generate more distorted, negative thoughts. A detailed
description of the ten forms of cognitive distortion that lead to depression, anger, anxiety, guilt and frustration can be found in Burns (1980).

A third premise of cognitive therapy is that patients have certain

underlying "cognitive schemata"—irrational, self-defeating attitudes —which predispose them to painful mood swings. In the example cited above, the patient's anger resulted from a dysfunctional assumption called "reciprocity": He reasons that if he is a good, hardworking person who always helps his fiancé she should reciprocate by treating him in the way he expects to be treated. When she reacts in an unexpected way he concludes that the reciprocity has broken down, that he has failed and/or that she is letting him down. Since these reciprocity contracts are generally assumed and not negotiated or openly discussed, he makes himself vulnerable to frequent feelings of bitterness and disappointment.

A second self-defeating attitude that appears to be operating can be called "emotional perfectionism" or "conflict phobia": He assumes that he is always supposed to have positive feelings and that he and his fiancé should never fight. Because he interprets arguments or disagreements as a sign of personal and romantic failure, he avoids confrontation instead of sharing his feelings. Thus his passive-aggressive behavior can be seen as not entirely volitional or malicious—although there certainly is a desire to inflict pain on his partner. Further, it does not indicate a lack of desire for intimacy and sharing. Instead, a cognitive therapist would conceptualize his actions as the automatic and involuntary consequence of self-defeating attitudes and assumptions which he has probably never verbalized or challenged. The patient is coached in ways of identifying these problematic underlying assumptions. This aspect of cognitive therapy can have a positive effect on the patient, because he can examine his behavior objectively and compassionately without feeling belittled or labeled. The concept of "passive-aggressive behavior" may sound pejorative and may create treatment resistance, whereas concepts such as "conflict phobia" and "automatic thoughts" are generally quite benign and nonjudgmental and appeal to most patients. For a detailed description of ways of identifying "silent" underlying assumptions, see Burns (1980).

The fourth principle of cognitive therapy is that patients can be trained systematically to modify underlying assumptions and negative thinking patterns in order to overcome painful mood swings, function more effectively, and enhance their ability to communicate and to experience intimacy. The treatment has several characteristics:
- The patient and therapist work as equals on a team. The therapist takes an active role and may do as much as 50% of the talking.
- There is an emphasis on self-help assignments which the patient carries out between sessions.
- The therapy focuses on solving problems in the here-and-now. While

this does not exclude the discussion of possible childhood factors that might have contributed to the patient's negative thinking patterns, such considerations are not usually considered necessary for emotional change.

- The therapy is structured, systematic, and usually (but not always) short-term. While the mean number of sessions can vary considerably, depending on the diagnosis, severity, and chronicity of the problem being treated, 15 to 30 sessions represent an average for a major depressive episode. For patients with more serious mood and self-image problems, such as those with a borderline personality disorder, weekly treatment for one to two years is not unusual.
- The aim of the therapy involves: training patients to identify upsetting situations and to become more aware of their negative feelings; helping patients pinpoint the cognitions that are associated with these negative feelings and identify the distortions in them; learning to substitute other thoughts that are more objective and realistic so as to bring about a shift in moods; becoming aware of the self-defeating assumptions and attitudes that predispose them to painful feelings and to develop a healthier personal value system; modifying self-defeating behavior patterns (such as defensiveness or procrastination) and enhancing communication skills.

The following vignette illustrates one of many techniques commonly used in therapy, the "Daily Thought Record" (Burns, 1980; in press, b). The patient keeps a daily journal of upsetting situations and feelings. S/he learns to write down the negative cognitions, called "automatic thoughts," and to substitute "rational responses." Then the patient assesses the outcome in terms of a change in mood or behavior. The patient described earlier wanted to work on reducing his resistance to disclosing his feelings with his fiancé. He found that even when she asked him about his negative feelings he tended to stop talking and feel tense. As illustrated in Figure 2, the first step in using the Daily Thought Record involved describing the problem in the space marked "Situation." Then he recorded his emotions as apprehension, frustration, guilt and embarrassment in the space marked "Feelings" and estimated their intensity as 50-80% on a scale of 0 to 100%. Next he wrote his negative cognitions in the column marked "Automatic Thoughts." Finally, he pinpointed the distortions in these thoughts and substituted more reasonable ones in the column marked "Rational Responses." This exercise gave him substantial relief, and he noted this in the space marked "Outcome."

Figure 2. The Daily Thought Record

Situation: I have trouble expressing myself. When Mary asks, "What's wrong?" I can't think of what to say. When I need help I find it difficult to ask for it. At times I feel morose, and she complains that the relationship is emotionally demanding. I fear rejection.

Feelings: Apprehension; frustration; guilt; embarrassment: 50-80%

AUTOMATIC THOUGHTS	RATIONAL RESPONSES
1. This relationship is likely to end. It may be at an end now.	1. (Fortune Telling Error) Each time we've had a crisis we've resolved it and strengthened the relationship.
2. I know that talking things out would improve the situation. I *shouldn't* be so inhibited.	2. (Should Statement) I'm making progress in learning to be more open, but it is nonsense to say I *shouldn't* feel inhibited. In fact, I *should* feel inhibited because I haven't overcome this problem yet!
3. I shouldn't feel so rejecting and angry.	3. (Should Statement) It's natural to feel angry with someone I love at times. Expressing these feelings can help our relationship become more spontaneous.
4. I don't have enough attractive qualities to sustain a relationship.	4. (Mental Filter) Not true! I have, in fact, been sustaining this relationship with Mary.
5. Any success in my relationship would be because of her and not the result of my good qualities.	5. (Disqualifying the Positive) On some level, love is always a gift that doesn't have to be "earned" or "deserved." But I do have many good points—as well as weaknesses—all of which make me quite human and eminently lovable.

Outcome: Much relief!

While this exercise can sometimes create a rapid mood switch, substantive, ongoing change requires repetition on a regular basis because the patient is likely to fall back into chronic, habitual ways of thinking. As a general rule, patients are advised that 10 to 20 minutes per day of such self-help exercise, five days per week for several months, along with once or twice weekly psychotherapy sessions, are necessary.

Dealing with the Passive-Aggressive Patient

There are numerous ways a patient who is afraid of expressing angry feelings directly might do so indirectly during a therapy session. If the therapist is alert to the warning signs and handles the situation sensitively and systematically s/he can avoid losing rapport and transform an

unproductive power struggle into a growth experience for the patient. Some of the common tip-offs that your patient might be developing negative feelings about the therapist or the treatment include:

1) S/he continually "forgets" to follow through on self-help assignments between sessions.
2) S/he acts argumentative and oppositional during therapy sessions and appears unwilling to give you the slightest satisfaction of making even an obvious point.
3) S/he makes sarcastic or cynical comments during therapy sessions.
4) S/he comes late to sessions, tends to get behind in paying bills or cancels sessions at the last minute.
5) S/he complains excessively during sessions, jumping from grievance to grievance without working systematically on any one problem.
6) S/he frequently protests that "You just don't understand my feelings."
7) S/he asks you about some new type of therapy or schedules a consultation with another therapist without reviewing this with you.
8) S/he continually challenges you to prove that you can be helpful but whenever you offer some helpful suggestions s/he thwarts you by saying "that wouldn't help me" or "I've already tried that." Then s/he asks you for more suggestions.
9) S/he appears upset but insists s/he doesn't *feel* like talking or s/he doesn't *have* to talk.
10) S/he comes to therapy intoxicated on drugs or alcohol or dressed inappropriately.

When you suspect the patient is harboring negative feelings, the obvious strategy is to encourage the expression of those feelings in a safe context. One helpful approach is to ask every patient for specific negative and positive feedback about the therapy at the beginning and end of each session. You could say, "I'd like to know if there was anything I said in today's (or last week's) session that hurt your feelings or turned you off or rubbed you the wrong way. I'd also like to know if there was anything we talked about that was especially helpful to you or that you reacted positively to. Let's start with the negatives first."

Once you encourage the patient to be assertive, it is crucial that you respond empathically—not defensively or argumentatively. Otherwise s/he will rightfully feel ambushed and it will be even harder to trust you and open up in the future. It can be helpful to respond initially to any

critical comment a patient makes with the three listening skills, regardless of whether or not you think the criticism is valid. They are:

1) *Empathy*: You show the patient that you can understand him or her accurately and sympathetically. There are two kinds of empathy and both are important.

A) *Thought empathy*: You paraphrase what the patient is saying. You repeat what s/he says and you reflect it back in a nonjudgmental fashion. Example: The patient says "You don't understand the way I feel." You respond, "I hear you saying I haven't understood how you feel. Can you tell me a little more about this?" Notice that you don't disagree with the patient or contradict him. A statement like, "But I *do* understand how you feel," will only come across as defensive and will convince the patient that you are not, in fact, a very good listener. Although one might think that therapists would not need to have this pointed out, we have frequently observed just this kind of non-empathic response in psychiatrists and psychologists at all levels of training. When you feel defensive or threatened by the patient, you will be the most likely to respond in an argumentative manner.

B) *Feeling empathy*: Once you have paraphrased what the patient is saying to you, you can usually make a pretty good guess about what his or her feelings might be. Share your impression in a nonjudgmental manner and ask the patient if you're reading the situation accurately. In the above example you could add, "If I haven't been understanding how you feel, I could imagine that you might be pretty frustrated and maybe a little bit annoyed with me. Do you feel that way?" It's crucial that you ask about negative feelings in a sensitive, nonconfrontational manner. The patient, on some level, is already probably blaming and condemning himself or herself for feeling angry. That prohibition is part of the cause of the passive-aggressiveness. Therefore, the more tactful, relaxed, and accepting the therapist is at this highly vulnerable moment, the easier it will be for the patient to open up. I find it helpful to ask the patient if s/he feels "hurt," "upset," or "irritated" rather than "angry," because many patients will deny feeling angry, but it is more acceptable to acknowledge feeling "hurt."

Once the patient has disclosed negative feelings, you can reinforce his or her assertiveness with a positive comment like, "I'm really glad you

shared that with me. Looking at these feelings isn't always comfortable but it can make our interaction a lot more meaningful. Tell me more about these feelings, would you?"

2) *The disarming technique*: You find some grain of truth in what the patient is saying, even if you're convinced it's partly or entirely distorted. Example: The patient says, "You're too business-like. All you seem to care about is having me fill out these self-help forms and doing homework assignments and paying your bill." You could respond, "It sounds like I've given you the impression I'm more concerned about the billing and the homework assignments than about you as a person. I can understand that you'd be feeling hurt and angry about that. You don't deserve to be treated in a cold or uncaring way. Can you tell if there are other things I've done or said that might have hurt your feelings?" Notice that when you disarm the patient, your statements must be 100% valid. Otherwise you'll sound phoney. It's also crucial that you present your statements in a genuine, non-sarcastic manner. By finding some truth in what the hostile patient is saying, you allow yourself to appear more vulnerable and less threatening. This frequently calms the patient—who may anticipate your attack—and leads to greater trust and a more relaxed and less rigid exchange of feelings.

3) *Inquiry*: You ask questions to gain more information about what the patient is trying to express. You can ask about other negative reactions the patient may have had, other people who have treated the patient unfairly, etc.

In addition to eliciting verbal feedback from the patient, you can utilize a form entitled "Patient's Report on the Therapy Session" which the patient can fill out after the session and give to the therapist at the beginning of the next session (see Figure 3). This form, which is modified from a psychotherapy rating scale developed by Dr. Jeffrey Young, asks the patient to rate the technical and interpersonal qualities of the session (Childress & Burns, 1981). The reverse side of the form (not included in Figure 3) asks the patient to write negative and positive reactions to the session and also to list the specific self-help assignments that are to be completed before the next session. This form can be helpful to patients who feel too threatened to share the negative reactions verbally when asked or who are so anxious that they cannot remember them when the therapist asks them directly. If the therapist gets less than optimal ratings in the bottom section of the form (which deals with factors like trust, warmth and understanding), it is evident that the patient has some

Figure 3. Patient's Report of Therapy Session

1. How much progress do you feel you made in this session in dealing with your problems? How do you feel about the session?
EXCELLENT   VERY GOOD   GOOD   SATISFACTORY   BARELY ADEQUATE   POOR
2. How pleased are you with the progress you've made in therapy thus far?
EXCELLENT   VERY GOOD   GOOD   SATISFACTORY   BARELY ADEQUATE   POOR
3. How well do you feel you are getting along, emotionally and psychologically, at this time?
EXTREMELY WELL   QUITE WELL   SATISFACTORILY   NOT WELL AT ALL   VERY POORLY

Using the scale from 1 to 4 below, rate the AMOUNT OF SUCCESS YOU HAD IN THE PAST SESSION in meeting each of these goals.

1	2	3	4
/	/	/	/
Unsuccessful	Somewhat Successful	Successful	Very Successful

—1) Better insight into and understanding of my problem(s).
—2) Ideas for better ways of dealing with people and problems.
—3) Help in being able to talk about what was troubling me.
—4) Encouragement and confidence to try things differently.
—5) Better self-control over my moods and/or actions.
—6) Greater ability to respond rationally to my self-defeating thoughts.
—7) Greater ability to evaluate some basic values and assumptions about what is important to me.
—8) Ways of scheduling my time better.

Using the scale from 1 to 4 below, rate the EXTENT TO WHICH YOU FEEL EACH OF THESE STATEMENTS IS TRUE TODAY.

1	2	3	4
/	/	/	/
Weak Feeling	Moderate Feeling	Strong Feeling	Extremely Strong Feeling

—— 1) The things my therapist says and does make me feel I can trust him.
—— 2) He often does not seem to be genuinely himself.
—— 3) He pretends that he likes me or understands me more than he really does.
—— 4) I feel that he really thinks I'm worthwhile.
—— 5) He is friendly and warm toward me.
—— 6) He does not really care what happens to me.
—— 7) He usually understands what I say to him.
—— 8) He understands my words, but not the way I feel.
—— 9) He really sympathizes with my difficulties.
——10) He acts condescending; talks down to me.

negative feelings that need to be ventilated before therapy can proceed effectively. Reviewing these ratings with the patient can be a springboard to better communication.

When eliciting negative feedback, the therapist must show a genuine concern and warmth and avoid projecting his or her tension with defensiveness. This can at times be difficult for novice and advanced therapists. You may find it difficult to acknowledge the truth in the patient's criticism because of your own perfectionistic tendencies and your own insecurities. If you feel threatened or uncomfortable, it's probably best to acknowedge this to the patient in a nonjudgmental fashion. You could say, "I feel a little upset about what you're saying because I suspect there might be some truth in it and I sometimes tell myself that I'm expected to be perfect, which I'm not. If we share these feelings we can develop a better understanding of each other. What would you think about that?" The selective use of self-disclosure by the therapist can be a relief to many patients who see the therapist as omnipotent, and it can also be a useful model for the unassertive, inhibited patient.

Like any therapeutic intervention, this one can backfire if the patient begins to see the therapist as unprofessional, disturbed or incompetent. If the patient does become critical or rejecting when you share your feelings, explore the patient's response, as in the following case.

Case Illustration

Sarah, a 30-year-old professional woman, had a long history of treatment by numerous therapists for severe depression and a borderline personality disorder. She had considerable difficulties in her relationships with friends and professional colleagues because of her tendencies toward blaming herself and others. She acknowledged a great deal of unexpressed anger in her personal and professional relationships, and in her sessions she expressed a persistent unwillingness to do any self-help assignments between sessions. When the therapist (D.B.) would inquire about this, she would often become hostile and threaten suicide. Her procrastination was not limited to her therapy but was a major stumbling block in her professional career. During one of these discussions, the therapist acknowledged feeling frustrated by Sarah's reluctance to participate in the self-help aspect of the treatment. She appeared threatened by this disclosure and became quite judgmental:

Sarah: A professional shouldn't feel angry with a patient.

D.B.: I take it it's upsetting for you that I'm feeling a little tense just

now. Are you saying I should always feel relaxed and objective and never have any negative feelings in my work with you? Or are you saying it's OK for me to have negative feelings but I should try to hide them from you? Or what?

Sarah: I see what you mean. It doesn't sound realistic that you'd *never* have angry feelings. But I'm afraid you'll reject me. I'm afraid that if I don't do the self-help assignments you'll give me an ultimatum and tell me to go and see another therapist.

D.B.: I can see now why my feelings are so threatening to you. You feel like you're in danger of being rejected. But suppose we had the understanding that it was OK to share these negative feelings and try to learn from them and that nobody was going to be rejected. Would that make things different for you?

Sarah acknowledged feeling a great deal of relief, and she even suggested developing a written contract specifying what she and her therapist could expect from one another. The key to the contract was that she would agree to do self-help assignments for several months to see if they would be helpful, and in exchange she was given the guarantee that she could express all the anger she wanted to during her sessions without any danger of rejection. Following this session, she reported a substantial reduction in her level of depression and the subsequent sessions were considerably less turbulent and more productive.

This case illustrates how the failure to do self-help assignments can be a common battleground between patients and therapists. Whether the therapist is treating the patient with medications, behavior modification, cognitive therapy, or marital or sex therapy, the issue of patient adherence is of considerable importance. If the patient cannot develop a collaborative relationship, the probability of a successful outcome is greatly diminished. The problem is particularly common when the patient is depressed, since motivational paralysis and inactivity are a central feature of the illness.

The first step in dealing with non-adherence is to identify the reason why the patient does not follow through on your suggestions between sessions. One of the authors (Burns, in press, b) has developed a memo called "The Concept of Self-Help" to help pinpoint the cause of the patient's resistance. This memo is given to each patient at the beginning of therapy. It explains that the willingness to help oneself between sessions is an important part of the therapeutic process and asks the patient to indicate whether or not s/he would be willing to participate in this

aspect of the treatment, and if so, for how many minutes per day, for how many days per week, and for how many weeks. This memo describes the kinds of self-help forms and activities that are commonly used in the treatment of depression and lists over 20 reasons why many patients find it difficult to try to help themselves. The patient is instructed to circle those that apply to him or her and to review them with the therapist during the therapy session. One common reason for not participating is the feeling of hopelessness—the patient feels so convinced he cannot recover that he sees no point in trying. Another is perfectionism—the patient feels he has to do his assignments perfectly and he fears the therapist's disapproval if he makes a mistake. Another would be coercion sensitivity—the patient feels that if she is expected or told to do something she has to resist doing it to save face and feel "free."

Patients have responded positively to this memo. It allows the therapist and patient to review the reasons for resistance nonjudgmentally and to develop specific strategies for overcoming the problem. For example, if the patient feels hopeless or convinced that the self-help assignments couldn't work, the therapist can suggest that the patient maintain this belief and test it by doing systematic self-help assignments daily for several months. In this type of experiment, it's important to set up reasonable criteria for "improvement" ahead of time. Improvement could be defined in terms of a reduction in the severity of depression on an instrument like the Beck Depression Inventory, or improving certain social skills, or solving a personal problem, etc. If the cause of the resistance is that the patient sees the request to help himself or herself as a coercive demand, the patient could be encouraged to make a list of the advantages and disadvantages of doing self-help assignments between sessions.

Another way of pinpointing the cause of a patient's resistance involves asking the patient to identify the "automatic thoughts" that cross his or her mind whenever s/he thinks about doing the self-help assignments. The patient can write these down during the therapy session, identify the distortions in them and substitute rational responses with the help of the therapist (Burns, 1980). If the patient has the automatic thought, "This couldn't possibly help me," the distortions would be fortune telling (making arbitrary negative predictions) and all-or-nothing thinking (thinking about improvement in black-or-white categories). The rational response might be, "I *feel* like this couldn't help me, but how can I know unless I try?" Or the patient might have the thought, "I *should* do these self-help assignments but I don't feel like it so I won't." The distortions would be emotional reasoning (thinking s/he has to feel like doing things)

and should statements (motivating himself or herself with shoulds, oughts, and musts), and the rational response would be, "It would be to my advantage to do it but I certainly don't have to. I probably won't feel like it until I've started, so I'll go ahead and get started even though I'm not in the mood." Or if the patient has the thought, "This is just like being in school. The teacher is giving me assignments," he could substitute the rational response, "I can do the assignments to find out if they help me, not because I'm being told to."

In addition to dealing with the patient's automatic thoughts, the therapist can pay attention to his or her own cognitions about the patient. It's easy to feel frustrated or annoyed with a patient who is slow to respond, argumentative, hostile, or unwilling to follow through on therapeutic suggestions. In these situations, it can be helpful for the therapist to share his or her thoughts and feelings with a colleague. It can be an enormous relief to discover that other therapists have similar feelings and also find these patients difficult. Furthermore, the therapist can frequently get suggestions that will lead to a breakthrough with a difficult patient.

It can also be helpful for therapists to write down their automatic thoughts and answer them just as the patients do. Figure 4 illustrates the cognitions of therapists along with their rational responses. If you

Figure 4. Therapists' Automatic Thoughts

AUTOMATIC THOUGHTS	RATIONAL RESPONSES
1. Jane hasn't done any self-help assignments for weeks. She probably wants to be depressed.	1. (Mind-reading) If she wanted to be depressed, she probably wouldn't be paying me good money to try to get undepressed. Find out why she has trouble doing the self-help assignments.
2. Fred is so argumentative. He wants to frustrate me.	2. (Mind-reading) Maybe Fred argues because he genuinely doesn't buy what I'm telling him. I can try to be more empathic and find out where he's coming from.
3. Mary's getting nowhere. What's wrong with me?	3. (Personalization) It may be that Mary's treatment will take longer than I expected. Ask her if she is dissatisfied with therapy. Ask a colleague if he would be doing anything differently. Maybe I'm doing OK.
4. I feel annoyed with Sarah. Sometimes I feel like wringing her neck. How unprofessional of me! My colleagues don't feel like this about their patients.	4. (Mind-reading) I can ask them and find out! Maybe it's natural to feel frustrated with a provoking patient. Try to learn from this experience instead of condemning yourself!

doesn't allow your patients to threaten your sense of self-esteem, you'll feel more relaxed and confident and you'll be in a better position to deal with their concerns objectively and effectively.

Once the therapist has written down his/her negative thoughts and answered them, s/he may begin to become aware that s/he has certain underlying attitudes that interfere with effective treatment. These include:

- *The help addiction*: I should always be able to help my patient solve a problem. If the patient is slow to respond or not cooperating with me, it means I'm a failure.
- *Perfectionism*: As a "professional," I should never feel annoyed, frustrated or insecure. I must always feel confident and sure of myself and know how to help my patient.
- *Personalization*: If any patient is angry or dissatisfied, this indicates some failure on my part.
- *The approval addiction*: I need to get every patient's approval. It's a threat to my self-esteem to have any patient dissatisfied or angry with me.

Passive-Aggressiveness in Interpersonal Relationships: Cognitive Antecedents and Consequences

Satisfactory functioning in interpersonal relationships calls for effective handling and resolution of conflicts. Whether in interactions with business associates or with friends, marital partners and family members, an individual is likely to be faced with situations in which his or her goals and preferences conflict with those of other people. The approaches one may take to resolve these inevitable conflicts can be constructive or destructive to a relationship such as marriage (Raush, Barry, Hertel, & Swain, 1974). Programs have been developed to train individuals in conflict resolution skills for the workplace (Welds, 1979); behavioral marital therapists (e.g., Jacobson & Margolin, 1979; Stuart, 1980) also use a variety of procedures for decreasing aversive control strategies, teaching problem-solving skills, and increasing mutually satisfying negotiation between spouses in conflict.

Cognitive factors can play a role in passive-aggressive behavior in interpersonal conflict at two points: the elicitation of anger toward another person and the selection of a passive-aggressive response rather than direct aggression, assertion, or submission. Ellis (1976) has suggested that irrational beliefs such as "I *must* get my way" are likely to

provoke one's anger when another person blocks one's goals. Seeing oneself as having a *preference* blocked may lead to moderate displeasure, but absolute standards can easily evoke a destructive level of anger and concomitant aggressive retaliation toward the frustrating party.

Once anger has been elicited, the choice of a passive-aggressive response may be influenced by the cognitive factors described earlier and outlined in Figure 1 (e.g., a judgment that the costs of direct assertion or aggression outweigh the benefits). Thus, our own clinical observations suggest that the cognitive precursors of passive-aggression are similar to those of direct aggression regarding the instigation of anger (e.g., "he had no right to step in front of me in line") and the intent to retaliate (e.g., "If he thinks he's going to get ahead of me, he has another thing coming!"), but also include inhibitory cognitions (e.g., "He'll beat me up if I push him out of the way") that attentuate aggressive expression of the anger.

Another cognitive factor that can lead to passive-aggression is the common tendency for people to confuse more constructive assertive behavior with socially disapproved aggression (Ludwig & Lazarus, 1972). Passive-aggression can represent an individual's attempt at not being aggressive (where *any* direct expressiveness is equated with aggression), while he or she still has a strong desire to prevail in the conflict with another person. The following case example illustrates this point.

Case Illustration

Bob grew up in a family where his behaving as a good and obedient son was reinforced strongly by his parents. He developed the belief that if only he did some good deeds in relationships he would be appreciated by others and would be free to use his free time as he wished. However, his wife Sue especially values time spent together and becomes upset when Bob takes long walks in the woods by himself, despite the fact that he shares household responsibilities and is attentive and affectionate when they are together. When Sue complains about Bob's solitary time, Bob considers her request for more time together unreasonable and feels quite angry. However, Bob does not express his feelings and preferences assertively, because he equates such direct expressiveness with hurtful aggression, a form of behavior he long ago learned was unacceptable. Consequently, when Sue talks to him about her dissatisfaction, Bob nods, says he understands, quickly gets distracted by some other activ-

ity, and fails to change the behavior that upsets her. Assertive expression on Bob's part could create an opportunity for negotiation between the spouses, but his passive-aggression leaves the issue unresolved.

Understanding the cognitive components of a person's behavior is vital to determining whether an act is in fact an instance of passive-aggressiveness. Defining a behavior as passive-aggressive only in terms of its tendency to oppose or block another person's goals neglects the appraisals and intentions of the actor. For example, failure to carry out a task requested by another person may reflect intentional opposition, as in passive-aggression, but it also may indicate that the person feels anxious and overwhelmed by the task, or that he or she is depressed and believes that one should *feel* motivated in order to carry out an assignment that involves effort (an instance of "emotional reasoning" where an individual equates subjective feelings with objective reality). A careful assessment of the individual's cognitions regarding another person's request will help differentiate passive-aggression from other responses that have a similar appearance at the behavioral level. The objectivity of restricting the definition of passive-aggression to observable topographical characteristics of the behavior is illusory. Even the impact of the act on its recipients is likely to be affected by the recipients' cognitive appraisals of the actor's intentions; e.g., retaliatory aggression tends to be greater when a victim of aggression perceives the act as unjustified rather than justified (Cohen, 1955; Pastore, 1952).

There is some evidence for the validity of the passive-aggressive's assumption that there are greater costs to *direct* aggression. Epstein (1980) found that direct aggressive requests elicited low compliance, high anger, and low sympathy from others, regardless of how reasonable the request was and how much sacrifice was involved in compliance. On the other hand, passive-aggression elicited more compliance, less anger, and greater sympathy when the request was more reasonable and required less sacrifice. In general, however, passive-aggressive behavior is perceived by others as negatively as is direct aggression (Epstein, 1980; Heisler & McCormack, 1982), and it is as unlikely as aggression to produce favorable behavioral responses from other people.

Another potential drawback of passive-aggression (as yet untested in research) is an erosion of trust within a relationship. Although direct aggression is aversive and likely to alienate significant others, the intent of the aggressor is clear; on the other hand, the relative ambiguity of passive-aggression necessitates that others be on their guards for indirect coercion. The vigilance and mistrust engendered in others by the pas-

sive-aggressive individual can seriously undermine an atmosphere of mutual give and take with the person.

Assertion training programs have been developed to substitute constructive, noncoercive behavior for aggressive, passive-aggressive, and submissive forms of unassertiveness (Alberti & Emmons, 1974; Epstein, 1981; Lange & Jakubowski, 1976; Smith, 1975). These programs typically include description and modeling of appropriate assertive responses by trainers, as well as rehearsal of these behaviors by clients with corrective feedback, coaching, and reinforcement by trainers. At the cognitive level, assertive "rights" are espoused by trainers, and clients' beliefs and assumptions that inhibit assertion or encourage forms of unassertiveness are challenged. Thus, modification of passive-aggression, as well as submission and direct aggression, involves both skill training and cognitive restructuring. Researchers such as Linehan, Goldfried, and Goldfried (1979) have demonstrated that cognitive restructuring can enhance the effectiveness of assertiveness training.

In summary, passive-aggression in interpersonal relationships is influenced by cognitive processes that elicit an individual's anger, induce a desire to oppose others, and inhibit direct expression of these feelings and impulses. The impact of passive-aggression may be less negative than that of direct aggression when it involves little sacrifice for the recipient of the act, but in general passive-aggression is destructive to relationships. Therapeutic approaches to problematic passive-aggression commonly involve attention to both skill deficits (behavioral deficits *and* excesses) and dysfunctional cognitions.

DIRECTIONS FOR FUTURE RESEARCH

Although the research studies cited in this chapter have shed some light on the antecedents and consequences of passive-aggression, there are many more unanswered questions that call for systematic research. Assertiveness and direct aggression have been the subjects of numerous investigations, but passive-aggression has only recently gained recognition as a construct worthy of study on its own. Consequently, the body of accumulated research on passive-aggression is small, and there is a need for studies in at least the following areas.

In order to test a cognitive-behavioral model of passive-aggression, we need to develop valid and reliable instruments to assess the component constructs. These would include measures of 1) the degree of perceived injustice and/or thwarting of goals, 2) negative versus positive intentions attributed to the thwarting person, 3) the perceived cost/benefit

ratios for assertive, direct aggressive, passive-aggressive, and submissive responses, 4) cognitions that may inhibit direct expression of thoughts and feelings (e.g., concern with disapproval and guilt), and 5) behavioral proficiency with assertive skills. Once these measures have been developed, it will be possible to conduct studies testing a cognitive-behavioral model by attempting to predict (concurrently and prospectively) passive-aggression from people's scores on the set of instruments. Multivariate statistical procedures such as multiple regression analysis can be used to test the relative contributions of the various cognitive and behavioral components to the prediction of passive-aggression.

Additional studies are needed of the impact of passive-aggression on recipients. Studies such as that by Epstein (1980) suggest that passive-aggression has generally negative social consequences but that under certain conditions (those involving low demands on the recipient) the passive-aggressive individual can gain compliance from another person with only moderate cost to the relationship. It will be important to determine what interpersonal consequences may actually reinforce this behavior and maintain it. Thus, passive-aggression should be studied as a *dyadic* problem as well as an individual phenomenon.

Finally, as we come to understand the factors involved in passive-aggressiveness and develop sound measures of these, we will be able to design more specific therapeutic interventions for modifying the relevant cognitive and behavioral components. Treatment outcome studies then can be designed to examine the separate and combined effects of cognitive and behavioral interventions.

REFERENCES

Alberti, R. E., & Emmons, M. L. *Your perfect right*. San Luis Obispo, CA: Impact, 1974.
Beck, A. T. *Cognitive therapy and the emotional disorders*. New York: International Universities Press, 1976.
Beck, A. T. Role of fantasies in psychotherapy and psychopathology. *Journal of Nervous and Mental Diseases*, 1970, *150*, 3-17.
Beck, A. T., Rush, A. J., Shaw, B. F., & Emery, G. *Cognitive therapy of depression*. New York: Guilford, 1979.
Blackburn, I. M., Bishop, S., Glen, A. I. M., Whalley, L.J., & Christie, J.E. The efficacy of cognitive therapy in depression. A treatment trial using cognitive therapy and pharmacotherapy, each alone and in combination. *British Journal of Psychiatry*, 1981, *139*, 181-189.
Burns, D. D. *Feeling good: The new mood therapy*. New York: William Morrow & Co., 1980. (Paperback: New American Library, 1981).
Burns, D. D. *Couples in love*. New York: William Morrow & Co., in press, a.
Burns, D.D. *The feeling good workbook*. New York: William Morrow & Co., in press, b.
Childress, A. H., & Burns, D. D. The basics of cognitive therapy. *Psychosomatics*, 1981, *22*(12), 1017-1027.

Cohen, A. R. Social norms, arbitrariness of frustration, and status of agent of frustration in the frustration-aggression hypothesis. *Journal of Abnormal and Social Psychology*, 1955, *51*, 222-226.

DeGiovanni, I. S., & Epstein, N. Unbinding assertion and aggression in research and clinical practice. *Behavior Modification*, 1978, *2*, 173-192.

Dember, W. N. Motivation and the cognitive revolution. *American Psychologist*, 1974, *29*, 161-168.

Ellis, A. *How to live with—and without—anger*. New York: Reader's Digest Press, 1977.

Ellis, A. Teachniques of handling anger in marriage. *Journal of Marriage and Family Counseling*, 1976, *2*, 305-315.

Epstein, N. Social consequences of assertion, aggression, passive aggression, and submission: Situational and dispositional determinants. *Behavior Therapy*, 1980, *11*, 662-669.

Epstein, N. Assertiveness training in marital treatment. In G. P. Sholevar (Ed.), *The handbook of marriage and marital therapy*. New York: Spectrum, 1981.

Epstein, N. Cognitive therapy with couples. *American Journal of Family Therapy*, 1982, *10*, 1, 5-16.

Heisler, G. H., & McCormack, J. Situational and personality influences on the reception of provocative responses. *Behavior Therapy*, 1982, *13*, 743-750.

Hollandsworth, J. G., Jr. Differentiating assertion and aggression: Some behavioral guidelines. *Behavior Therapy*, 1977, *8*, 347-352.

Hollandsworth, J. G., Jr., & Cooley, M. L. Provoking anger and gaining compliance with assertive versus aggressive responses. *Behavior Therapy*, 1978, *9*, 640-646.

Jacobson, N. S., & Margolin, G. *Marital therapy: Strategies based on social learning and behavior exchange principles*. New York: Brunner/Mazel, 1979.

Lange, A. J., & Jakubowski, P. *Responsible assertive behavior*. Champaign, IL: Research Press, 1976.

Linehan, M. M., Goldfried, M. R., & Goldfried, A. P. Assertion therapy: Skill training or cognitive restructuring. *Behavior Therapy*, 1979, *10*, 372-388.

Ludwig, L. D., & Lazarus, A. A. A cognitive and behavioral approach to the treatment of social inhibition. *Psychotherapy: Theory, Research and Practice*, 1972, *9*, 204-206.

Millon, T. *Disorders of personality: DSM-III, Axis II*. New York: Wiley, 1981.

Millon, T. *Modern psychopathology: A biosocial approach to maladaptive learning and functioning*. Philadelphia: W. B. Saunders, 1969.

Pastore, N. The role of arbitrariness in the frustration-aggression hypothesis. *Journal of Abnormal and Social Psychology*, 1952, *47*, 728-731.

Raush, H. L., Barry, W. A., Hertel, R. K., & Swain, M. A. *Communication, conflict and marriage*. San Francisco: Jossey-Bass, 1974.

Rush, A. J., Beck, A. T., Kovacs, M., Hollov, S. et al. Comparative efficacy of cognitive therapy and pharmacotherapy in the treatment of depressed outpatients. *Cognitive Therapy and Research*, 1977, *1*, 17-37.

Smith, M. J. *When I say no, I feel guilty*. New York: Dial Press, 1975.

Stuart, R. B. *Helping couples change*. New York: Guilford, 1980.

Welds, K. Conflict in the work place and how to manage it. *Personnel Journal*, 1979, *58*, 380-383.

5

An Existential-Experiential View and Operational Perspective on Passive-Aggressiveness

Alvin R. Mahrer

I want to answer two questions. The first one is this: From the perspective of an existential theory of human beings, what do we mean by the phrase "passive-aggression," and how do we make some conceptual sense of persons who are described that way? The second question is: From the perspective of an experiential theory of psychotherapy, how do we work therapeutically with persons who are described as passive-aggressive?

An existential theory of human beings (Mahrer, 1978) gives us the conceptual foundation for understanding persons we describe as passive-aggressive. It even provides a conceptual foundation from which a theory of psychotherapy may be developed. But it is not a theory of psychotherapy. For that we turn to experiential psychotherapy (Mahrer, 1983). The theory of experiential psychotherapy is the working child of

I want to express my appreciation to Patricia Gervaize and the other members of my Psychotherapy Research Team for assistance in the preparation of this chapter.

an existential theory of human beings. For understanding persons whom we describe as passive-aggressive, the key word is existential; for therapeutic methods and procedures, the key word is experiential.

In an important sense, passive-aggression is a serious phrase, with some conceptual grounding and theoretical significance. It has real meaning from a kind of psychoanalytic/psychiatric theory of human beings (e.g., American Psychiatric Association, 1980; Friedman & Kaplan, 1967; Klein & Davis, 1969; Millon, 1981; NIMH 1966, 1967; Pasternack, 1974). From within that perspective it has conceptual meaning and it is entitled to respect. However, when we shift to an existential theory of human beings, the phrase has no conceptual grounding, no genuine theoretical meaning. When we are reasonably rigorous and conceptually tough, the existential theory of human beings has no place for that phrase. It has no meaning in any serious way; it belongs to a psychoanalytic/psychiatric theoretical vocabulary, and not ours. That is what happens when we acknowledge differences in our theories of human beings.

One option is to stop right here, and to admit that we agree on the conceptual considerations for having nothing in common to talk about. I admire that option, but I do not want to choose it. A second option is to assert that we all really know what we mean by passive-aggressive, so let us not get side tracked with all sorts of definitions. After all, we all agree that it refers to more or less passive ways of expressing aggression (cf. Bach & Goldberg, 1974; Friedman & Kaplan, 1967; Pasternack, 1974). Who could object to such a simple, descriptive, conceptually inoffensive statement? The problem is that this is the nondescript tip of the same old psychoanalytic/psychiatric conceptualization. That option generally leads us from passive ways of expressing aggression into the whole psychoanalytic/psychiatric approach, complete with their notions of psychopathology, their ideas about aggression, their psychodiagnostic classification system, and so on. I reject the psychoanalytic/psychiatric meaning of passive-aggression, even when it is wrapped in an apparently inoffensive definitional ribbon.

The option I choose comes from a recognition that the phrase "passive-aggression" and the meaning to which it refers have a fascinating, diverse, long, and distinguished history (see Millon, 1981). I would like to compromise by offering a meaning which has some components com-

mon to many theories of human beings and some components restricted to an existential theory. To the extent that this meaning has some common goodness-of-fit with other meanings, we can have something to talk about. I believe that there is a fair measure of goodness-of-fit and that we do have something we can talk about.

Passive-aggression refers to a) certain ways of being and behaving, coupled with b) certain kinds of accompanying experiencings, occurring within the context of c) certain kinds of external worlds. This is the easy part of the meaning. Here are the referents for the key word, i.e., "certain":

Passive-aggressive ways of being and behaving (Figure 1) are typically illustrated by the following:

1) The person behaves in ways which are helpless and needy. This behavioral subpackage may be supplemented by temper tantrums, and these generally occur within the context of being helpless and needy.
2) The person behaves in passively infuriating ways ranging from thinly disguised anger to apparently helpful cooperativeness. These ways of being are clothed in innocent passivity, and the effects are interfering, damaging, and infuriating.
3) The person is negativistic, obstructionistic, uncooperative and stubborn in ways which are passive, indirect, and irresponsible. Specific behaviors include dawdling, intentional inefficiency, and procrastination.
4) The person behaves in ways which are superficially compliant and acquiescent, with undertones of whining, complaining, and grumbling.
5) The person behaves in ways which are passively complicit in the delivery, or neglect of stopping the delivery, of interference, damage, harm, hurt, and violence.

Passive-aggression refers to the above certain ways of being and behaving which, according to the existential meaning, must be accompanied with the following certain kinds of experiencings (see Figure 1):

1) The person is experiencing a sense or feeling of control and domination, and this occurs within a context of being (experiencing as) the passive little child, the victim, the hurt and mistreated one, the one who is innocent, sick, handicapped.
2) The person is experiencing a sense or feeling of aggressive provocation, and this occurs within a context of being (experiencing as) the

passive little child, the victim, the hurt and mistreated one, the one who is innocent, sick, handicapped.

3) The person is experiencing a sense or feeling of resisting, defying, refusing to be dominated or controlled. Again, this occurs within the context of being (experiencing as) the passive little child, the victim, the hurt and mistreated one, the one who is innocent, sick, handicapped.

The third part of the existential meaning includes the constructed presence of certain kinds of external worlds (see Figure 1):

1) The external world includes a victim, someone who is constructed by and the target of the person's passively aggressive and controlling ways of being and behaving.

Figure 1. Deeper Domain of a Person With "Passive-Aggressive" Operating Domain, Behaviors, and External World.

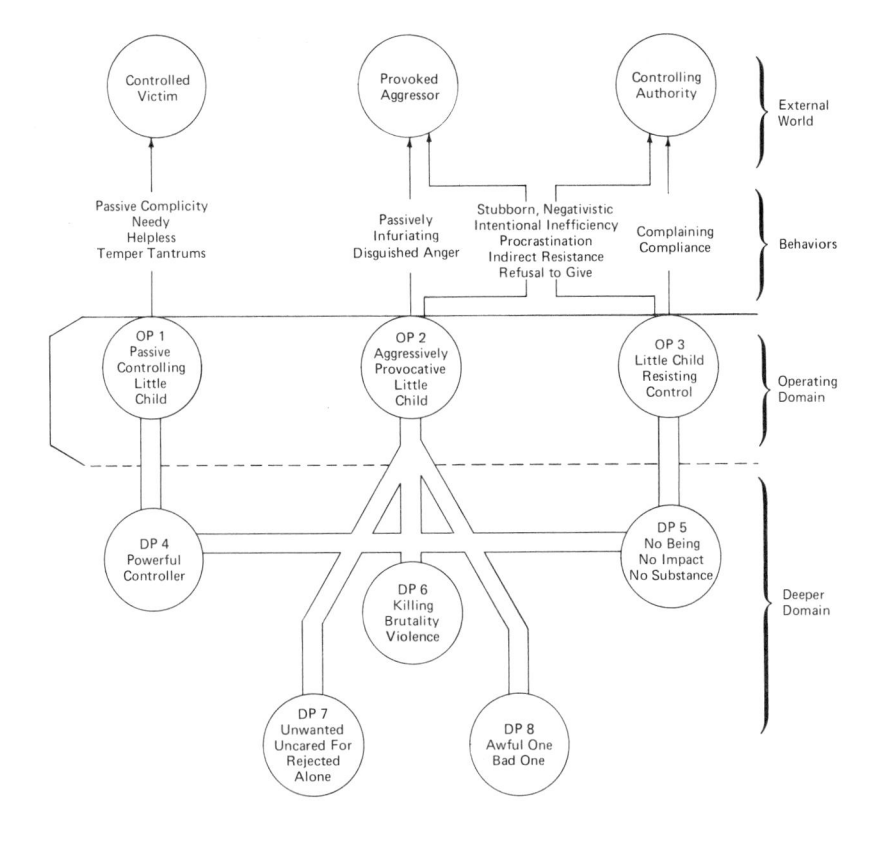

2) The external world includes a provoked aggressor, someone who is constructed by and the target of the person's ways of being and behaving.
3) The external world includes a controlling authority, someone who is constructed by and against whom the person can be resistive, defiant, and rebellious.

These three parts of the package must go together, and each is both the cause and the effect of the others. For example, in order for passive-aggressive experiencing to occur, there must be a proper external world, i.e., there must be someone who plays the proper role of aggressively controlled victim, provoked aggressor, or controlling authority. Sometimes the external partner is all too readily available, and then the person responds with appropriate behavior and experiencing. At other times, the external partner must be constructed and moulded into being the appropriate way, and bringing this about is the function of the proper behavior which itself is brought about by and provides for the proper experiencing. The three parts of the meaning work together in a smoothly functioning package, and the net result is the right experiencing with the right behaviors and the right external world.

What do we mean by the phrase "passive-aggression"? It refers to a person who functions and operates on the basis of potentials for experiencing passive control, aggressive provocation, and resistance to control. It refers to a person who exists in a constructed world of aggressively controlled victims, provoked aggressors, and controlling authorities. And it refers to a person whose ways of being and behaving, as described above, serve both to construct these appropriate external worlds and to provide for these experiencings.

The Question of Common Deeper Personality Processes

In its more general form, the question is this: To what extent are passive-aggressives understood as sharing common deeper personality processes (or psychodynamics or unconscious mechanisms)? Worded in our vocabulary, the question is: To what extent may persons, described as having "passive-aggressive" operating potentials, ways of behaving, and external worlds, be understood as sharing common deeper potentials?

To both questions our answer is: none, or virtually none, or very little indeed. If we consider a group of persons who fit our meaning of passive-

aggressive operating potentials, ways of behaving, and external worlds, we have few or no guesses about their deeper potentials. Instead, our theory suggests that the deeper potentials of these persons differ markedly from one to another. There are at least two considerations for this position. One is that deeper potentials can be served by a broad array of operating potentials and, symmetrically, any operating potential may serve a broad array of deeper potentials. Second, the more specifically and concretely this particular person's deeper potentials are understood and described, the more idiosyncratic they become. We may start with global words such as "the deeper experiencing of being unwanted and rejected," but these words refer to thematic classes of experiencings whose highly specific and individualized meanings vary enormously from particular person to particular person.

In contrast, other approaches hold to the presumption that there is a large measure of commonality to the deeper personality processes of passive-aggressives (e.g., Friedman & Kaplan, 1967; Kemp, 1977; Millon, 1981; Pasternack, 1974; Wolberg, 1977). Where these other approaches set out on a search for the nature of the underlying deeper processes or internal psychodynamics, we do not. Where they define treatment programs based on the presumption of expected deeper processes, we do not. Differences on this question have serious theoretical and practical implications for conceptual understanding, issues of etiology, research hypotheses, research methods, ways of listening to these persons, and treatment methods and goals. It is a most central question indeed.

From our perspective, then, there is no conceptual basis for presuming a passive-aggressive entity, constellation, syndrome, or classification. Our meaning expressly declines the idea of any underlying psychodynamic root or common personality processes. Accordingly, we regard the presumption of a passive-aggressive entity (constellation, syndrome, or classification) as a conceptual will-o-the-wisp. We do not set forth on investigations of whether passive-aggression is a mental disorder which is common (e.g., Pasternack, 1974) or rare (NIMH, 1966, 1967), whether "it" occurs more in women or men (e.g., Friedman & Kaplan, 1967), how it compares with other so-called diagnostic entities (e.g., Whitman, Trosman & Koenig, 1954), what the distinguishing characteristics are of the illness (e.g., Small, Small, Alig, & Moore, 1970), the characteristic response of "passive-aggressives" to drugs (e.g., Klein & Davis, 1969), or any other questions flowing from a presumption of a passive-aggressive entity, constellation, syndrome, classification, or personality disorder.

ETIOLOGY

Meaningless Versions of the Question of Etiology

From our existential perspective, the question of the etiology of whatever is meant by passive-aggression must be approached carefully. There
are versions which simply lack conceptual meaning from our theoretical
perspective.

The meaningless version of the question is: What is the etiology of
the entity (constellation, syndrome, classification, or personality disorder) known as passive-aggression? Because we have no such thing in
our theoretical framework, this version of the question stands as conceptually meaningless.

The version of the question becomes a little more meaningless when
it presumes the existence of a distinguishing set of etiological causes to
the passive-aggressive entity. Our theory leads us to decline the presumption of a passive-aggressive entity or disorder, and also the presumption of a distinguishing set of etiological causes of that entity or
disorder.

The meaninglessness of the question reaches almost ridiculous pro-
portions when it is presumed that the truly basic etiological roots are
biological. For example, in speculating on the basic etiological roots of
passive-aggression, Millon (1981) speaks of such neurological and phys-
iochemical bases as heightened reticular activity, sympathetic system
dominance, and anatomically dense or well-branched neural pathways.
I regard such versions of the question of etiology as meaningless in that
a) I decline an assumption of a passive-aggressive entity or personality
disorder; b) I decline an assumption of a distinguishing set of etiological
roots or causes to "passive aggression"; and c) I decline an assumption
that basic causes, factors, variables, concepts or constructs are biological
in nature (Mahrer, 1978). All in all, these are regarded as meaningless
versions of the question of etiology, at least from my theoretical perspective.

Meaningful Versions of the Question of Etiology

There are two meaningful versions of the etiological question which
make conceptual sense from an existential perspective. The one I want
to answer in this chapter is: Given an infant or child with particular
deeper potentials and disintegrative relations among and between these

deeper potentials, how does that person come to have the operating potentials, ways of being and behaving, and external worlds which we define as passive-aggressive? Once there are deeper potentials, how may we understand the development of passive-aggressive operating potentials, ways of being, and external worlds? Another meaningful version of the etiological question is: How do we describe the development of these deeper potentials; where do they come from; how do they come about? I regard this second version as meaningful but outside the scope of this chapter.

Let us begin, then, with an infant or child or person with deeper potentials that have disintegrative relationships. The deeper domain given in Figure 1 is an appropriate beginning. The etiological question is: Given that deeper domain, how may we understand the ways in which that person comes to have the operating potentials, the behaviors, and the external world indicated in Figure 1?

A means of providing for the painful experiencing of the deeper potential. Starting with disintegrative deeper potentials, the person will develop the passive-aggressive package as a means of experiencing the deeper potential; because the deeper potential is surrounded with disintegrative relationships, the experiencing will be hurtful, unpleasant, painful. It is as if some way must be found to experience the painful deeper potential.

The child starts with a deeper potential for experiencing power and control, but in a way which is painful and unpleasant (DP4, Figure 1). In order for this experiencing to occur, the child may become a passively controlling person (OP1) who behaves in helpless and needy ways which both secure and aggressively control some external victim. Thereby the person gains a measure of the deeper experiencing of power and control.

Given a deeper potential for experiencing killing, brutality, violence and assaultiveness (DP6), the child may likewise develop an operating potential for passive control (OP1) and, by means of temper tantrums, aggressively control the appropriate victim to provide for the painful experiencing of the deeper violent brutality (cf. Cole, 1980).

Starting with a deeper potential for experiencing the painful sense of being unwanted, uncared for, alone, rejected (DP7), the child may develop an operating potential for aggressive provocation (OP2), behave in passively infuriating ways which construct an external world of provoked aggressors. There is then a measure of deeper experiencing of being unwanted, uncared for, alone, and rejected.

A means of establishing a disintegrative relationship with the externalized form of the deeper potential. The story begins with disintegrative relationships between the child and the deeper potential. Then the child constructs some agency or individual who is the externalized form of that deeper potential, and establishes the same disintegrative relationships with that individual as are present between the child and the deeper potential.

If the deeper potential is the experiencing of assaultiveness, brutality, and violence (DP6), the passive-aggressive package is a way of constructing an externalized form of that deeper experiencing, and to provide for the same disintegrative relationships. The child may develop an operating potential for aggressive provocation (OP2) and behave in ways which are stubborn, negativistic, and passively infuriating. This not only constructs a provoked aggressor, the externalized form of the deeper brutal assaultiveness, but also establishes a painfully disintegrative relationship between the child and the external individual.

A means of denying (hiding, disproving) the deeper potential. Given the disintegrative deeper potential, the passive-aggressive package can serve as a means of denying the nature of the deeper potential. It is a way of proving or showing that one is not the way the deeper potential is.

For example, how can a child deny (hide, disprove) the bothersome inner truth of having no substance, of being a vacuum, with no impact or effect (DP5)? One way is by interacting with authority figures who try to control him, while he is defiantly resistive, fighting the control every inch (OP3). By behaving in indirectly resistive ways, by refusing to give what the controlling authority wants, by procrastinating, the child denies that he is without substance, proves that he is a force to be reckoned with, disproves that he is a nothing.

Starting with deeper potentials which are disintegrative, here then are three ways in which the passive-aggressive package develops. This is our answer to the etiological question of how to understand the development of passive-aggressive operating potentials, ways of being and behaving, and external worlds.

THERAPEUTIC STRATEGY AND PROCESS

Every psychotherapy counts on one or two key ingredients, axes which bring about the kinds of changes important to that psychotherapy. Some count on establishing just the right kind of therapist-patient relationship, e.g., the effective transference or the effective mixture of

client-centered facilitating conditions. Some rely on just the right sort of insight or understanding. Some modify the contingent relationship between the behavior and the right cues or stimuli. Experiential psychotherapy salutes a fourth axis of change. We offer the person an opportunity to undergo therapeutic experiencing (Mahrer, 1983). Indeed, we invite the person to undergo five kinds of therapeutic experiencing which occur more or less in sequence (Figure 2). For the person

Figure 2. The Sequence of Steps in a Session of Experiential Psychotherapy.

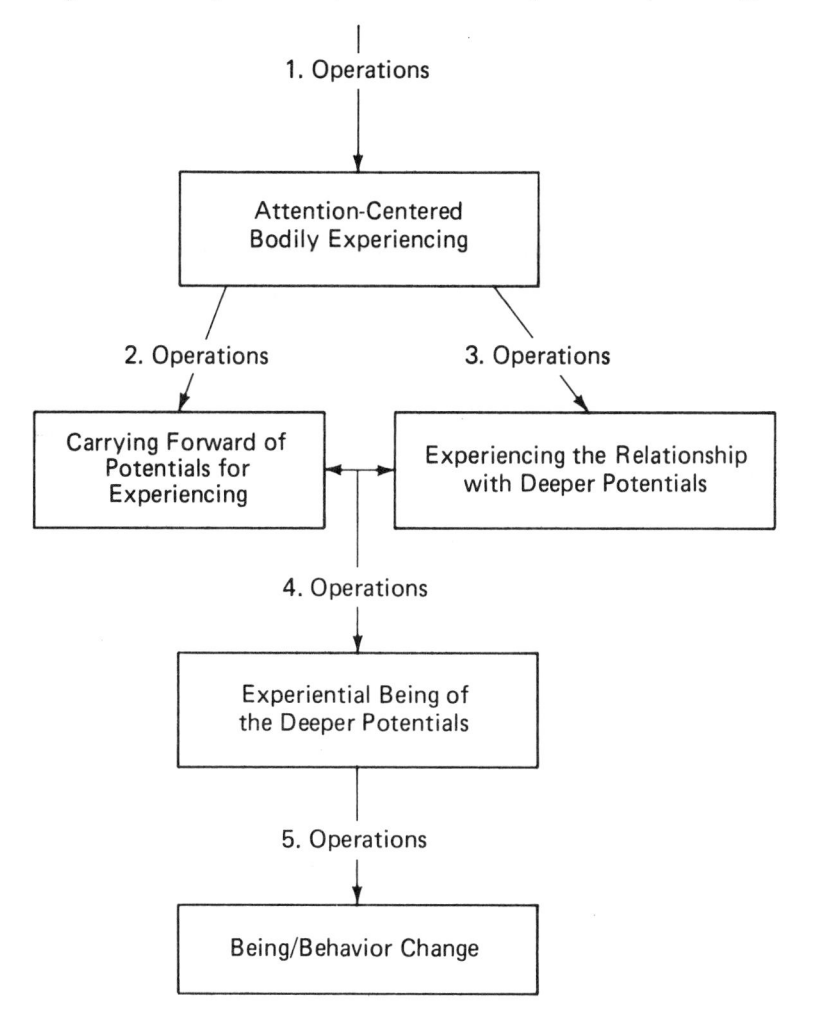

who is described as passive-aggressive, just as for any other person, the invitation is to enter into a process of therapeutic change by means of a sequence of five kinds of experiencing which occur in a sequence each session.

The Sequence of Experiential Steps in Each Session

An experiential session is open-ended, and generally takes two to three hours. As indicated in Figure 2, there is a sequence of steps.

1) *Attention-centered bodily experiencing.* The first step consists of the patient's allowing most of his attention to focus on whatever is so personally meaningful that bodily sensations reach at least a moderate level of intensity. Instead of attending to the therapist, instead of talking to the therapist, the patient's attention goes mainly to some personally meaningful center. In this way, the patient enters into some kind of experiential state. To help this occur, the patient's eyes are closed, and the therapist serves mainly as a teacher of what to do and how to do it. Accordingly, the patient may be attending to a) something quite imminently present and compelling right now, e.g., the nasty way the boss yells at him; b) some deep-seated personal problem, one which has been plaguing him throughout his life, e.g., always sensing that something is wrong or flawed with his very core; c) changes occurring in him and his life, good or bad ones, e.g., becoming increasingly short-tempered; d) internal, bodily states and phenomena, feelings and thoughts, e.g., being scared and tense, with knots in the stomach; e) compelling figures in his world, e.g., the father who is always there, and whom the patient can never really please; f) incidents, recent or remote, in which feelings rose significantly, e.g., starting to cry when his mother yelled at him for losing the keys.

While the therapist helps, it is the patient who selects the right attentional center. For the person with the passive-aggressive package, anything at all may be the right center of attention for this session right now, provided that it is accompanied with at least moderate bodily sensations such as tension in the chest, butterflies in the stomach, dizziness or lightheadedness, or any other kind of moderate bodily sensation, either pleasant or unpleasant.

2) or 3) *Carrying forward of potentials for experiencing.* When the patient's attention is on some meaningful center, and when bodily sensations are at least moderate, some kind of experiencing is occurring. For example, with most of his attention on the controlling authority and with tension

in the chest region, the patient may be experiencing a sense of resistance. At this point, the therapist has options (Figure 2). One of these is to carry forward whatever experiencing is here now, to amplify it, let it come forth further. No matter what it is, regardless of its nature or content, the aim is to carry forward that experiencing. Now, for example, the patient is experiencing resistance even more, with greater amplitude and saturation.

3) or 2) *Experiencing the relationship with the deeper potential*. After the first step, or in concert with the second step, the therapist may elect to promote the experiencing of the relationship between the patient and a deeper potential. It is as if the deeper potential were to come to life, and the patient and deeper potential were to have it out with one another, to love and hate one another, to engage in a full-feeling, two-way, back-and-forth encounter. Consider such a live encounter between the deeper potential for powerful control (DP4, Figure 1) and the passively controlling little child (OP1, Figure 1). Picture the two of them having it out with each other. That is what occurs in the third step. The experiencing moves toward a clashing peak and then opens into a relationship of closeness and welcoming, acceptance and integration, from one to the other.

4) *Experiential being of the deeper potential*. So far, the patient remains a passive-aggressive person, complete with passive-aggressive potentials for experiencing. The operating and deeper experiencings have been carried forward (heightened, amplified), and the relationships with the deeper potentials have been opened up and softened, but the person has never budged out of the operating domain (Figure 1). The fourth step consists in the momentous disengagement from the operating domain, from the substantive, continuing identity in which he or she has existed. The very core of the person is to enter into being the deeper potential. He is to become the new identity, the new being. He is to undergo the profound shift into being the person who is the deeper potential, the one who has been carried forward and enlivened (step 2), the one whose form has transformed from its disintegrative face to its integrative face, the one into which the relationship is now open (step 3). He is no longer, during this fourth step at least, a passive-aggressive person with passive-aggressive operating potentials, passive-aggressive ways of being and behaving, and living in a passive-aggressive world.

5) *Being/behavioral change in the extra-therapy world*. In the previous steps, the person has undergone some changes. They may be slight,

brief, and small, or they might be bigger, longer, and more momentous. But some changes have taken place. The fifth step is the risking of possible changes in ways of being and behaving. In this step, the person risks considering new ways of being and behaving, ways which come from the former deeper potentials. Also, the person risks giving up the former passive-aggressive behaviors and passive-aggressive external worlds.

For the person with the passive-aggressive package, each therapeutic session proceeds along these steps, more or less in that sequence. It is the same sequence of steps for all patients. There is nothing special about patients with operating potentials, behaviors, and external worlds which we describe as passive-aggressive.

The Directions of Change: Aims, Goals and Objectives

In experiential psychotherapy with persons who are described as passive-aggressive, what are the aims, goals, objectives, and directions of change? There are two ways of answering this question. One way is given in Figure 2. In terms of the theory of practice of experiential psychotherapy, the directions of change, the aims, goals, and objectives are given in the process of moving through the five sequential steps of therapy. The first aim is to achieve attention-centered bodily experiencing (Figure 2). Why? For what purpose? The reason and the purpose are to open the way toward the carrying forward of experiencing (step 2) and toward the experiencing of the relationship between the patient and the deeper potential (step 3). Each step is explained and justified as leading the way to the next step in the logically tight and self-contained, circular series of steps which comprise the working sequence of experiential psychotherapy. The final step opens the way for a new beginning with the first step, and around we go. This is one way of answering the question.

The second way of answering this question comes from the existential theory of personality. If a person has the passive-aggressive package, what can the person become? If the person undergoes the steps of experiential psychotherapy, what are the directions of change? What are the aims, goals, and objectives of undergoing the experiential process? Why should a person undergo the steps of the experiential process? Existential theory gives us these answers:

a) *Toward the good or integrative form of the deeper potential.* The very content or nature of the deeper potentials will undergo a radical shift.

It is truly a dramatic change. The content or nature of the deeper potentials changes from a form which is disintegrative (bad, frightening, menacing, chaotic, ominous) to a form which is integrative (pleasant, welcomed, friendly, harmonious). It is as if the essential structure of the deeper potential shifts radically from its bad, disintegrative face to its good, integrative face. The consequence is a profound change in the content or nature of the person's inner personality structure. Here is a new person.

For example, in its disintegrative form, feared and avoided by the passive-aggressive person, the deeper experiencing occurs as the awful state of having no impact on others, of having no substance or presence, of being a dead vacuum (DP5, Figure 1). The direction of change, the aim or goal or objective of experiential psychotherapy, is toward the radical shift into its integrative new form. For this particular person, it may consist of the qualitatively new experiencing of letting others be, being free of the essential urgency of having to confirm or validate one's presence and existence. The core of the experiencing can shift from its bad, disintegrative form to its good, integrative form (OP5, Figure 3).

In its bad, disintegrative form, the deeper potential may consist of the painful inner sense of being unwanted, uncared for, rejected, utterly alone (DP7, Figure 1). For this particular person, this can metamorphose into a good, integrative form in which there is a whole new experiencing of independence and autonomy (OP7, Figure 3). In the same way, every deeper potential can undergo the radical shift from its continuing bad, disintegrative face to its altogether new good and integrative face (see Figure 3). The direction of change, the aim or goal or objective is this same metamorphosis into the good, integrative new form of the deeper potential. This is the conceptual legacy of an existential theory of personality change.

b) *The former deeper potentials move toward becoming part of the operating domain.* One radical shift in the deeper potentials involves the above transmutation from its disintegrative to its integrative form; the second is that the changed deeper potential now becomes a part of the operating domain (Figure 3). The person operates from it, functions and behaves on the basis of it, experiences it. In this crucial and critical sense, the operating, behaving, functioning, experiencing person is now a qualitatively new and different person who is no longer a passive-aggressive person.

c) *Toward new ways of being and behaving.* There are two reasons why

the stage is set for new ways of being and behaving. One is that the former *deeper* disintegrative potential is now an *operating* integrative potential. This shift from deeper to operating means that changes occur. When the deeper potential becomes an operating potential for experiencing independence and autonomy (OP7, Figure 3), then the person will be ready 1) to be and behave in new ways which build and construct the kind of external worlds in which independence and autonomy can be experienced, and 2) to be and behave in new ways which provide directly for this new experiencing.

The second reason is that the former deeper *disintegrative* potential is now an operating *integrative* potential. Instead of being surrounded with feelings of tension, avoidance, and fear, relationships with other potentials are characterized by mutual openness, welcoming, and acceptance. These are indicated by the plus sign in the overlap between potentials in Figure 3. Accordingly, two further classes of behavior now tend to occur. 3) The person can relate to, be aware of, accept, and welcome other operating potentials. As the part which is independent and autonomous, he can accept his own aggressiveness (OP6, Figure 3), his own tendency for experiencing wickedness (OP8, Figure 3). 4) The person can gracefully shift from one potential to another, even when these potentials are quite different from and perhaps opposite to one another. Here is an easy shift from playfully aggressive ways of being and behaving (OP6) to being and behaving in ways which let others be (OP5), and back again. All in all, the person who had formerly behaved in passive-aggressive ways (Figure 1) now behaves in new and changing ways (NB4-NB8, Figure 3).

d) *Toward enhanced feelings of exictement and aliveness, and inner peacefulness and harmony.* The person moves in the direction of two distinct kinds of pleasant feelings or bodily sensations. With the sheer heightening of experiencing, there are new feelings of excitement and aliveness, a bodily felt tingling and overall vitality. As the person is experiencing, is being and behaving, there are these newfound feelings of excitement and aliveness. With integrative (welcoming, accepting) relationships among potentials, there is likewise a heightening of inner peacefulness and harmony, a sense of inner oneness and wholeness. These are good and pleasant new bodily felt feelings. In short, the formerly passive-aggressive person enjoys new feelings and bodily sensations.

e) *Toward a receding away of passive-aggressive operating potentials, ways*

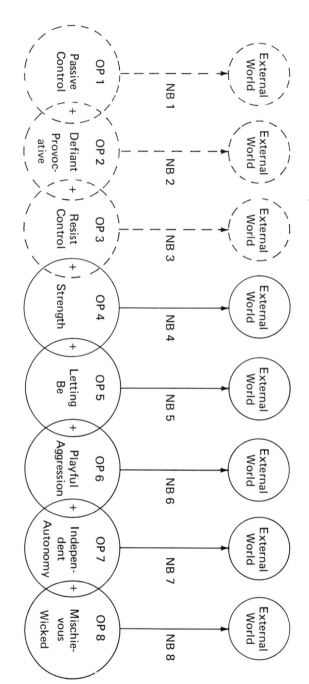

Figure 3. Directions of Change for a "Passive-Aggressive" Person. Operating Potentials, Behaviors, and External Worlds.

of being and behaving, and external worlds. All of the changes so far open the way for a new person to emerge and remove the conceptual roots for the old person to remain. Accordingly, the passive-aggressive person tends to recede away. The old passive-aggressive operating potentials go away; the new person simply does not experience that same sense of a passively controlling little child, an aggressively provocative little child, or a little child who is resisting control (OP1, OP2, OP3, Figure 1). There is a washing away of the former passive-aggressive behaviors. No longer does the person construct and live in the same old passive-aggressive world; there are fewer controlling authorities, provoked aggressors, and controlled victims. These changes are indicated by the dotted circles in Figure 3.

If the old operating potentials remain, their nature and their reason for being change. This is the risk, namely that the former passive-aggressive person will either no longer exist or, if s/he does, s/he will be significantly changed. This is why the former operating potentials are indicated by dotted circles, the new external world is also indicated by a dotted circle, and there are new behaviors (NB1-NB3, Figure 3). In either case, one of the directions of change, one of the aims, goals, and objectives, is the receding away of the former passive-aggressive operating potentials, ways of being and behaving, and external worlds.

These changes (or aims and goals) mean that a new person tends to come forth and the former passive-aggressive person tends to recede out. The directions of change which are yoked to an existential theory of human beings and also to an experiential theory of psychotherapeutic practice may be contrasted with those of other approaches and theories. For example: "Treatment consists mainly of exploratory psychotherapy to resolve dependent conflicts and to allow new measures to cope with frustration" (Pasternack, 1974, p. 68), or "Major goals of therapy are to guide these patients into recognizing the sources and character of their ambivalence, and to reinforce a more consistent approach to life" (Millon, 1981, p. 271).

Undertaking the Method of Experiential Psychotherapy Versus "Treating" Passive-Aggression

In its more rigorous form, there is a sequence of steps which comprise the experiential method. To the extent that the patient and the therapist undertake this method, the patient and therapist will undergo the five kinds of experiential changes described above, and there will occur the

directions of change we have just discussed. There are many ways in which this undertaking of the method of experiential psychotherapy contrasts with some other theories and approaches in which the therapist sets out to "treat passive-aggression."

In experiential work, every session starts with whatever attentional centers the patient finds meaningful. These may or may not have anything to do with the so-called passive-aggressive package. In this method, there are no "problems" of "passive-aggressives."

In experiential work, the meaningful attentional centers are important in and of themselves. Through them we move into the next steps of the experiential process. We do not try to figure out the psychodynamic meaning or the symbolic significance of the patient's "problem" or "complaint" or "symptoms."

In experiential work, the meaningful attentional centers may be accompanied with feelings which are unpleasant and painful or, on the other hand, feelings which are warm and lovely, rollicking fun and hilarious. Work does not consist of getting at "the problem," some serious entity which the patient is supposed to "have."

In experiential work, we start each session with meaningful attentional centers which will likely change from session to session. Indeed, not only is the patient quite free to locate new attentional centers, but the very work of therapy itself will bring forth new attentional centers as beginning points for therapeutic work. This is in contrast with the identification of an initial complaint or the presenting clinical picture or the pretherapy test results or the patient's symptoms or the so-called initial problem.

In experiential work, the important data occur in the therapy session itself. These consist of a) the nature of the operating and deeper potentials; b) the nature of their relationships; and c) the nature of the constructed external worlds (see Figure 1). Other approaches value other kinds of data, much of which may be gathered by means such as psychodiagnostic assessment and evaluation, mental status examination, psychometric and projective testing, demographic and case history data-gathering methods.

In experiential work, the broad contours of the directions of change are given by the existential theory of human beings, as discussed above. The specific objectives and directions of change emerge from the personality structure and resources of this particular person who started out with the passive-aggressive package. The existential theory is linked to a method of experiential therapy which enables the kinds of changes

to occur which are ready to occur because this particular person is the way this person is. In contrast, many approaches include a therapist outfitted with a powerful intent to get the person to be the way the therapist wants the person to be.

These are a few of the differences between what the experiential therapist does and what many therapists do who follow other approaches. We undertake the method of experiential therapy in concert with a person whom we agree to refer to as currently having the passive-aggressive package of operating experiencings, ways of being and behaving, and constructed external worlds. In contrast, some other approaches consist of therapists who set out to treat the passive-aggressive pathology.

How do we work therapeutically with persons who are described as passive-aggressive? I have discussed the sequence of steps in each session and the directions of change. The purpose of this final section is to illustrate some specific therapeutic procedures in working with the passive-aggressive package of a particular person. I shall describe only some of the actual therapeutic procedures because of considerations of space.

Stanley is in his early thirties. He was in experiential psychotherapy for 14 months. There were 127 sessions, usually two a week, with most of them around two or two and a half hours or so. The excerpts are taken from the third and fourth sessions. Throughout experiential work, both patient and therapist recline in large, comfortable chairs, their legs and feet on hassocks. The patient's eyes are closed all the time; the therapist's eyes are closed most of the time.

Throughout these opening sessions, Stanley's operating and deeper potentials, his ways of being and behaving, and his constructed external worlds are given in Figure 1. After 20 or 30 more sessions, the operating potentials were virtually gone, the former passive-aggressive ways of being and behaving were essentially absent, and the external world no longer included controlling authorities, provoked aggressors, and controlled victims. In short, Stanley no longer fit the meaning of passive-aggressive. The purpose of this case study is to illustrate, by means of excerpts, some of the actual therapeutic procedures used in the third and fourth sessions in the process away from the passive-aggressive package and toward the changes indicated in Figure 3.

Attention-Centered Bodily Experiencing

Every session starts with the preponderance of the patient's attention on some meaningful center, accompanied with at least moderate bodily sensations. In this first step, the therapist is the teacher who tells the patient what to do and how to do it. With most patients, it is relatively easy to do successfully. With Stanley it is difficult. How can a therapist give instructions without falling into being his partner in a role rela-tionship game in which the therapist is the controlling authority, the provoked aggressor, or the controlled victim? Stanley is an accomplished craftsman at forcing individuals into these roles, and a therapist who offers instructions in what to do and how to do it is beautiful grist for Stanley's passive-aggressive mill. Here is a technical problem in the practice of experiential psychotherapy.

There are two ways in which the experiential method solves this prob-lem. One is that the instructions are paradoxical in that the more the patient carries them out the less the patient is aware of the therapist. Thus the therapist may be firm in insisting that the patient place the predominance of attention on some meaningful center and not on the therapist. The therapist may repeat the instructions each time the patient fails to follow them well. The net result is that the patient is concerned with (attending to) something or someone other than the therapist, bodily sensations are at least moderate, and the patient is less and less aware of and attentive to the therapist. In the opening phase of these two sessions, Stanley tried several times not to follow the instructions. But after repeated and insistent provision of the same instructions, he began following them and soon was engaged with persons and situa-tions other than talking with and to the therapist.

The second way of solving this problem is that the instructions give the patient wholesale freedom of choice to follow the method or not. If the patient wishes to place attention on any meaningful center, that is fine. If the patient is ready to go into an experiential state, that is fine. If the patient is willing to talk to, be with, be concerned with and attend to anything (except the therapist), that is fine. However, if the patient chooses not to follow the instructions, the choice is entirely his, and experiential work ends for this session. All of the choice, the freedom, and the responsibility for undergoing the work or for ending the session for today lies with the patient. In this first step, the therapist is nothing but the teacher of the method with a patient who is willing and ready to proceed. Stanley fully understood this option and proceeded with the

work. These are the two ways of solving the technical problem of patients, especially including those with the passive-aggressive package, who may be inclined to invite the therapist into carrying out the passive-aggressive games in which the therapist is the controlling authority, the provoked aggressor, or the controlled victim.

In the following, Stanley's attention is predominantly on his boss, an architect in the small firm where Stanley has worked for a few years. Furthermore, what he is saying is accompanied with moderately strong bodily sensations. This is attention-centered bodily experiencing as it starts out in one of the sessions:

Pt. (with a fair measure of closed in tightness and lightly bubbling annoyance): The deadline . . . he wanted the drawings done by this Monday. I know I upset him. If I had enough time to work on them without his changing the . . . uh, the . . . well, the things he wants. I think sometimes he is OK. Lots of the others complain about him. . . . I know I do OK. Just that . . . he gets mad at me. (The instant he says this there is a quick little laugh, then a quick veering away.) But he gets that way sometimes with all of us . . .

The attention is perhaps most centered, and the level of bodily sensations highest, when he says, "He gets mad at me," and then has that little laugh. At that instant, Stanley may be with a provoked boss, having tense little scary sparks in his chest wall, and experiencing a bubble of provocative defiance (OP2, Figure 1).

The next excerpt also comes from the beginning of one of these early sessions. In meeting the criteria for attention-centered bodily experiencing, most of his attention is on the interaction with his wife, Rachel, and there are moderate bodily sensations occurring as he is doing this. Light bodily sensations of a kind of drawing up of the skin are occurring across the whole upper body. Stanley is talking mainly to himself about all of this, and very little attention is directed toward the therapist.

Pt. (petulant and complaining): I can't eat eggs like that. My stomach churns and I throw up. I get weak and sick. She knows that. I guess I like when she stays home from work and puts cold washrags on me when I. . . . We had a fight, well, not a fight. She said she'd be late for work. But those eggs just wipe me out and I have to be taken care of. Rachel's good. She said she was sorry. Hard

to remember 'cause my whole body was shaking. God, those loose eggs. I'm getting nauseous just thinking about them.

In the following, there is a bodily sensation of a hot heavy ball in the stomach region as his attention is on the boss:

Pt.: Ray wants me and another guy to come in on Saturday to talk over the timetable for the restaurant. He is a workaholic and sets the rules. Every time I come to talk to him about my work he, well, he just listens I guess. But then he just tells me to do it his way. I have ideas and he . . . always yells at me for being late. Or not late so much. Well, sometimes . . . I'll do it. Jobs are hard to get and he is someone you just don't argue with. I try to tell him that he's the boss. But . . . I wish I didn't have to come in on Saturday . . .

As the patient is saying all of this, the therapist's attention is likewise on whatever the patient is attending to. It is as if both patient and therapist are saying the words, and the therapist's attention goes to whatever is denoted and connoted as the patient has that little laugh, or attends to the nauseousness and the loose eggs, or does not want to come in on Saturday. The therapist listens by sharing the patient's attentional center or whatever center is there when the patient is talking. In the same way, the therapist shares whatever bodily sensations are occurring right now in the bodies of patient and therapist, sensations such as a hot heavy ball in the stomach region, or a drawing up of the skin across the whole upper body, or whatever bodily sensations are occurring. This stance or posture of the therapist is referred to as experiential listening (Mahrer, 1983). Most of the work of experiential therapy occurs with the therapist in this stance or posture in which he or she shares much of the patient's immediately ongoing external world, ways of being and behaving, operating and deeper experiencings. The therapist is either outside, talking to the patient and giving instructions on the next step, or joined with the patient in posture of experiential listening.

By following the initial instructions, the patient finds some meaningful center upon which most of his attention can be focused so that at least moderate bodily sensations are occurring. This is the important first step in the sequence. Now we can proceed.

Carrying Forward the Potentials for Experiencing

As indicated in Figure 2, one option is for the therapist to carry forward whatever potentials for experiencing are now occurring. What are some techniques for bringing this about?

The therapist clarifies the situational context. Let us go back to the first excerpt above, when Stanley is attending to the boss: ". . . I know I do OK. Just that . . . *he gets mad at me* . . ." With those words, there is a sharp little laugh. In this immediate instant, the therapist has a concrete image of the boss. As the patient laughs, the therapist sees the boss infuriated, hopping up and down, eyes wide with sputtering, frustrated fury.

The technique consists of holding that image, making it more present and real, more clarified. By being in this actual scene, by clarifying the image of the boss, whatever experiencing is momentarily present will carry forward.

T: Yeah! Really mad! Look at him! He's hopping up and down and he's so damned mad he's . . . he can't say anything. . . . Look at those eyes! (A little more of Stanley's attention goes to the boss in this instant.)

Pt.: He tightens his jaw. I mean he clenches his jaw when he gets . . . frustrated a bit.

T: I want to see him clearly. I mean right here and now when he's mad! What he looks like. How he is. His face, he's . . . he's . . . can't see his body and what it's like. Show me, help me.

Pt.: Well, he's mad. He gets that look on his face.

T: The look, the look. Like he's going to explode.

Pt.: Yeah. (Now the image of the boss's face becomes quite real, and it is as if the therapist is facing the infuriated boss.) . . . I guess I really got him upset. (Stanley laughs mildly.)

T: (It is getting funny.) Look at the guy!

Pt. (laughing mildly): I don't think he knows how to take me. He tries hard to be reasonable. I mean not get emotional. I have that effect on him. I get him emotional. (The laughing increases.) I guess I drive him crazy! He sort of gets near me and . . . his jaw tightens. Like his blood pressure goes up. He looks like he's going to pop! (Stanley is now thoroughly enjoying himself, laughing rather hard, and there is a carrying forward of a kind of mischievously aggressive provocativeness.)

The therapist is the behaving-expressing potential. Experiencing also carries forward when the therapist behaves and expresses what the potential is ready to behave and express. Not only is the therapist able to do this, but the therapist can do this within the situational context of whatever is present. In the above context, for example, the therapist can express the mischievously aggressive provocativeness directly at and to the boss. In this technique, the therapist actually undergoes the burgeoning experiencing:

T (with a wickedly delightful laugh): Hey boss! I think you're gonna pop! Ha ha! I gotcha!

Pt. (drawing back a little): I wouldn't say that . . .

T (completing what Stanley does not say): . . . 'Cause . . . 'cause if I did . . . (laughs hard) . . . I think I can drive you CRAZY!

Pt. (rising feeling): I've never done that!

T: Boss. Hey boss! I'm gonna drive you CRAZY!

Pt. (almost happy): Maybe I'd think it . . .

T: Can you hear, boss? I think it. I think I can drive you out of your gourd!

Pt. (obviously enjoying this): I know that I bother him. I try to be friendly sometimes, but I think I rub him the wrong way. He gets a look sometimes. I think I get scared of him. He scares me. He used to play football . . .

T: (The therapist now has a new image of the big tough ex-football player trying to catch the defiant little kid who is much too fast for him.) Try to catch me, big tough ex-football player! C'mon, just try to catch me. Nyaa, nyaa! Ha!

Pt.: (Laughing.) He'd have a heart attack!

T: Christ yes! Clunk! Dead! And on the gravestone: Here lies the boss, son of Igor and Brunhilde. Driven into the grave by Stanley Z!

Pt. (in open, sheer experiencing): How's that! Now I gotta find someone else! I can't drive your gravestone crazy. Maybe I can get it to rot! Or crumble. How could I do such a thing? Who'd think that I . . . this'd never happen. (Hard laughing.) I wish I had such an effect! It may take some time, but I can drive anyone crazy! Like in my own way. I do it. Don't try to mess with me or I'll do things! No one'll really know. Sort of like it just comes from me. I'd like to warn him sometimes. Quietly, not messing with any one. If you are mean to me, well I'll drive you crazy. I mean it may take a while, and I can do it. It sounds like a threat and it is! Maybe I should tell him that but if I did it, well he'd . . . no one'd believe

me. I hate to look at him, direct . . . (And now, a direct confronting of the boss.) You always seem to pick on me. You've been that way since I started. For really nothing! Like I did something to you. You seemed to torture me and treat me like I was your boy. Just someone for you to tease and pick on. I don't like being treated like that. But you never stop. Like you enjoy picking on me all the time. I can't be an equal to you. I don't know why you do that! I just come in the room and you . . . you want to tease me and ridicule me in front of everyone. I wish I could get back at you. I wish I could. (He stops, right on the verge of tears. The carrying forward of the aggressive provocation (OP2, Figure 1) opens the way for the experiencing of the deeper potential (DP7). Accordingly, the patient is now on the verge of that deeper sense of being unwanted, rejected, alone.)

The therapist welcomes full experiencing. Experiencing is carried forward by means of a welcoming attitude toward fuller and fuller experiencing, by welcoming heightened amplitude and saturation. This is accomplished by a) sensitively selecting whatever the patient is being and doing which promotes fuller experiencing in the therapist; b) allowing the level of experiencing in the therapist to become fuller; and c) repetition of the felinged words and behaviors on the way toward fuller experiencing.

Let us return to Stanley's attending to Rachel and the eggs:

Pt.: I can't eat eggs like that. My stomach churns and I throw up. I get weak and sick. She knows that. I guess I like when she stays home from work and puts cold washrags on me when I. . . . We had a fight, well, not a fight. She said she'd be late for work. But those eggs just wipe me out and I have to be taken care of. *Rachel's good. She said she was sorry.* . . . (As the therapist is with the patient, these last words are suddenly accompanied with a tightening up across the chest.)

T: Rachel's good. She said she was sorry . . . (And with fuller experiencing.) Rachel's good. She said she was sorry. Yes, that does something. Again, again!

Pt.: Rachel is good. She is good. She said she was sorry!

T (even more fully): Yeah! Yeah! Rachel is good! She said she was sorry!

Pt.: I like when she says she is sorry! I like that! *She should be sorry!* (These last words are filled with even more energy.)

T: She should be sorry! Be sorry! More! More! She should be sorry! Louder! More feeling!!

Pt.: Be sorry! I want her to be sorry! (Breathing hard, yelling.) I don't like eggs like that! You know that! Dammit! You should be sorry! You should be!!! (Now there is a pause, and his voice almost hisses.) You're going to be sorry, Rachel! You do what I want, do you hear me? (We began with the passively controlling little child (OP1, Figure 1) and now there is the emerging of the deeper sense of powerful control (DP4).)

The therapist identifies earlier experiential scenes. We can now identify earlier scenes or situational contexts in which the emerging deeper experiencing started to occur. Experiencing is carried forward by identifying these earlier scenes and allowing the experiencing process to carry forward within the context of these earlier scenes. Identification is accomplished by describing what we know about the nature of the emerging deeper experiencing, and by describing what we know about the parameters of the earlier scene or situational context. Let us return to where Stanley has said, "You're going to be sorry, Rachel! You do what I want, do you hear me?" At that point, Stanley stopped. The therapist begins describing the earlier experiencing and the earlier scene:

T: You're going to be sorry. You do what I want, do you hear me? This sense, maybe for a second or so, sense of having that person, someone, in my power. Special feeling. Control over them. Strength. That person is going to do what I want. A year ago, maybe a long time ago, being a child, some time.. With someone. Someone did something. Hurt me. Mistreated me. Their fault. Some time. The other person mistreated me . . . when is this? Where? Somebody is here . . .

Pt.: (He fills in the early scene, and continues the experiencing.) My Mom and Dad were divorced. I'm sitting in the kitchen and I threw up. Bean soup. She gave me bean soup. I thought she was going to hit me. But she just looks at me real funny. I felt something then. When she looks at me. Remember it just as clear. I'm very little. I look at her, and I remember thinking that she can't do anything to me. She looks little. But I felt something. Like cold. No, like I had a thing. I felt OK in my stomach. But my body feels funny. Like I have no arms or legs. My chest and in me it is hard. Real big and strong. She didn't say nothing. I felt stronger than

her. I watched her. That's it! I just look at her and I felt hard inside. Removed. Like I was just watching her and she couldn't do nothing to me. Something inside felt . . . indestructible. Yes, indestructible. It's the first time. That's the first time I ever felt like that. I remember thinking how good that was. Maybe cause Mom didn't get mad at me. Yell at me . . .

Once the person attends to a meaningful center, with at least moderate bodily sensations, one of our options is to carry forward whatever experiencing is here. These are some of the techniques for accomplishing this. Now the person is undergoing heightened experiencing of those potentials which we agree to call passive-aggressive, and there is also a carrying forward of the deeper potentials.

Experiencing the Relationship With Deeper Potentials

When the patient starts by attentional centering, the other option is for the therapist to promote the experiencing of the relationship between the patient and the deeper potential. As indicated by the negative signs in Figure 1, Stanley's relationship with his deeper potentials consists of turning away from them, denying them, pushing them away, regarding them as uncanny and menacingly sinister. The feelings are bothersome, unpleasant, and painful. Promoting the relationship with these deeper potentials means that there is a heightening of the experiential, feelinged, interactional relationship between the deeper potential and the patient, and also between the patient and the deeper potentials. In the course of this experiential relationship, patient and deeper potential meet one another, touch and joust, love and hate, push and shove, encounter and confront one another. The ineluctable consequence is a welcoming acceptance, a softening, a graceful and easy openness, an harmonious oneness; in short, the experiential relationship becomes more integrative.

The heart of the technique is for the therapist to become the voice and agency of the deeper potential. The therapist allows himself to merge and fuse into the deeper potential, to welcome the sinking into it and to welcome its filling of him so that the therapist now relates to the patient as the voice and agency of the deeper potential. It is as if the patient's deeper potential were to come alive, have an identity, and engage in an interactive experiential encountering relationship with the patient (Mahrer, 1983).

Let us pick up where Stanley was interacting with the boss. At the

close, there was a carrying forward of the aggressive provocation (OP2, Figure 1) and an increasing imminence of the deeper experiencing of being rejected, uncared for, alone (DP7):

Pt.: . . . You seemed to torture me and treat me like I was your boy. Just someone for you to tease and pick on. I don't like being treated like that. But you never stop. Like you enjoy picking on me and ridiculing me in front of everyone. I wish I could get back at you. I wish I could. (He stops. At this point, Stanley is quite close to the deeper potential for being rejected, uncared for, alone. He is on the verge of tears. As the therapist becomes the voice and identity of the deeper potential, the experiencing of the relationship begins.)

T: Well, Stanley, you may as well shut up. Everyone hates you sooner or later. You're always all by yourself. Everyone thinks the same thing about you. No one likes you or even wants you around! (Bodily sensations heighten, and the encounter moves ahead.)

Pt. (near to tears): He picks on me . . . (A final stab at putting the blame on the provoked aggressor.)

T: And now you're all alone and hated. It's always like this.

Pt.: (Stanley cries.)

T: No one wants you around, ever. (Stanley cries harder and harder.) Maybe he'll fire you. Hell, you ask for it, and then you'll really be alone. Jobs are hard to get.

Pt.: It's not my fault.

T: Yes it is, little boy. It's your fault.

Pt. (louder): No!

T (firmly): It's always your fault. It always ends up the same way . . . no one ever wants you.

Pt.: (Stanley sobs for a minute or so. Then he is silent.) . . . I thought I could go through something. I'd have something happen and something big and I thought it would take maybe a year but then I'd be different. I thought I'd blow up and get mad about something and then I'd be better, I'd be different. (But the deeper potential knows this is illusion. Here is the last wisp of hope for a magical burst of transforming energy followed by the idyllic state in which there is no more rejection, no sense of being unwanted or uncared for. It is as if the deeper potential knows the folly of such hopes.)

T: And then there would be flowers and sunshine and wonderful people who love and cherish you . . .

Pt.: (He falls into sobbing.) I may as well be dead . . . (Much more

sobbing.) I'm finished . . . (Silence. Then, the tone is somewhat lighter.) It's like everyone went away.

T (miffed): Hey! Wait a minute! I gotta be rejected, remember? Where is everyone? Come back? I need you! Where the hell are they? Dammit! Dammit to hell! The kid's alone! He says he's finished! Nobody's listening to me! How the hell is the kid going to feel miserable! He needs you all so he can feel shitty, you know, rejected and alone?

Pt.: My face feels funny. My skin feels scorched. It's very strange! My skin is like leather and hot. Like it's all loose and . . . I feel . . . (Big long sigh.) This is weird! It's really weird. My body feels like one thing inside, and my skin feels like it's not my skin. It feels like I'm inside my skin and my skin is parched . . . hot, scorched, and like (laughs lightly) it's maybe three or four inches from my body. Like I can move around a little and my skin just stays there. But I can feel it like it's still mine. This is weird! If I move too much it's like maybe it'd hurt. I mean my skin. It's tough and leathery and all around me. I never had anything like this!

With Stanley being the aggressively provocative little boy (OP2, Figure 1), and with the therapist as the voice and agency of the good integrative form of the deeper sense of being unwanted, uncared for and alone (DP7, Figure 1), there is a heightening of the experiencing of the interactive relationship between the two. At first it becomes painful and scary, and then it moves toward a more integrative experiencing, a closer and more open relationship.

Experiential Being of the Deeper Potential

To the extent that there has been a carrying forward of deeper potentials (step 2, Figure 2) and an integrative softening of the relationship between the patient and the deeper potential (step 3, Figure 2), the way is now open for Stanley to undergo the experiential being of the deeper potential. In this step, the very heart and center of his sense of I-ness is to disengage from and leave behind the whole identity of the person he has been and is. Stanley is to emerge out of the entire operating domain (Figure 1) and, in a profoundly radical metamorphosis, be and exist as the deeper potential. There are several techniques for undertaking this shift. Here are two of these techniques.

New experiencing in redivived critical moments. Experiential work illu-

minates earlier moments in Stanley's life, moments in which the deeper potential could have occurred, or started to occur. These are critical moments when, in an instant, Stanley might be and exist as the deeper potential or, instead, run from it, block it, deny it, follow a way of being which becomes the operating potential. The technique consists of returning to these critical moments and, this time, being and existing and experiencing as the carried forward, integrative, new, good form of the deeper potential.

In the kitchen, with mother, there was a critical moment in which Stanley was close to being the deeper experiencing of powerful control (DP4, Figure 1). We return to that moment and have the opportunity of choosing to be that deeper potential. The moment is returned to by describing every detail of that scene: what the kitchen looks like, the objects and colors and smells, what mother looks like, her body posture and her words, everything about the immediate scene. Little by little the details are illuminated, and both therapist and patient are here, living in this moment. The therapist defines the nature of the deeper experiencing, including the sense of being big and strong, the inner firmness and strength, the internal intactness, and the words Stanley said earlier in beginning to express this new experiencing: ". . . Real big and strong . . . I felt stronger . . . I felt hard inside . . . she couldn't do nothing to me. Something inside felt . . . indestructible. Yes, indestructible . . ."

The invitation is for Stanley to disengage from the ordinary, continuing operating domain, the person whom he is, and, instead, to exist and be and experience as this deeper potential. The therapist leaves the choice to him. In deciding to go ahead, the instructions show him what to do and how to do it. In essence, he is to be in that critical moment, be the deeper potential, and experience fully. We take up where he is beginning:

Pt.: I own you. I can get you to do whatever I want. Yes. Yes. Mommie! Mommie! I got you. I control you! (The therapist is here with Stanley, saying this to her, experiencing this.)

T (with full feeling): I control you! Do what I say!

Pt.: (His voice takes on a firmer quality.) You are going to do what I want! Yes, I see the way you look now. I see you. Oh yes! Yes! It's me! Me! I am the one! Do what I want! I feel evil and . . . and mad. I am strong! God, I am! You know it, don't you? You've always known it. You're scared of me now, Mommie! Get down on your knees and say you're sorry. Get down!!! DO IT!!!

T: DO IT!!! NOW!!!

Pt.: Nobody gets to me, Mommie! No one! Do you hear! Huh? Apologize
   for never wanting a child! DO IT! MORE! YES! YES! CRY! GO
   AHEAD! You never wanted a child! You never wanted to have a
   man! You wanted to have an abortion and you hated me before I
   was even born!!! You wanted a divorce from him AND FROM ME!!!
   ADMIT IT YOU BITCH! Yeah, cry! It's true! Cry! Admit it! ADMIT
   IT!!! (He is screaming in a booming voice. Then he starts laughing,
   and the laughing is screeching, laced and punctuated with words
   like "I know . . . I've always known . . . you can't fool me . . .")

Stanley is being and experiencing as the deeper potential. Here is one
way of enabling the patient to undergo the experiential being of the
deeper potential.

Doing to them what they did to you. A second technique is also known
as reversal (Perls, 1971), accusing the accusers (Shorr, 1972), and the
method of converse consequences (Loevinger, 1966). Within experiential
psychotherapy, one way of constructing external individuals is for these
persons to be the voice and the agency of the patient's own deeper
potentials. For example, if there is a deeper control in the patient, then
from childhood on there is always some external figure who is the controller; if there is a deeper harsh rejection, then from childhood on there
is always some external figure who is the rejecting one. Typically it is
unthinkable for the patient to reverse the process and to be the active
one who controls the controller or rejects the rejecter. Yet this is the
technique through which the patient undergoes the experiential being
of the deeper potential.

In step 3, Stanley gained a measure of integrative relationship with
the deeper potential for experiencing the sense of being unwanted, uncared for, rejected and alone (DP7, Figure 1). In its more integrative
form, this is the experiencing of independence, intactness, autonomy
(OP7, Figure 3). However, it is the boss who is the rejecting one, the
one who does not care, the independent and autonomous one. In order
to gain the experiential being of this deeper potential, the instructions
show Stanley how to do to the boss what the boss does to him. Stanley
is ready:

Pt.: You miserable little slime. I don't give a fucking damn for you. You
   are miserable. I have never cared for you, never. I have never given
   a damn about your puny business. You are nothing but a grasping

slob. You and your stories about football. They are sad little ex-
aggerations. You're not 20 anymore. You're not on the team any
more. You're a sad sack, and none of us gives a fucking damn
about you or your business. We want our pay checks and a chance
to get the hell away from you and your "team." The team is over,
boy! It's all over! I don't like you! I never have. . . . You're just a
sad ex-football player who can't make it in the adult world. You
poor slob. (He stops, breathes deeply and slowly, and continues.)
I feel tingly all over my body. Like I'm in my body. My body. I feel
clean . . . nice . . . I feel like a person. Fresh. I like this . . . I see
you so clearly. Clearly . . . I feel good. Light sort of, and floaty.
I never felt like this . . . yeah . . .

Here are two techniques whereby Stanley disengages from the continuing, substantive personality in which he exists, and enters into a
new existence as the deeper potential. From here we move on to the
final step of the session.

Being/Behavior Change in the Extra-Therapy World

The patient has carried forward experiencings (step 2), has experienced the relationship with deeper potentials (step 3), and has experienced the very being of the deeper potential (step 4). To the extent that
Stanley has undergone these changes, the invitation is to be and behave
in new and different ways in the extratherapy world. I am referring to
concrete changes, specific new and different ways of being and behaving; also, I am referring to changes which are accompanied with a sense
of risk, i.e., a little excitement, a little nerve-edged titillation mixed with
a little fright.

Here is the risked consideration of actual, specific new ways of being
and behaving, coming from the new Stanley who carries forward experiencing a little further, who now has a more integrative relationship
with the deeper potentials, and who can exist and be the deeper potential. Here is risked possibility of new behavioral possibilities, the heightened sense of choice to be and behave in ways which were not possible
before the session. Of the various techniques, I shall illustrate two.

Playfully being the disintegrative form the the deeper potential. Throughout
his life, Stanley made sure that he never fully existed as a thoroughly
unwanted, uncared for, absolutely rejected, completely alone, agonizing
person (DP7, Figure 1). Instead, he spent his life as an aggressively

provocative little child (OP2) doing painful things with provoked aggressors such as his current boss. During the session he gave this deeper experiencing a taste of life, he achieved a somewhat integrative relationship with it, and he even existed within it. Now he is ready to risk the consideration of letting it come forth into the real extra-therapy world.

T: Listen, Stan, I'll tell you just how you can really feel alone and rejected, miserable, really rotten. First you got to stop going to work.

Pt.: That's silly, I have to work!

T: No, wait! Listen! Just stop going to work. Then you'll be home all the time. Stay home. Then you can be hard to get along with, and make Rachel take care of you because you're so damned unhappy and sorry for yourself. You do that pretty well.

Pt.: She wouldn't like that.

T: See! Now you got it. Make life miserable for her. She has to do the shopping and cooking 'cause you're feeling rotten. And after about, oh maybe three months . . .

Pt.: She'd leave me.

T: Right! Now, here's phase two. Listen carefully. You then fall apart. Don't bathe, don't eat. Stay in bed. Curl up like a baby, and cry. You have to cry hard and loud so that others in the building will hear you. Open the door and windows.

Pt. (lightening up): I thought about that. It sounds too real. It could happen. I could do it, I know. It's been, around the corner. Never wanted to think about it. Actually, I think I do a pretty fair job as it is, now. (He is playing with the possibilities of actual changes in ways of being and behaving, and he moves into the good, integrated form of this potential, the sense of independence and autonomy.) . . . I'm thinking about Rachel. She mentioned maybe I could work with another guy, Henry. He's an architect too. I think maybe that Henry and I could work together. And I think we could get along. Maybe I could quit. I could tell them off. I've been rotten there, I know. I've been awful. I don't wanna . . . I don't know. I think maybe I could just leave there. Rachel's always wanted me to quit. I maybe could talk with her about that. Henry and I could start our own firm. The two of us. I've liked doing little renovations, and Henry has this remodeling place. I could work with him, think I've always wanted. . . . I'll talk with her about that. I like him. Rachel's wanted more security. Wanted to be more with me. I think I could. Something more on my own, with Henry.

Like to have a hand running my own shop with Henry. Might be OK. Seems maybe possible. To have my own place. I love Rachel. I know I've been . . . I haven't . . . well, hell, I want to do more things with her. I think I'd like to talk maybe with her about this, all of this. . . .

Being the new way which emerged in the session. Each step in the experiential process is a stage on which new ways of being and behaving are played out. Stanley was being a new and different way. Here comes the question of generalizability or transferability or simply being this way in the extratherapy world. For example, during the course of the session, Stanley allowed himself to be a strong person (OP4, Figure 3), and this was accompanied with quite pleasant bodily sensations and feelings. Suppose that he entertains the possibility of being and behaving in this way, but now in the actual extratherapy world? The therapist refers back to the way Stanley was with Mommie:

T: I loved being this way. It was great! "Admit it you bitch! Yeah, cry! It's true! Cry! Admit it! . . . You can't fool me." Wow, that was wonderful! My whole body felt great!

Pt.: Uh huh. Me too!

T: Let's see. I want to do this really. Get them to admit it. No more going along with the lies. I got it! I'm going to throw a party for my Mommie, my aunts, and my grandmom. Over my Mommie's house. And I'm going to blow the whistle on all this shit I've been taking all my life, right? You know all those nasty little remarks and innuendos about Rachel? Well, no more! They either take their claws off of her or . . . no! They have to apologize to her. Yeah! They got to say they're sorry. They've been blaming her for years, and all that shit about babies. They never stop. OK. From now on, they stop! . . . And I'm going to get tough. Strong. Go to the Y and start training. Kung-Phooey or whatever. Get strong and lethal. And make Rachel do all those great sexy things you've always dreamed about. Make her blow you, and beat her up a couple of times. A new whip'll help . . .

Pt. (laughing): Can I talk now?

T: Ask nicely.

Pt.: I want to talk with my Dad. I did a terrible thing. I always . . . when I was a kid he always took me places and showed me buildings. He was an engineer. Not a very good one. He loved buildings. I thought I'd make him happy . . . and he wasn't at all. But the

thing is. I never. He never said he wanted me to be an architect. I started school and did it for him. Then I've been mad at him 'cause he still doesn't think much of me. He still is a . . . well, depressed and feeling sorry for himself. What a damned shame. My fault, a little. I guess I got to do some admitting to him. But I never talk with him alone. My mother. She's always there. I never . . . we talk about him. She talks about him and I just let her and listen. I got to tell her no and talk to him. I mean for me. I have to talk to him. Maybe it won't make any difference to him, but for me. I want to admit that I never really wanted to be an architect. Like maybe he never really wanted to be an engineer. I thought it would make him happy. I feel funny. Like I am all excited. I want to talk to my Dad! (Laughs.) Yeah!

CONCLUSION

Denouement

In this chapter I have tried to present my own version of a humanistic-existential theory of what this theory understands as passive-aggression. I know that there are different meanings of "passive-aggression," thankfully, and that there are different theories of what we mean by passive-aggression. I have also tried to present my own version of an experiential approach to therapeutic work with a person who represents what I mean by passive-aggression. In the spirit of moving forward the humanistic-existential theory of passive-aggression and the experiential approach to therapeutic work with these persons, I would like to know of other psychotherapists who are similarly concerned with the matters discussed in this chapter.

REFERENCES

American Psychiatric Association. *Diagnostic and statistical manual of mental disorders*. Third Edition. Washington, D.C., 1980.
Bach, G. R., & Goldberg, H. *Creative aggression*. Garden City, NY: Doubleday, 1974.
Cole, M. *Violent sheep: The tyranny of the meek*. New York: Times Books, 1980.
Friedman, A. M., & Kaplan, H. I. (Eds.) *Comprehensive textbook of psychiatry*. Baltimore: Williams & Wilkins, 1967.
Kemp, D. E. Curing "moral masochism." In M. James (Ed.), *Techniques in transactional analysis*. Reading, MA: Addison-Wesley, 1977, pp. 387-394.
Klein, D. F., & Davis, J. *Diagnosis and drug treatment of psychiatric disorders*. Baltimore: Williams & Wilkins, 1969.
Loevinger, J. Three principles for psychoanalytic psychology. *Journal of Abnormal Psychology*, 1966, 5, 432-443.

Mahrer, A. R. *Experiencing: A humanistic theory of psychology and psychiatry.* New York: Brunner/Mazel, 1978.

Mahrer, A. R. *Experiential psychotherapy: Basic practices.* New York: Brunner/Mazel, 1983.

Millon, T. *Disorders of personality: DSM-III, Axis II.* New York: John Wiley, 1981.

NIMH Document. *Outpatient psychiatric clinics.* Public Health Service Publication No. 1854, 1966.

NIMH Document. *Patients in mental institutions.* Public Health Service Publication No. 1818, 1967.

Pasternack, S. A. The explosive, antisocial, and passive-aggressive personalities. In J. R. Lion (Ed.), *Personality disorders: Diagnosis and management.* Baltimore: Williams & Wilkins, 1974. pp. 45-69.

Perls, F. S. *Gestalt therapy verbatim.* Toronto: Bantam, 1971.

Shorr, J. E. *Psycho-imagination therapy.* New York: Intercontinental Medical Book Corporation, 1972.

Small, I. F., Small, J. G., Alig, V. B., & Moore, D. F. Passive-aggressive personality disorder: A search for a syndrome. *American Journal of Psychiatry,* 1970, *126,* 973-983.

Whitman, R. M., Trosman, H., & Koenig, R. Clinical assessment of passive-aggressive personality. *Archives of Neurology and Psychiatry,* 1954, *72,* 540-549.

Wolberg, L. R. *The technique of psychotherapy.* New York: Grune & Stratton, 1977.

6

Passive-Aggressiveness: An intrapsychic, interpersonal, and transactional dynamic in the family system

Florence W. Kaslow

A perusal of the family therapy literature yields few indexed references to passive-aggressiveness. Consequently, searching for an existing framework or model within the family systems approach upon which to build a clinical portrait of passive-aggressiveness as a dynamic within the family system could lead to great frustration. Thus, this emerges as a tentative, speculative formulation which attempts to draw upon some ideas articulated in DSM-III and in the theory and practice of family therapy. Hopefully, it will stimulate others to consider this dynamic further since, given the frequency with which we do encounter passive-aggressiveness in family therapy, it merits further consideration.

Appreciation is expressed to Gloria Weeks, M.S.W., staff member at the Florida Couples and Family Institute, for her able assistance in the preparation of this manuscript.

All case material is sufficiently disguised to protect the identity and privacy of the patients involved.

CLINICAL PROFILE: THEORETICAL PERSPECTIVE

In the following we have recast the psychiatric literature on the individual into a family systems perspective. Let us see where that leads. Regarding the passive-aggressive personality, DSM-III (American Psychiatric Association, 1980) states that "the essential feature is a Personality Disorder in which there is resistance to demands for adequate performance in both occupational and social functioning; the resistance is expressed indirectly rather than directly" (p. 328). The implication in the first part of the definition seems to be that the problem is an intrapsychic one; it is *within* the personality of the individual and in some characteristic way a definite feature of the person's very being. However, the definition then refers to resistance to demands for performance. Such phraseology usually connotes opposition to something expected from an external source, probably another human being—real in the present or remembered vividly, even if inaccurately, from the past. The inclusion of the phrase "in both occupational and social functioning" catapults the personality disorder into the interpersonal sphere, moving outside of the intrapsychic domain and one's private self into the social unit of the family and/or peer network and the work world. From a family systems perspective, relationships are conceptualized in terms of circular rather than linear causality and impact; thus, if the "resistance is expressed indirectly rather than directly" it is nonetheless communicated to, and likely to disturb, one or more family members. Given that the expression may be covert and have the effect of exerting pressure on others to either become more demadning or take over to get the task accomplished, leaving them feeling subtly undermined and therefore resentful, this passive withholding can constitute a quietly powerful and controlling maneuver. Also, since the message is indirect and often unspoken, the passive resister can seem so nice and soft-spoken, while the "demanding" party who wants something done or requests an answer gets louder and appears more shrewish to the outside observer. This irony compounds the dilemma; how can one justify disliking or being angry at such a seemingly nice, low-keyed person who others may see as the hapless victim of excessive tirades?

DSM-III goes on to state that the passive resistance is expressed even when "more self-assertive and effective behavior is possible" (p. 328). This is possible, but not probable, from a family systems perspective. Although the family member may sense, or even cognitively know, that more assertive behavior is permissible, he or she may realize, accurately, that greater conflict and eventual loss of power will ensue from assertive

responses, whereas through passivity leverage and some control are acquired. It is suggested here that passive behavior is deemed to be more effective in some critical arenas of interpersonal relations than assertive actions would be; otherwise it would not be resorted to. Seeming passivity, or doing nothing, can be a powerful and hostile stance; it makes others exceedingly uncomfortable and often forces them into taking the initiative to say or do almost anything to break the uncomfortable silence and/or impasse. We therefore agree completely with the next DSM-III sentence that "The name of this disorder is based on the assumption that such individuals are passively expressing covert aggression" (p. 328). Whereas overt aggression would be criticized and disregarded, covert passive hostility is much harder to recognize and argue against. It is less apparent and more insidious; the perpetrator often seems a beleaguered victim or scapegoat in the family context. Yet, when the dynamics are visualized and then diagrammed in a circular feedback loop and causal cycle, it is evident that he or she is also a provacateur. Such aggression is hard to deal with; the target person often is uncertain that his/her perception of its depth and reality are accurate; other family members may not notice it or may subtly promote it since the passive one is also acting out their unexpressed negative feelings and they are quietly cheering on the sidelines.

Next DSM-III informs us that "Individuals with this disorder habitually resent and oppose demands to increase or maintain a given level of functioning" (p. 328). As will be shown later, the repetitive nature of the problem not only is intrapsychic, but also becomes a feature of the family's transactional pattern and contributes to keeping the system stuck. The thought of change may be even more abhorrent than the tedium and discomfort of the repetitive, demanding, passive resistance cycle. Being oppositional by doing little or getting into trouble for nonperformance can be a superb attention-getting mechanism. In a family system that does not usually recognize good behavior and/or supportive interactions, even negative attention may be preferred to no attention.

Quite another advantage of passive-aggressiveness is that it may provide an excellent channel through which the adolescent, who has been told "not to make waves," can express his rebellious urges without as great a risk of inducing punishment. And what a marvelous way for the seemingly less powerful member of a marital dyad to sabotage his/her more outspoken, domineering spouse. What delight must ensue for those who can upstage an authoritative spouse, parent, or sibling by embarrassing them through being late, never arriving at a special event, or failing to get an important task done when guests are expected!

DSM-III states that "this occurs most clearly in work situations, but is also evident in social functioning." As shown above, it is also manifest in family relationships and it is not uncommon in school situations. Passive-aggressive college students may reenact the family scenario with certain professors—attempting to inveigle them by saying on the last day of the semester that their goals for the course remained unfulfilled and implying the instructor is at fault, although they remained uncommunicative when asked earlier in the term what their objectives were. Similarly, although notice of when a term paper is due may be given 10 to 12 weeks in advance, passive-aggressive students are likely to come into class the week before the deadline and ask for an extension—testing out and "trapping" the naive instructor by questioning whether he/she is really as flexible and concerned about students' well-being as he/she purports to be. In the same way, they challenged their parents with meta messages about "if you really loved and understood me, you'd let me get away without fulfilling my commitments." They have never learned to assume responsibility for their own performance.

My experience with such students (and family members) has been that it may be best to answer the query, "What happens if it isn't in or done on time?" with, "Then it is not acceptable"—without further explanation. The implications are convincingly clear! (Of course, an exception should be made when really serious extenuating circumstances intervene.)

In each of these circumstances, we concur with DSM-III (p. 328) that "the resistance is expressed indirectly, through such maneuvers as procrastination, dawdling, stubbornness, intentional inefficiency, and 'forgetfulness.'" How can one fault a mate or child who apologizes convincingly and says, "I'm so sorry; I forgot," even if the omission had serious consequences? After all, a devoted parent or spouse can never be 100% sure the "forgetting" was deliberate; if he or she were, then self-respect would dictate confrontation and this would threaten the tenuous homeostasis of the marital or family system. It seems better to overlook the perfidy and assume it was a lapse in memory.

Stubbornness is perhaps the least passive of the machinations in the above list and the one most apt to incite anger and reprimands. A perpetually obstinate family member's impact on others can be extreme—even to the point of provoking rejection in the form of "either do it or move out" or in the form of child or spouse abuse.

An example given in DSM-III is that "a housewife with this disorder fails to do the laundry or to stock the kitchen with food because of procrastination." Clearly she is reneging on her ascribed nurturing-care-

taking functions. What is not clear in such a unidimensional portrait is:
1) what appreciation she receives for food-shopping and preparation;
2) what value is placed on her role as laundress; 3) whether other family
members dawdle in responding to her requests; 4) whether nurturing
is valued or disparaged in the family and social context. Without this
knowledge, we do not know the interactive meaning of the symptom/
syndrome or if it is utilized for leverage, to gain power, or to convey
displeasure. On the other hand, it may represent a behavior which has
acquired its own "functional autonomy"; that is, it may have become
an end or objective in and of itself, even though initially the actions
were undertaken for quite another reason. This important concept was
formulated by Gordon Allport, who stated "functional autonomy re-
gards adult motives as varied, and as self-sustaining contemporary systems, growing out of antecedent systems, but functionally independent
of them" (Allport, 1961, p. 227). To the extent that passive-aggressiveness has become an internalized, entrenched, habitual way of acting and
reacting for an individual, it will probably elicit repetitive symmetrical
or complementary reactions from all other members of the family and
contribute to the "stuckness" of the system (Bateson, 1936, 1958). More
will be said about this cyclical interaction later.

The first explanatory-descriptive passage in DSM-III concludes with
the sentence "For the diagnosis to be made, it is essential that this
pattern of behavior occur in a variety of contexts in which more adaptive
functioning is clearly possible." In family systems terms, the repetitive
behavior occurs at the transactional level as well as at the intrapsychic
and interpersonal levels, thereby becoming a somewhat rigidified element in the family's homeostasis. From a growth perspective, if more
adaptive behavior were possible and the person could dislodge him-
self/herself from the impasses such behavior helps lock tightly into place,
it would be utilized. More effective actions might well be possible—but
for someone else!

Regarding *associated features*, DSM III states, "Often individuals with
this disorder are dependent and lack self-confidence." In systems terms
in seeking a mate, they are likely to link up with someone upon whom
they can be dependent, an apparently strong, self-sufficient person who
will be a rescuer or caretaker. In return for the protection they receive,
they are supposed to be appreciative and compliant and definitely nonconfrontational. The passivity is perpetuated; however, there is accompanying rage and frustration which gets repressed. When the accumulated
fury can no longer be held in, it breaks through in unexpected verbal
or physical aggressiveness. Since such an outburst is likely to place the

relationship in jeopardy, and the passive/dependent partner fears being abandoned and left to fend for himself/herself, he or she is likely to apologize.

For example, let us consider Mr. and Mrs. Green. In marital therapy Mrs. Green was trying to change the nature of their Doll's House marriage (Ibsen, 1879); Mr. Green, in turn, had become annoyed and worried that he and the children were no longer enough for her, which constituted a terrible wound to his narcissism. Mrs. Green finally became enraged and shouted, "You can no longer keep me a puppet-paper doll, only doing what you allow me to do, dancing as you pull the strings. I will no longer be treated as if I am stupid and incapable and kept in a gilded cage."

Mr. Green then stated firmly and derisively, "Considering what a wonderful world I've created for you, that you are the envy of all of our friends, how can you be so ungrateful? If you are so capable, you're free to leave your beautiful gilded cage." Imperiously he stalked out of the room.

Frightened by the passion of her resentful outburst, and fearful of the threatened dire consequences of having to manage on her own, Mrs. Green wept piteously. Exhausted and devastated at the thought of losing her lovely home (gilded cage), her adoring husband (guardian of her cell), and her carefully circumscribed and envied status in the community, she prettied up her tear-stained face, dashed on her husband's favorite cologne and went to him, docilely and seductively saying, "I don't know what possessed me; I didn't mean all those horrible things I said. You're the most wonderful husband in the world and I will do anything you want and be whatever you want. Just don't leave me. My life would be meaningless without you."

Mrs. Green's passive, acquiescent nature and quiet beauty had attracted Mr. Green. He needed a spouse whom he could dominate and take care of according to his specifications. When she wanted to expand her thinking and behavioral repertoire and become more assertive in seeking self-fulfillment, Mr. Green was not ready to renegotiate the unwritten, unspoken marital contract (Sager, 1976). Unconsciously, he wanted to keep his wife a doll-bride, having her remain almost static in time. He did not want her to grow and change, assume initiative or think for herself; he loved her as she was. This is a common element in reenforcing a passive/dependent partner's characteristic way of being in the world.

The above case material is a little at odds with part of the description in DSM-III, even though they seem to reflect an interpersonal rather

than a purely intrapsychic context. It is stated that "Typically, they [passive-aggressive personalities] are *pessimistic* about the future but have no realization that their behavior is responsible for their difficulties. Although the individual may experience conscious resentment against authority figures, he or she never connects his or her passive-resistant behavior with this resentment" (p. 328). In the Green case we see the *systems elements of circular causality*—she attracts him partially because of her passive-compliant personality; he likes it and wants to perpetuate it. When she wishes to discontinue this pattern, he resorts to being authoritarian to subvert her effort to change. Overwhelmed at the potential consequences of defying him openly, and uncertain that her desire to be more self-actualizing is valid, she backs off. The repression of her desire for greater autonomy, at least for the ensuing time period, combined with her dawning awareness of his negation of her selfhood, causes tremendous resentment to build within; this resentment is like a potentially explosive volcano, likely to erupt again with aggressive force when the tremors within can no longer be contained. The linear causality posited in DSM-III emerges as too simplistic and inadequate an explanatory model for such complex system dynamics.

DSM-III goes on to indicate that "frequent complications include major depression . . . and alcohol abuse or dependence." Clinically this is congruent with a family systems perspective. This is vividly shown in the case below.

THERAPEUTIC STRATEGY AND PROCESS

Therapeutic strategy will be illustrated in the case of Bob S., who was 23 when he first came to see me. He had been referred by a student in the graduate school setting in which I taught. She had been dating him and was concerned about his prolonged depressed mood.

History

Bob was one of three children. His brother, Stan, was a year older and sister Sue was three years younger. Bob remembered his Dad, who had died four years earlier, as kindly, fairly affectionate, quiet and somewhat ineffectual. Mom was seen as powerful, manipulative, and ambivalent—encouraging him to be a bright, achieving student, yet discouraging his efforts during adolescence to individuate and become self-directing in terms of choice of activities, friends, use of time, and career goals. He perceived Stan as the outspoken sibling who had been

gutsy enough to "do his own thing" and be his own master, but knew his disobedience had caused their parents, particularly Mom, great anguish. Stan had been labeled the "bad" son, headstrong and belligerent. He had extricated himself by going away to Chicago to get his MBA and had settled in the midwest after graduating when he acquired a junior executive position in a large corporate firm.

Bob had not wanted to irritate his mother; in fact, throughout his childhood and adolescence he had consciously wanted to please her by being good—in order to continue to get whatever approval and positive sanctions for his behavior and thoughts he could from her, as he felt this was necessary for his survival. During the pregenital and latency years he had realized her love was contingent upon his being "good," which for him meant being quiet, respectful, agreeable, and pleasant. Just "being" was insufficient to warrant nurturing and spontaneous affection. Being uncertain of his mother's love, and fearing the wrath she showed when Stan became too intractable, Bob exhibited a great deal of passive, compliant behavior. His reality-testing had been accurate. Nice Dad did not protect Stan from Mom's derisive attacks; if anything he meekly backed her up with telling the boys, "You should mind your mother." Dad maintained the precarious balance in the family through an acquiescent "peace at any price" modus operandi—he knew he either conformed to his wife's dictates or the family he so valued would break asunder. Although his idealized image of his loving, harmonious family did not coincide with the reality of the family's dynamics and functioning, Mr. S. had deluded himself into thinking "some how things will get better."

Dad had been a senior in college when he married Mrs. Silver. He entered medical school the next year; she became pregnant. During his second year, she again became pregnant and required more help and attention from him than he could supply and still keep up with his studies. He took a leave of absence, got a job with regular hours and a good salary, and helped his young wife with the child-rearing. As the family size increased and their financial needs grew correspondingly, he found himself unable to leave his secure job and return to medical school. He resented this disruption of his life ambition but superficially was resigned because he wanted to be a good husband and father. His wife believed him to be somewhat of a failure—unable to juggle everything and become a successful doctor.

Twenty-year-old Sue was pretty and sweet. She seemed to acquiesce to her mother's expectations yet often did what she wanted to outside of the home. Her major defense was to rarely discuss what she thought,

felt or did, so as not to antagonize her mother. Mom thought Sue was cooperative and quiet, and so Sue escaped criticism and had formed an unobtrusive but fulfilling alliance with her Dad. She was popular at school and Mom approved of her high achieving friends, so she did not become a focal child for Mom's frustration and belligerence.

During high school, Bob became aware of his artistic talents in sculpting. Under the tutelage of several fine teachers, he came to realize that he was very bright and articulate and decided that his dream was to go to law school. He joined the debate society and began to develop proficiency in intellectual argumentation. He became more optimistic, hoping that he could logically talk to his Mom about *his* desire to go to law school rather than to medical school, for which he had been scripted. (He was to replace Dad in *her* dream to have a doctor spouse.) He also decided to ask to be allowed to convert part of their basement into an art studio in which to sculpt—a medium in which he found tremendous relief from his pent-up tensions and obsessive-compulsive traits. He wanted to utilize his wonderful manual dexterity which Mom saw as essential for the skilled surgeon in this artistic pursuit instead.

Although during his 16th and 17th years, Bob had tactfully and cogently explained his desires and ambitions, he found them negated each time he opened up the subject. An art workshop in the basement would be expensive to install; it would become too messy to tolerate. Law school was ridiculous; she insisted they had agreed he would go into a good premedical program and he was not to renege on his word. The whole family would be disappointed and he owed this to them. Although at a preconscious level he knew that he had not agreed but had been swept along by her enthusiasm for this career goal for him, Bob did not have the courage and fortitude to buck her and be disloyal to the family goal and image (Boszormenyi-Nagy and Spark, 1973). He entered a premedical program, felt restless and dissatisfied and found himself becoming sad, less energetic, more detached. Several frantic assertive efforts to tell his Mom "lay off, it's my life and I have to do what's right for me," led to forceful reproaches accompanied by the threat of refusing to pay his tuition if he transferred to being a political science/pre-law student. Bob's doubts about his own gender identity surfaced in the form of loss of appetite and sleeplessness. He began going to student hangouts more regularly for a few beers. His father had a stroke and rapidly deteriorated during Bob's senior year; he died a few months before Bob's graduation. Bob made a "death bed promise" to "take care of Mom and not aggravate her."

His ensuing reactive depression was severe; he felt trapped and unable

to spring the release latch. He resorted to drinking daily, barely managing to finish his last semester. In August, before he was scheduled to enter medical school, he made a final thrust to share his grief with his mother and siblings to pull himself out of the quicksand into which he had sunken. Each was dealing with the loss separately and each was unwilling to discuss his/her agony. Bob's mother's response was "Pull yourself together. What's done is done. You will start medical school in two weeks and make your father and me proud. He would prefer that to your tears."

Bob's long-term underlying sense of hopelessness and helplessness about his ability and right to make his own choices (Seligman, 1975) broke through and inundated him. His depression deepened; he felt flooded with despair. The day before he was to begin medical school, he collapsed and was hospitalized through emergency room admission. He had successfully, though unconsciously, (S. Freud, 1938) defied his mother—passively asserting control of his own destiny through becoming emotionally and physically ill.

After several weeks of tests, which revealed no organic difficulties, Bob was placed on an antidepressant and discharged from the hospital. It was too late to enter school and catch up with the class. He realized that along with his and mother's disappointment over this unexpected turn of events, he also felt relieved and maybe even victorious. Mom exhorted him to reserve a place in the next year's class; Bob promised to, yet kept putting it off. During the next six months he drifted, feeling pessimistic and without direction. He took a job as a salesman on the road, seeking a foundation of wisdom or an anchor during his travels and a way not to have to live home constantly with his mother and sister. He found neither. Returning to his home town, he took a position at the courthouse and began dating. That is when he sought therapy.

Therapeutic Process

His request was for individual therapy, and, given his age and expressed desire to break away from his mother's continuing pervasive influence, that appeared to be the treatment of choice. He was in a state of agitated depression—taking his medication some weeks, resorting to heavy drinking others. In therapy the main themes were his existential despair, his lack of a sense of self (the boundaries between him and mother were unclear), his resentment at being dictated to and expected to fulfill someone else's ambitions. He realized that to succumb and do so against his will meant emotional suicide to him and so he was resisting

becoming "my son, the doctor"; yet, he was paying a high price because his resistance had immobilized him. Conversely, he also realized that to refuse to follow the pathway his parents had charted for him led to his being branded an ingrate and a failure. Being listened to in therapy as he poured out years of accumulated frustration and rage, feeling permission to cry and scream, and sensing he could express his ambivalent desire to please his parents while still wanting to be himself and "do my own thing" without being considered weird or wicked enabled him to relax a little and take in the support for his strivings for independence and self-actualization (Maslow, 1968). In the first phase of treatment, his twice weekly sessions were conducted using a psychodynamic/insight-oriented approach and were very ego supportive, although a family systems perspective was maintained throughout. We contemplated the impact of his changing attitudes and behaviors on his significant others (Sullivan, 1953) and considered the influence of their ideas, values, and expectations on him. He navigated his way through I-Thou issues and considered what kind of balance he wanted to achieve between autonomy (self-determination) and homonomy (self-surrender to the needs of the larger environment or forces in nature) (Angyal, 1965).

Eager for self-knowledge and exceedingly bright, Bob made good headway. A strong therapeutic alliance evolved and he was able to permit stripping away of such defenses as repression, avoidance, denial and reaction formation (A. Freud, 1954). He became aware of the escapism and self-destructiveness inherent in his heavy drinking and his somatization of unexpressed anguish to the point of collapse. As he came to experience this as the result of anger turned inward and then felt free to ventilate and examine the rage in therapy and to release it in a more aggressive and forceful tennis game, his spirits lifted; the depression and drinking which had masked the anger abated considerably. He took on managerial responsibilities at the courthouse and found his rational thinking and pleasant yet competent demeanor earned him the respect of subordinates and colleagues.

After five months of therapy, his resolve to become an attorney had strengthened; however, he still felt powerless to tell his mother he was planning to apply to law school, to take the LSAT Examination, or to move into his own apartment.

This marked the transition into the second phase of therapy. His brother was coming east from Chicago for an extended holiday and three family sessions were scheduled for the family. Bob was coached on how to prepare them and was anticipating the sessions with a mixture of

eagerness and apprehension. He recognized and dealt with the other family members' ambivalence, reassuring them that the goal was "not to lay a guilt trip on anyone," but rather to invite them all to share whatever they could in enabling him to continue to make progress.

During the first session each family member told his or her story, offering his/her unique version of the family's history, dynamics, and critical incidents (Duhl, 1981; Kantor, in press). They were able to hear and relate to their varying perspectives on the same life event and the different meanings each attached to it. Stan commented on the novelty of their articulating feelings and not interrupting or contradicting one another with remarks like, "You should not feel that way," or, "That isn't the way it happened," which had been typical earlier.

Bob whispered, "I wish we could finally talk about Dad's death and funeral." This stimulated a much-delayed discussion of Mr. S.'s untimely death. The therapist was able to evoke some of the unresolved grief and free them to talk about their privately held sense of loss and reach out to one another in a more sharing/caring way as they attempted to cope anew with the mourning process. As they were about to depart, Mrs. S. volunteered, "It's as if therapy can open a whole new window on the world." Bob hung back as they left and said, "Wow, it just might work!"

The second family session revolved around issues and feelings evoked as a result of the prior meeting. The central theme of separateness and connectedness emerged. Although the (grown) children expressed their desires for clearer boundaries and the right to be more self-determining without feeling Mom's disapproval and unwillingness to give up control over their lives, they also talked about their mutual liking and admiration for one another, their continuing devotion to and concern for Mom, and their respect for Bob for recognizing the depth of his depression and being willing to become involved in therapy. He drew sufficient encouragement from this to unveil, positively and enthusiastically, his enjoyment of the court environment and his desire to become a lawyer. He asked that they consider his needs and wants and indicated that their endorsement of his plan was important to him, that he would rather proceed with it than without it.

His clarity and positive assertion of his dream (Beavers & Kaslow, 1981) were in marked contrast to his former pathetic, passive entreaties for permission and approval. Before concluding his impassioned monologue, he turned to Mom and said, genuinely and sympathetically, "I'm sorry I couldn't become the doctor you wanted. I just couldn't; even my love for you can't make it right for me." Mrs. S.'s eyes misted

and there was a brief but poignant silence. She broke it by saying wistfully. "I wanted it so much that I failed to hear your longings. Can you forgive me?" Bob went and hugged her and everyone present resonated to the power of the interchange and its enlightening, freeing consequences.

The third session might have been anticlimactic except for the fact that once Mrs. S. became "unstuck" from her frozen position, she was able to assess why she had forced Bob into complying with her demands to achieve scholastically and become a doctor. After a weekend of intensive soul searching, in preparation for the final scheduled family therapy interview, she realized her vicarious projection—she had aspired to being a doctor but her parents and much of society had crushed this objective in women of her generation. She had displaced the desire by marrying a man with the same aspiration, hoping to realize it vicariously, and then, unwittingly, had snuffed out his quest—interfering with his fulfillment as others had impeded hers. Her revealing exploration of her personal memory lane led her to comprehend vividly that for years she had been relying on Bob to bring the dream to fruition—for her! She came to the third session eager to recount her lucid picture and also to say that, in turning inward, she had found the sparks of her own longings still simmering. She had called several hospitals for appointments pertinent to positions in their administrative offices and was seriously contemplating returning to college to pursue a Masters in Hospital Administration.

Follow-up

With the unhealthy enmeshment threads disentangled, Bob was able to enter law school and three years later is doing well as a quietly assertive, considerate, and optimistic third-year law student who serves as a dorm counselor in order to earn his room and board away from home. Sue and Stan are able to communicate with each other, Bob, and Mom with greater candor and to express a wider range of emotions. Mrs. S. has completed her graduate work and is the recently hired administrator of a small suburban hospital. She and Bob talk by phone several times a week and are pleased with their new, mutually respectful mother-son relationship. When Bob believes she puts him down or tries to boss him around, he either says, "Ouch, you're up to your old shenanigans" or resorts to legal discourse.

Bob continues to maintain telephone contact with the therapist and comes in for a session about once every three months to continue to

solidify his gains. His plan is to terminate totally once he completes law school and is settled into a job that he finds challenging. He has grown into a confident, high achieving young professional—unbound from his earlier passive-aggressive patterns of behavior.

Commentary

DSM-III (329) continues regarding *predisposing factors* that "Oppositional Disorder in childhood or adolescence apparently predisposes to the development of this disorder." In the Silver family, Sue also manifested a subtle oppositional disorder, masking her annoyance and distress toward her dominant mother and submissive father by tuning them out, becoming secretive, and slyly pursuing her own course. Because Bob was targeted as the most likely to succeed academically and in personality seemed most vulnerable to his parents' demands, he became the scapegoat for his mother's frustrations and his father's longings. To survive the pressure, he developed a passive-aggressive style of relating; to the extent that it was ego-dystonic, he vacillated between trying to rid himself of the uncomfortable role of symptom bearer through becoming assertive and trying to ingratiate himself to all by being docile and compliant.

Bob, like Mrs. Green, met the DSM-III diagnostic criteria of expressing resistance in two or more of the following ways: procrastination, dawdling, stubbornness, intentional inefficiency, and forgetfulness. However, when viewed from a family systems perspective, it becomes evident that the behavior had become part of a patterned way of "being in relationships"—it had taken on interpersonal and transactional as well as intrapsychic meaning and import. Effective treatment involved first- and second-order change in the family's way of relating.

THE CLINICAL PROFILE RESUMED

Symmetry and Complementarity

Earlier in this chapter reference was made to the fact that marital and family relationship systems get "stuck." Let us elaborate this from a different vantage point than the DSM-III perspective utilized as a point of departure so far—that of symmetrical and complementary interaction (Bateson, 1936). Watzlawick, Beavin and Jackson, who utilize Bateson's work in *Naven* as a foundation for their seminal discourse in *Pragmatics of Human Communication* (1967), posit that dyadic partnerships may be

based either on equality or difference. In symmetrical relationships, in which equality is the cornerstone, partners frequently mirror each other's behavior. They tend to think and act in similar fashion, minimizing all differences. This can lead to much agreement and validation, repression of conflict, and/or boredom from too much sameness. It can also provoke a continual battle for control while the partners deceptively sustain an illusion of equality.

In complementary relationships, each partner's behavior complements the other's; the interaction is predicated on maximization of difference. This is exemplified in the reciprocal nature of the Greens' attachment in the Doll's House marriage depicted earlier. According to Watzlawick et al. (1967, p. 163), "there are two different positions in a complementary relationship." One partner assumes the "superior, primary, or 'one up' position"; the other occupies the corresponding "inferior, secondary, or 'one down' position." Whether this is the pattern which evolves specific to a given marital pair, or whether it is essential for survival, as in mother-baby bonding, the two roles are mutually intertwined and satisfying for as long as the "goodness of fit" remains intact. The person in the one down position is often the more passive, dependent, acquiescent member of the dyad (although a healthy child may be dependent in an age-appropriate manner without being excessively placid and compliant).

If the passive individual becomes stronger and more assertive, the dominant member negates or severely criticizes the thrust toward independence. The passive partner may retreat in order to regain the safety and security inherent in the one down position or he/she may ultimately become sufficiently outraged to subtly undermine the domineering partner through procrastination or withdrawal. (Bob S. did both.) Another mode may be an unexpected aggressive attack.

Only when one member escalates the fray by exaggerating the behavior the other disparages can they begin to break out of the impasse. The runaway behavior has to be sufficiently extreme to break the stultifying impasse. Pollack, N. Kaslow, and Harvey (1982) talk in terms of types of "interactional knots" which serve to maintain the homeostasis of the system, no matter how depressing and discouraging the repetitive cycling may be. Dell (1982) and others who posit a non-homeostatic view attest that symptoms and problems persist because of the pattern or organization of interactions in which they occur. He indicates that the problem behavior or pattern continues because the same (unworkable) solution is attempted repetitively.

Bateson (1936) seems to have given a slightly different explanation for

the stuckness in a relationship. In his study of two clans in New Guinea, he repeatedly observed that symmetrical rivalry persisted when and because it co-occurred with complementarity in the relationship. Pollack et al. (1982) also have found that when complementary and symmetrical relationships co-occur in the interactional context, this serves to maintain the interactional/transactional pattern repetition and lock people into tight knots. Although their hypothesis relates interactional knotting to the perpetuation of depression in the family system, their model seems to be equally applicable to passive-aggressiveness. Table 1 depicts this in graphic form.

To elucidate, considering the Greens, in Type 1: Interpersonal sphere—they shared in presenting an affective portrait of the idyllic couple and a world view on the importance of harmony; behaviorally, for him to be dominant, he needed and found a submissive spouse. The coexistence of these two dynamics kept the system from being toppled. When Mrs. Green threatened to disrupt the complementarity, Mr. Green stabilized it by re-asserting at a heightened level his role in their recip-rocal relationship and reminding her of their desire for a similar life-style.

In some families, a youngster who has responded to a volatile, abusive father by becoming passive to ward off impending verbal or physical attacks may eventually, as he grows physically larger and stronger, identify with the aggressor and become hostile and rebellious. The act-ing-out adolescent may be experiencing covert encouragement from his mother, who silently goads him into defying her husband—something

Table 1
Two Types of Interactional Knots Maintaining Passive-Aggressive
Behavior as a Problem in Families

	INTRAPERSONAL FIELD	INTERPERSONAL AND TRANSACTIONAL FIELD
Type #1	Affect (C)	Affect (S)
Domain of	Behavioral Competence (S)	Behavioral Competence (C)
Type #2	Affect (S)	Affect (C)
Domain of	Behavioral Competence (C)	Behavioral Competence (S)

Note: "S" and "C" refer to symmetry and complementarity, respectively.

Figure 1. A Positive Complementary Feedback Loop

Expresses understanding of son's disgruntlement

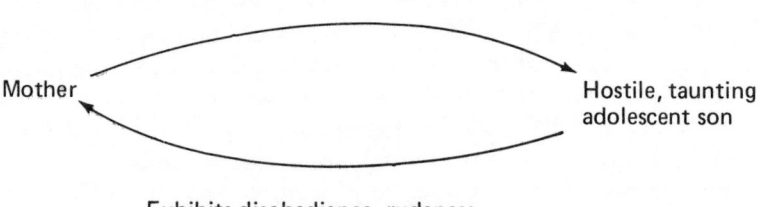

Exhibits disobedience, rudeness,
angry-aggressive behavior

she lacks the courage to do. Superficially, she expresses understanding of his disgruntlement and sets in motion a positive complementary feedback loop that becomes self-sustaining. This is depicted in Figure 1.

Another positive complementary feedback loop, illustrated in Figure 2, can be equally effective in maintaining a redundant pattern. These are labeled positive because they reinforce the existing modes of relating. Here both parents unite in disciplining their passive-aggressive son; rather than breaking the pattern which is their intent, they perpetuate it through repetitive symmetrical transactions.

A family therapist asked to treat either of these deeply entrenched, repetitive, circular patterns would need to challenge the continual reapplication of a nonworkable solution. Here, generating an accurate systemic hypothesis, reframing the role of the scapegoat into that of the family savior, and/or using a potent paradoxical injunction may constitute a successful intervention strategy (Selvini Palazzoli, Boscolo, Cecchin, & Prata, 1978).

Figure 2. A Positive Complementary Feedback Loop

Aggressively reject and
discipline undesirable behavior

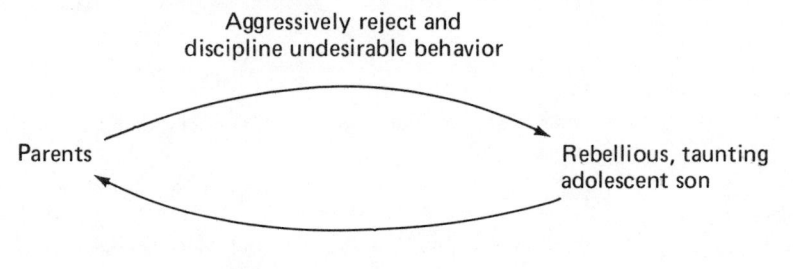

Exhibits similar rude, rejecting, hostile,
aggressive behavior

CONCLUSION

In this chapter, I have attempted to delineate and illuminate passive-aggressiveness as an eloquent, expressive dynamic in a couple's or family's interactional and transactional functioning. In the general discussion of the etiology and the clinical profile, as well as in the case presentations, what has emerged is a family systems perspective view of passive-aggressiveness as both a proactive and reactive characteristic way of behaving that can be cause and/or effect. This flows from an explanatory model that posits circular causality and feedback loops in interpersonal relationships.

Individuals were seen to perpetuate seemingly unsatisfying and demeaning complementary relationships because of linked symmetrical ones which inhibit escalation and the resultant pressure to self-correct or re-equilibrate differently that would be necessitated if the existing system were permitted to break down, that is, become truly dysfunctional. We have posited herein, along with Pollack et al. (1982) that runaway sequences in either the complementary or symmetrical domain comprise the pathway toward affective learning and differentiation. "Moments of relationship distortion are necessary to the [unknotting] process because they stand as invitations to the participants to interact differently. . . . the participant's experience of increasing distress is inextricably tied to the subsequent relief" (p. 179). Ultimately, only extreme escalation of either topples the entrenched pattern, thereby creating a vacuum to be filled with something new, generating the need for change and serving as a conduit for evolving a new interactive process.

Similarly, Kantor's (in press) thinking is quite congruent with the hypothesis being advanced here. He indicates that unresolved identity crises in a couple can lead to divorce *or* to the profound need to evolve new strategies for effectively reaching goals. Where the latter course of action is pursued, it will be essential that the spouses find ways to vary their customary action-reaction styles, enriching their lives through experimentation with new behaviors, thought patterns, and evaluative feedback inputs leading to a new, fulfilling creative synthesis.

Thus, the therapist consulted by a couple or family caught in a "ritual impasse," the "recurrent, episodic playing out of the family identity crisis," in this instance the dominant/passive-aggressive syndrome, has the task of helping them dynamite asunder the cords that bind them in their "wasteful, destructive exercise in mutually induced despair" (Kantor, in press). To do this, one must help them individuate by demarcating boundaries (Minuchin, 1974) and asserting their separate realities, help-

ing family members insist that their inner meanings, values and longings not be ignored, and that they be validated and appreciated for their thrust in the direction of self-actualization—as individuals and as a family group. The therapist must link up as a powerful change agent, in accordance with his/her own theoretical persuasion, in order to enable them to muster the determination, energy, creativity, and sense of humor necessary to change this or any other continuously recycled pattern of interactive behavior. The therapist must also know when to disengage from the family—respecting their ability to keep up their momentum and growth and not perpetuate a new dependency—this time on the therapist.

REFERENCES

Allport, G. W. *Pattern and growth in personality.* New York: Holt, Rinehart & Winston, 1961.
American Psychiatric Association. *Diagnostic and statistical manual of mental disorders.* Third Edition. Washington, D.C., 1980.
Angyal, A. *Neurosis and treatment: A holistic theory.* New York: Wiley, 1965.
Bateson, G. *Naven.* Cambridge: Cambridge University Press, 1936.
Bateson, G. *Naven.* Second Edition with added "Epilogue, 1958." Stanford: Stanford University Press, 1958.
Beavers, W. R., & Kaslow, F. W. The anatomy of hope. *Journal of Marital and Family Therapy,* 1981, 7 (2), 119-126.
Boszormenyi-Nagy, I., & Spark, G. *Invisible loyalties.* New York: Harper and Row, 1973.
Dell, P. Family theory and the epistemology of Humberto Maturana. In F. W. Kaslow (Ed.), *The international book of family therapy.* New York: Brunner/Mazel, 1982, pp. 56-66.
Duhl, F. J. The use of the chronological chart in general systems family therapy. *Journal of Marital and Family Therapy,* 1981, 7 (3), 361-374.
Freud, A. *The ego and the mechanisms of defense.* London: Hogarth Press, 1954.
Freud, S. *The basic writings of Sigmund Freud.* New York: Random House, 1938.
Ibsen, H. *A doll's house.* (1879).
Kantor, D. Critical identity image: A concept linking individual, couple, and family development. In J. K. Pearce & L. J. Friedman (Eds.), *Family perspectives on psychotherapy.* In press.
Maslow, A. *Toward a psychology of being.* New York: Van Nostrand, 1968.
Minuchin, S. *Families and family therapy.* Cambridge: Harvard University Press, 1974.
Pollack, S. L., Kaslow, N. J., & Harvey, D. M. Symmetry, complementarity, and depression: The evolution of an hypothesis. In F. Kaslow (Ed.), *The international book of family therapy.* New York: Brunner/Mazel, 1982, pp. 170-183.
Sager, C. J. *Marriage contracts and couple therapy.* New York: Brunner/Mazel, 1976.
Seligman, M. E. P. *Helplessness: On depression, development, and death.* San Francisco: W. H. Freeman, 1975.
Selvini Palazzoli, M., Boscolo, L., Cecchin, G., & Prata, G. *Paradox and counterparadox.* New York: Aronson, 1978.
Sullivan, H. S. *The interpersonal theory of psychiatry.* New York: Norton, 1953.
Watzlawick, P., Beavin, J. H., & Jackson, D. O. *Pragmatics of human communication: A study of interactional patterns, pathologies and paradoxes.* New York: Norton, 1967.

The Organizational Profile

7

Passive-Aggressive Behavior in the Business Setting

David F. Bush

We are all too familiar with stories of individuals employed by large corporations or government agencies who are labeled as "deadwood" or "burned-out." Not only are many of these persons ineffective in their jobs, but their behavior may also impair the effectiveness of their co-workers. An outcome of these employee behavior patterns, many of which could be classified as passive-aggressive, is reduced organizational productivity.

Employee productivity was not as critical during the era of an expanding economy, and as a result personnel regulations were enacted which made dismissal of employees more difficult in large organizations. However, accountability is becoming increasingly important in the economy of the '80s. Fortunately, many organizations have become enlightened about the potential payoff of behavioral science interventions and have become willing to invest in the development of their human resources through training, counseling, and organizational change.

This chapter will examine passive-aggressive behavior in the business context, discussing the manifestations of these behavior patterns in the business setting, their impact on the organization, the contributions

organizations make to such behaviors, and the detection and reduction of such behaviors.

Several comments should be made about the perspective from which this chapter is written. First of all, it is the perspective of a behavioral scientist who serves as a consultant to managers who are concerned with increasing the effectiveness of their organizations. Thus, the client is the business organization rather than individual employees. Furthermore, interventions must be "sold" to the organization in terms of good outcomes for the organization or, that hackneyed expression, the "bottom line." For example, it is easier to persuade a corporate official that an intervention intended to enhance employee communication skills, such as listening, will have a positive effect on productivity than it is to persuade him or her of the importance of an intervention expressed in "mental health" terms. Unfortunately, "mental health" terminology and treatment still carry a stigma in much of the business world. Thus, a great deal of reframing of psychological concepts must be performed to enable the consultant to communicate effectively and persuasively with the management client. For this reason, I have generally dealt with passive-aggressive behaviors in the business setting in terms of problems in communication (listening, assertiveness), decision-making, motivation, and conflict resolution.

In working with business organizations, we should not overlook the possibility that characteristics of the organization itself may increase the likelihood of passive-aggressive behavior. Among the interventions that will be considered in this chapter are selected approaches to modifying those organizational characteristics which seem to contribute to the frequency of passive-aggressive behavior. The discussion of passive-aggressive behavior in the business setting will begin with a description of the forms of passive-aggressive behavior in business organizations, then move to a consideration of diagnostic approaches and intervention strategies, before finally examining a case study.

ORGANIZATIONAL MANIFESTATION

There is no single business culture, since there is no singular classification of business enterprise nor a single type of organizational structure. Thus, we find, for example, that different approaches to leadership are effective or ineffective in different types of industry which are characterized by different organizational structures. For example, business organizations vary a great deal in structure, ranging from hierarchical to matrix. In those businesses which are characterized by numerous

strata, we find that expectations for behavior are often stratum-dependent. Certainly more social skills are required of the manager of industrial relations than a mechanic in the truck fleet. Similarly, an office of many people performing similar clerical tasks may be an ideal place for someone to "hide" from work, particularly if he or she has found the work to be nonrewarding, either intrinsically or extrinsically, while a salesperson in a highly competitive market has little opportunity to hide. While such avoidance of work has recently been discussed in the context of tedium and burnout (Pines, Aronson, & Kafry, 1981), many of the case examples discussed by these authors present examples of passive-aggressive behavior.

Many writers in the field of management have discussed contrasting styles of management, ranging from the simplistic two-state approach of Theory x and Theory Y (McGregor, 1960) to the more complex grid approaches which stress comparative emphasis which the manager places upon the needs of the employees and the need for production. These styles of management usually encompass an approach to leadership, decision-making, and conflict resolution. Decision-making approaches can range from simply adhering to the same policy, to erratic, impulsive changes, to an inability to decide characterized by procrastination, buck passing, or bolstering. Janis and Mann (1977) have labeled the latter pattern "defensive avoidance." They see it as a response to high levels of conflict involved in the decision-making, creating great stress. Decision-makers simply avoid the stress by avoiding the decision. But in avoiding the stressful decision, decision-makers may avoid a number of activities critical to their jobs. As more and more information is sought by the insecure decision-makers, the delay may create a chain reaction that is costly to the company. Such procrastination is easy to recognize. On the other hand, the decision-maker may try to have a superior make the decision, "passing the buck." Then, if the machine that was selected does not work or the sales approach fails, it was the boss's decision. Those who use bolstering simply attempt to deceive themselves by exaggerating the advantages of one of the less-than-desirable alternatives, since they have concluded that they are unlikely to find a more satisfactory alternative. However, this "resolution" may lead to continued ambivalence. The "defensive avoider" may continue to frustrate others by foot-dragging, not having information needed by other members of the management team, and making excuses. While some employees may defensively avoid decisions because of compulsiveness, others no doubt do so out of a passive-aggressive pattern.

Filley (1978) has recently noted that, although most business organi-

zations continue to use power-oriented approaches to conflict resolution, a problem-solving approach is more appropriate since it facilitates co-operation in future work of the organization. He argues that this is particularly true in situations where creative problem-solving is required. A problem-solving approach or a no-lose solution (Gordon, 1977) approach to conflict resolution not only leads to organizational effectiveness, but also encourages assertive self-expression. Power-oriented approaches, on the other hand, encourage indirect expressions of aggression, since frustration is increased, superiors express aggression, and open expression is forbidden. These dynamics are not at all unlike those described by a number of writers (Kaplan & Sadock, 1981; Millon & Millon, 1974; Millon, 1981) as underlying the passive-aggressive personality disorder.

For example, consider the successful micro-computer corporation whose chief executive was described by its recently resigned president as a strong king with no strong barons, thus violating Machiavelli's rule that "the strongest kingdom had the strongest barons and a strong king" (Chakravarty, 1983). This autocratic and abrasive leader's company had "one of the highest rates of turnover in the industry" (Chakravarty, 1983). Clearly, extremes of conflict resolution by domination lead to high turnover, but what of those who remain? How many will exhibit more and more passive-aggressive behavior because direct expressions of their frustration are blocked while at the same time they are unable to leave?

SYSTEM ANALYSIS AS DIAGNOSIS

This section will discuss how the business world may give rise to passive-aggressive behavior by looking at different corporate environments which are characterized by structure, roles, and norms which may contribute to this problem. We will also examine approaches to the diagnosis of passive-aggressive behavior in a corporate setting. Much of this discussion will be concerned with ways in which performance appraisal systems can be used to detect passive-aggressive behavior. A new measure designed for corporate applications will be presented and discussed.

When the development of business organizations is examined, there are at least three perspectives to consider, namely, 1) the organization-environment interface, 2) the group-to-group interface, and 3) the individual-organization interface (Lawrence & Lorsch, 1969). The third perspective is of greatest relevant to our concern with passive-aggressive behavior. The interaction between the individual and the organization

can be perceived as the interaction between two systems, each containing three subsystems. One system, A. the individual, arrives with a developmental history and at any time is characterized by motives, values, and perceptions, all relevant to working in the second system, B. the business organization. The organizational context of the employee, as a system, consists of three types of subsystem variables: 1) task variables; 2) formal organizational variables; and 3) the expectations of others (Lawrence & Lorsch, 1969). The employee's work behavior is the performance of certain tasks within the context of both the expectations of other employees (B-2) and formal organizational characteristics (B-3). The employee's behavior both influences and is influenced by these factors. Among those expectations and formal characteristics that have an important potential for influencing the likelihood of passive-aggressive behavior are organizational leadership styles. In considering leadership styles we will see that human relationships and effective performance may be at odds in certain leadership styles.

Leadership styles do not usually exist in isolation. A democratic manager is hard to find in an autocratic company and the reverse is equally unlikely. That is part of the reason that Blake and Mouton (1969) indicated that meaningful organizational change must start at the top. The leadership style that characterizes the individual-organization interface has many implications for the behavior of the employees. When a manager attempts to select a leadership style, it is best that the objectives of the manager be considered (Tannenbaum & Schmidt, 1973). If a continuum of leadership is considered from boss-centered leadership to subordinate-centered leadership, seven scale points along the continuum that reflect different managerial approaches to decisions may be identified (Tannenbaum & Schmidt, 1973). These approaches range from "Manager makes decision and announces it" to "Manager permits subordinates to function within limits defined by superior" (Tannenbaum & Schmidt, 1973, p. 164). Some consultants have simplified this scale to the expressions, "tell," "sell," "consult," and "join." While "sell" suggests that the manager attempts to be persuasive, it does not suggest that he or she is listening to the employee in any meaningful way. Only the middle three points on the Tannenbaum and Schmidt scale suggest that the manager is truely listening, for the two most subordinate-centered involve providing the group with ground rules and allowing them to formulate the decision. To adequately detect passive-aggressive behavior patterns and attempt to deal with them constructively, a manager must be listening. The passive-aggressive tendencies will probably be maximized in organizations characterized as either authoritarian or dem-

ocratic, as rigidly structured or structureless. In other words, we are proposing a curvilinear relationship between employee freedom and passive-aggressive coping. Tannenbaum and Schmidt (1973) and a number of other studies have supported the contention that a relatively high level of subordinate-centered managerial behavior is associated with 1) increased employee motivation; 2) increased employee acceptance of change; 3) increased quality of managerial decision; 4) increased teamwork and morale; and 5) increased employee development. However, these same studies note that it is not at all helpful to provide the employees with more freedom than they are prepared to handle with excessive anxiety. The manager must monitor the employees in such a way as to make sure that they are challenged.

The manager who listens skillfully is an attentive observer and an ideal client for the organizational psychologist or management consultant who is called in to attempt to solve organizational problems. Too often the job of the consultant is to teach the client these observational skills so that the manager will fully understand and accept the consultant's diagnosis of the organizational problem (Schein, 1969). Listening skills are among those most frequently sought in the training of managers, since ineffective listening is commonplace. In what ways do poor listening skills on the part of the manager lead employees to use more passive-aggressive coping? To answer this question, we must look at two different types of managerial poor listening. One type of manager is a poor listener because he or she is tuned out. This person may be "burned-out," but he or she may also be passively "tuning out." The other type of manager may be a poor listener because he or she is not easily listened to. The manager may express himself or herself in a way that conveys unwillingness to listen to anything other than that which he/she has already decided upon. The manager may convey a sense of the employee's being unimportant, usually by nonverbal behaviors such as not looking at the employee, interrupting, or changing the subject. He or she may strongly and forcefully present his/her views (tell) and offer subordinates little opportunity to ask questions or offer alternative solutions. The *Monthly Letter* of the Royal Bank of Canada (1979) described a situation in a U.S. manufacturing plant which illustrated the consequences of such managerial behavior.

> The plant had a serious quality control problem which took months—and relatively huge amounts of money—to identify and solve. Then a young tradesman, on the brink of resigning, told the personnel manager he had known what was wrong from the be-

ginning. Why hadn't he said something about it? Well, he said, he had approached both his foreman and the plant engineer, "but they wouldn't listen. I stopped trying to tell them when they made me feel like a jerk"

This employee did not respond in a passive-aggressive manner, but how many do? This employee was willing to risk not finding another job rather than tolerate treatment that reduced his self-esteem. Others, however, may be less assertive and express their frustration in passive ways. Stalling, procrastination, and the other behaviors discussed so often in this volume can result. Teamwork and basic cooperation are replaced by conflict that festers and continues to erode morale and productivity.

Examinations of an organization which reveal such patterns of managerial behavior suggest several interventions throughout management. These organization development (OD) interventions will be discussed briefly in the next section. Now we will turn from the organization to the individual by examining an important management tool called performance appraisal.

Performance Appraisal

Performance appraisal has received a great deal of attention in recent years for several reasons, including legal problems such as Equal Employment Opportunity Commission (EEOC) compliance and employee motivation (Lefton, Buzzotta, Sherberg, & Karraker, 1977). Lefton and his collaborators base their approach on two dimensions of managerial behavior: dominance-submission and hostility-warmth. But more importantly, they stress the importance of uncovering the employee's views of the job. "It's no exaggeration to say that *if you cannot probe effectively, you cannot do an effective performance appraisal*" (Lefton et al., 1977, p. 142). They note that probing not only examines what the employee thinks, but "also helps *raise the other person's receptivity*." Thus it helps motivate the employee. An effective performance appraisal increases both employee receptivity and managerial receptivity, since it forces the manager to be a more effective listener. The employee is encouraged to express his or her feelings openly rather than in a passive manner.

Behaviorally-based approaches to performance appraisal offer an opportunity for direct detection of passive-aggressive behavior patterns. These performance appraisal approaches have been recognized for sev-

eral years (Kearney, 1976) and the various proposed formats that have been introduced have not been without controversy (Kane & Bernardin, 1982; Kingstrom & Bass, 1981). Cederblom (1982) has argued that there are three important factors in the performance appraisal interview: the supervisor's knowledge of the subordinate's job; the supervisor's supportiveness of the subordinate; and the supervisor's encouragement of the employee's participation in the interview. Certainly, these managerial behaviors should both allow discussion of passive-aggressive behaviors and facilitate their reduction.

Schneier and Beatty (1979a, b, c) have argued that an effective performance appraisal system must combine behavior-based and effectiveness-based measures. They point out that performance appraisal systems that examine only the degree to which the employee fulfills objectives may miss behavioral problems. Employee performance may be assigned to one of four categories: 1) low performance on both behavior-based and effectiveness-based measures; 2) high performance on behavior-based measures and low performance on effectiveness-based measures; 3) low performance on behavior-based measures and high performance on effectiveness-based measures; and 4) high performance on both measures. This combined system, which embodies both behaviorally-anchored rating scales (BARS) and management by objectives (MBO), leads to more precise problem diagnosis and more specific feedback to the employee. While the passive-aggressive employee may be expected to fall into category 1, people who are assigned to category 3 may also exhibit passive-aggressive behaviors. In fact, pilot work with the scale presented in Figure 1 has revealed that employees whose profiles indicate frequent passive-aggressive behavior may also satisfactorily meet performance effectiveness objectives, while leaving the manager and co-workers frustrated by day-to-day behavior. Although they are technically competent, these employees will receive poor evaluations on office popularity contests and bars performance appraisals. Clearly, employees in quadrant 3 represent a consequence of passive-aggressive behavior in the business setting.

Job Behavior Style Profile

Figure 1 presents *The Employee Job Behavior Style Profile* (TEJ-BSP) which is designed to be completed by the manager or supervisor and may be used as a component in performance appraisal (Bush, 1982). This instrument asks the manager to review his or her observations of the employee's behavior over the past appraisal period (three months to a

Figure 1. The Employee Job Behavior Style Profile (TEJ-BSP)

In your interactions with the employee, have you observed the employee behaving in the following ways? Please respond to the statements below using the following scale:

NA = not applicable
0 = never (never)
1 = seldom (a few times a year)
2 = occasionally (a few times a month)
3 = frequently (once a week)
4 = very often (almost daily)

1. Employee withholds important information ....NA 0 1 2 3 4
2. Employee withholds cooperation when requested ....NA 0 1 2 3 4
3. Employee keeps you waiting unreasonably long for   NA 0 1 2 3 4
   requested information ....
4. Employee makes excuses ....NA 0 1 2 3 4
5. Employee "forgets" appointments ....NA 0 1 2 3 4
6. Employee "forgets" task deadlines ....NA 0 1 2 3 4
7. Employee accidentally breaks equipment ....NA 0 1 2 3 4
8. Employee "arbitrarily" does not complete tasks in   NA 0 1 2 3 4
   manner requested ....
9. Employee misunderstands instructions or directions ....NA 0 1 2 3 4
10. Employee listens poorly, missing key points ....NA 0 1 2 3 4
11. Employee complains about reasonable requests for   NA 0 1 2 3 4
    increased performance ....
12. Employee misplaces material for projects ....NA 0 1 2 3 4
13. Employee fails to make promised arrangements ....NA 0 1 2 3 4
14. Employee forgets to bring documents to meetings ....NA 0 1 2 3 4
15. Employee is stubborn about making requested changes ....NA 0 1 2 3 4
16. Employee "puts off" making decisions or completing tasks ....NA 0 1 2 3 4

year) and indicate the frequency of those behaviors by marking the appropriate category. Since the scale contains only 16 items and fits on one page, the manager is not overwhelmed and can complete it for a fairly large staff in a short period of time. By using behavioral frequencies rather than vague impressions, the TEJ-BSP avoids the perpetuation of stereotypic responses.

A careful inspection will reveal that these items reflect the five essential dimensions of passive-aggressiveness listed in DSM-III (American Psychiatric Association, 1980). Thus, each can be scored and plotted on a profile that reflects these five dimensions (see key, Figure 2). Using the criteria suggested by DSM-III, when a profile has a mean score greater than a 4 rating on two dimensions, the employee should be considered to be displaying levels of passive-aggressive behavior that suggest poor coping and disruptive behavior. Mean scores beyond 4 may represent

Figure 2. Scoring the TEJ-BSP: Creating the Profile

DSM-III Criteria:
1. procrastination ....measured by three items
2. dawdling ....measured by seven items
3. stubbornness ....measured by five items
4. intentional inefficiency ....measured by nine items
5. "forgetfulness" ....measured by five items

TEJ-BSP loadings:

Item number	DSM-III Criterion number
1.	3 and 4
2.	3 and 4
3.	1, 3, and 4
4.	2 and 4
5.	2 and 5
6.	2 and 5
7.	4
8.	4
9.	2 and 4
10.	2 and 4
11.	2, 3, and 4
12.	2, 4, and 5
13.	1 and 5
14.	5
15.	3
16.	1

potentially serious pathology. If an employee is rated at a 2 level on at least two of the dimensions, the employee should be considered a prime candidate for training sessions that emphasize assertiveness, self-awareness, listening skills, and decision-making skills. If three or more dimensions register at a mean of 2 or greater, the manager should definitely consult a corporate psychologist to develop an approach for counseling the employee or for referral to a psychologist or psychiatrist.

At this time, the TEJ-BSP has been pilot tested in three business organizations and is currently being used by managers and consultants in several corporate settings. In one setting the manager reported low scores on all items for his employees, but reflected that his own scores might be much higher. In another setting, the manager reported ratings of 4 and 3 for several employees who were classified in category 3 above, namely, those who produce effective outcomes but behave in an annoying manner.

Fundamental Interpersonal Relation Orientation (FIRO-B)

Work group behavior is influenced by the composition of the group and an important characteristic of those group members is their interpersonal orientation (Schutz, 1958). Schutz bases his approach on the assumption that as interpersonal needs are more satisfied within the group, compatibility increases and so does group productivity. Conversely, as group members are less satisfied, the likelihood of conflict increases and group members seek satisfaction for their interpersonal needs from other sources. FIRO-B is based on two concepts: *interpersonal needs*, which include inclusion, control, and affection, and *behavioral expression*, which includes the expression of these needs and the desire for their satisfaction. Figure 3 presents a 3 by 2 matrix of these concepts. Each cell in the matrix is conceptualized as having scores that range from low to high.

Higgins (1982) has discussed the productivity implications of these dimensions by relating them to task and maintenance roles in the group. While high scores on dimensions one and three are seen as being desirable for all group members, high scores on dimension 2 are appropriate only for those in leadership positions. The strengths of needs and their expressions are measured in the FIRO-B system by a questionnaire which has been used in many organizations to analyze work groups to determine where incompatibilities may exist that could adversely affect productivity. Employees who register high scores on the desire for inclusion and affection in conjunction with low scores on the expression of these needs, particularly if they desire control, should be checked for passive-aggressive behavior using other instruments, such as the Employee Job Behavior Style Profile or more conventional clinical instruments.

Psychological tests that detect passive-aggressiveness will not be discussed in the present chapter because of its primary concern with the business setting. However, Meyer (1983) has discussed diagnostic considerations for the use of the MMPI, the 16PF, and the WAIS in detecting

Figure 3. Dimensions of Interpersonal Relation Orientation Used in FIRO-B.

INTERPERSONAL NEEDS	NEED EXPRESSION	DESIRE FOR SATISFACTION
1. need for inclusion	initiate interaction	others initiate interaction
2. need for control	seek to control others	others allow you to control
3. need for affection	initiate affection	receive affection

the passive-aggressive personality disorder. Evidence from such a battery may be useful in determining the severity of the passive-aggressive tendencies observed by the means described earlier in this section.

STRATEGIES FOR INTERVENTION

This section will discuss interventions suitable for business organizations in which passive-aggressive behavior may have been found to be a source of reduced organizational effectiveness and/or employee satisfaction. These situations usually lead to some type of organization development (OD) intervention. OD is the general name given to programs of planned change conducted within business organizations; these are typically long-range efforts focusing on improving problem-solving processes through increasing the collaborative nature of the organizational culture with the assistance of an applied behavioral scientist acting as a change agent (French & Bell, 1973). "OD is a normative-reeducative approach to change" (Higgins, 1982, p. 334). Huse (1975) has suggested a typology for OD interventions which is based on different levels of personal involvement. The major headings are: 1) system-wide approaches; 2) individual-organization interfaces; 3) concern with personal work style; and 4) intrapersonal analysis and relationships. Although individuals may be assessed in the *system-wide* approach, the primary concern is with the organization-environment interface. Clearly, however, a number of environmental factors may influence the individual as well, such as changing market conditions or a recession. Nonproductive employees, passive-aggressive or not, will be less tolerated under such financial market conditions.

Individual-organization interfaces have already been discussed in the context of diagnosis. They involve a number of steps which may be of some help in reducing passive-aggressive behavior. Job design and role analysis can aid in creating a better person-job match. The creation of flexible working hours can also suggest that the organization is responsive to employee needs. Huse (1975) also lists behavior modification and management by objectives, results, and rewards under this heading. Both of these approaches are useful, since they focus employee concern on outcome contingencies. However, care must be taken in the latter to match objectives and rewards to the employee very carefully. With the former, the effectiveness of the intervention may be dependent upon the degree to which the contingent outcomes can be regulated both on and off the job.

Concern with personal work style is a category which provides an em-

phasis on individual employees as members of a work team. The techniques in this category stress the improvement of interpersonal relations. The most commonly discussed intervention in this category is called *team-building* (Dyer, 1977). Two others that are useful interventions where passive-aggressiveness is indicated are *process consultation* (Schein, 1969) and *third-party intervention* (Walton, 1969). Each of these interventions is useful in dealing with the passive-aggressive employee, because they attempt to facilitate group problem-solving approaches to resolving disruptive interpersonal relations within the group.

Team-building consists of two phases: diagnosis and intervention. Diagnosis utilizes three types of data to identify problems: 1) employee surveys, such as Dyer's (1977) *Team-Building Checklist*, 2) interviews, and 3) productivity data to identify the problems. The interventions attempt to create individual awareness of the group processes, the contributions each member makes to these processes, and ways in which these processes can be improved. Open and clear communication is stressed in the group intervention. Perhaps most importantly, the group learns to continue the process of data gathering, self-examination, and corrective action.

This approach is seen in the popular Japanese import called *quality circles*. A number of American corporations, including Honeywell, have effectively used this approach. A skilled consultant assists the team members in starting the process. Whether the consultant is internal or external, the process involves teaching the group to conduct democratic problem-solving. The consultant does not impose an agenda on the group, but instead encourages the members to formulate their own objectives and to honestly express their own values. The employees are encouraged to attempt to solve the problems that they perceive to be important. If a supervisor meets with the group, he or she is not allowed to bring that role into the quality circle meeting. In most applications, these meetings occur for one hour per week on company time.

Passive-aggressive behaviors would no doubt be noted by the members of such a group. The advantage of the group process used in such team-building sessions is the opportunity for the facilitator to encourage each group member to express his or her own views on group problems. In this way the passive-aggressive employee may be persuaded to utilize more direct expression of frustration and anxiety.

The fourth type of intervention in the Huse (1975) typology, *Intrapersonal analysis and relationships*, consists of a number of approaches that attempt to increase personal awareness, encourage new attitudes, and change behavior patterns. These approaches have the greatest similarity

to clinical psychological interventions of any discussed thus far, in that the employee may be removed from the immediate work group for these interventions. These interventions have the advantage of being accepted as means to personal development within the business community. They tend to be viewed as approaches to self-improvement rather than as a means of treating an "illness." Thus, they receive greater acceptance than interventions labeled "psychotherapy."

The interventions in this category include: life and career planning, laboratory training, encounter groups, personal consultation, transactional analysis, the Gestalt approach, assertiveness training, active listening, and role-playing. OD practitioners will vary in their use of these interventions as a function of familiarity and comfort with each. However, each can be adapted to help in cases of employees exhibiting passive-aggressive behavior. Life and career planning involves the employee in a careful assessment of both self and environment, combined with an examination of short-term, long-term, and intermediate objectives. Since this planning is frequently conducted in a counseling situation, it provides an opportunity to encourage awareness of passive-aggressive patterns and their consequences, as well as an opportunity to examine the consequences of alternative ways of coping. Furthermore, since there are ample advantages for the organization, it is possible to persuade management of its cost-effectiveness.

Group processes, including laboratory training, sensitivity training, encounter groups, and role-playing all have their risks in working with the passive-aggressive. The group facilitator must be highly skilled, since the ever-present danger of emotions becoming too strong may be enhanced by the frustrations the group may have experienced with a member's passive-aggressive behavior. The intense social situation may contribute to less effective coping rather than improvement. Carefully planned role-playing exercises may be useful to assist the passive-aggressive employee in feeling the frustration of dealing with another person's passive-aggressive behavior. The effectiveness of such exercises is enhanced if they are videotaped, played back, and discussed. If the facilitator is able to stop the tape at key points and ask the participants to reflect, important insight may be gained. This video technique may also be used for *behavior modeling*, an OD process which involves presenting an appropriate response on tape so that the participant can compare the videotape of his or her performance with that of the model.

Transactional analysis and the Gestalt approach have been popular in OD circles for some time, and are therefore perceived as acceptable approaches, since their personal development potential has been

stressed. Personal counseling can be approached in the same way. If the professional counselor is labeled as one who deals with work-related problems rather than as a psychologist or psychiatrist who treats the "mentally ill," both the business and the employee will be more willing to listen, since they'll be less threatened. Both TA and Gestalt can be useful in dealing with passive-aggressive behaviors, since TA is useful for helping people understand the relationship between their interpersonal behavior and intrapersonal dynamics and the Gestalt approach is useful in dealing with feelings of aggression and anger.

TA, assertiveness training, and active listening are repeated in many management training activities. The communication involved in all three overlaps some of the key problems of the employee who utilizes a passive-aggressive coping style. Assertiveness training is beneficial because it helps the employee develop self-awareness and direct expression of needs, in contrast with the indirect expression of poorly understood needs characteristic of the passive-aggressive employee. Active listening habits are also incompatible with the social style of the passive-aggressive employee. Again, training in paraphrasing and other active listening skills is made more effective when videotaped feedback is used, since it provides an opportunity to discuss various perspectives on "behavior" that is "out there." The active listening skills also have rapid payoffs in terms of greater social skill, since other employees will usually show appreciation for the new attentiveness of the formerly "tuned out" coworker.

This examination of OD interventions that may be helpful in cases of passive-aggressive employee behavior has not treated any of these approaches in depth, since there were so many to cover. Clearly, determination of the appropriateness of these interventions depends on both the characteristics of the organization and of the employees involved. Only a selection of these approaches would appear in any case study, like the one which follows in the next section.

CASE STUDY: JOAN AND THE NEW MANAGER

Joan B. is a 24-year-old Caucasian female employee of a data-processing department in a large corporation. She is an identical twin who had completed two years of college. She first came to my attention when I was consulting with the manager of her department. Her manager was asked to complete The Employee Job Behavior Style Profile for his staff. Upon scoring them, I discovered that one of his employees had received high ratings on two of the five dimensions including ratings of 4 (almost

daily) on items 1, 2, and 4 and a 3 rating (once a week) on item 11. These items suggested that the employee was frequently stubborn and intentionally inefficient, two of the criteria of passive-aggressiveness listed in DSM-III. Further inquiries were made about the employee and a series of interventions was planned. The background information proved interesting, since it suggested that the employee was capable but not contributing to the work group in accordance with her potential.

When the manager arrived about two years ago, he discovered that the department had been poorly managed in many ways and found Joan to be a reasonably competent employee who was also generally uncooperative and resisted authority. He later discovered that she had been in the habit of "going over the head" of her boss whenever she experienced any conflict with him. The previous boss had been managerially incompetent and generally ineffective. His immediate superior had even encouraged her bypassing of her manager. Furthermore, she was perceived as the most competent employee in a work group that consisted of relatively incompetent employees.

When the manager arrived, he instituted policies that upset the existing status hierarchy within the group. Within six months he had taken a young clerk who had the least status in the department and trained her to work with the computers. He then hired a new person from outside, who with subsequent training moved into the number two spot in the department. Then a second new person was added and given training to upgrade his skills. All three of these people were given promotions and raises commensurate with their new skills.

During this period Joan and the other employees, whose employment preceded that of the manager, did not approach the manager for additional training. Instead, they persisted in the normative behavior of isolated, noncooperative work. The old behavior patterns were no longer rewarded, but resisted change. Joan and one other "old-timer" expressed frustration with the new emphasis on training and the fact that other employees had passed them in terms of department status. Joan would initiate "games" with the manager by asking questions to which she knew the answer and focus excessive attention on details during training seminars on new software conducted by the manager. Her disruptiveness reached the level that the manager felt forced to stop these training sessions for the entire staff and replaced them with small-group "on-demand" sessions for those who seemed highly motivated.

Joan also refused to share her expertise with other employees. The manager encouraged the establishment of a norm of assisting co-workers. He stressed the sharing of skills and the helping of co-workers. She

was frequently observed to refuse requests for assistance from co-workers. On one occasion, Joan submitted a new program to the manager which he quickly discovered did not work. Rather than correct the defective program himself, he returned it to her with a note attached which asked her to "debug" it and resubmit it to him. She responded with complaining. She had expected that he would fix it for her. She complained to co-workers that the manager simply did not want to risk trying to fix it himself. The next time she submitted a defective program the manager followed the same procedure. It appeared, in the context of her other behaviors, that she was attempting to challenge the manager in a passive manner by testing his skills, since the mistakes in the programs seemed intentional. Since the manager did not reinforce this behavior, it gradually disappeared.

One of the interventions attempted in this case was a form of behavior modification conducted by the manager. A specific set of behaviors was created which would be rewarded by social warmth and expressions of approval by the manager. These included expressions of openess and sharing with fellow employees, cooperation and helping other employees, answering questions from other employees, taking responsibility for a mistake (not making so many excuses), and the prompt performance of reasonable requests without complaint. Her behavior changed noticeably, but still contained disruptive elements. Therefore, it was decided that a team-building intervention would be helpful to enhance overall group productivity and cooperation. Weekly group sessions were instituted which had a more general problem focus, rather than strictly aimed at software problems. Team spirit and cooperation were stressed. Examples of good teamwork were praised and their contributions to increased productivity were discussed.

Specific interventions aimed at Joan's problems have included sending her to training seminars in transactional analysis and assertiveness. TA was selected since she frequently engages in "game" transactions; it was hoped that such a seminar would help provide her with some insight into her own behavior. The assertiveness training was also selected to assist her in replacing her frequent use of indirect expressions of aggression with more direct expressions of her needs.

While this example may not represent a severe case of the passive-aggressive personality disorder, it certainly represents a passive-aggressive coping style which was disruptive in a business setting and which has been effectively dealt with through a set of behavioral interventions. Furthermore, this example fits that category characterized by technical competence combined with a lack of interpersonal skills which

produces employee dissatisfaction with day-to-day behavior. These OD interventions, like many that are effective in corporate settings, involved helping the manager and the employees change the organizational climate. In this case, much of the consultant's intervention was in the form of teaching the manager approaches to changing employee behavior which would be classified in the "sell" and "consult" types of leadership discussed earlier (Tannenbaum & Schmidt, 1973), rather than the extremes of "tell" or "join." One can argue that at least some of Joan's problem behavior can be attributed to the ineffective leadership of the previous boss. Clearly, the leadership style of the new manager has reduced her passive-aggressiveness at work and enhanced her performance as a productive and cooperative member of the staff.

REFERENCES

American Psychiatric Association. *Diagnostic and statistical manual of mental disorders*. Third Edition. Washington, D.C., 1980.

Beatty, R. W., Schneier, C. E., & Beatty, J. R. An empirical investigation of perceptions of ratee behavior frequency and ratee behavior change using Behavioral Expectations Scales (BES). *Personnel Psychology*, 1977, *30*, 647-658.

Beckhard, R. *Organization development: Strategies and models*. Reading, MA: Addison-Wesley, 1969.

Blake, R. R., & Mouton, J. S. *Building a dynamic corporation through grid organization development*. Reading, MA: Addison-Wesley, 1969.

Bush, D. F. *The Employee Job Behavior Style Profile*. Unpublished manuscript, 1982.

Cederblom, D. The performance appraisal interview: A review, implications, and suggestions. *Academy of Management Review*, 1982, *7* (2).

Chakravarty, S. N. Albatross. *Forbes*, January 17, 1983.

Dessler, G. *Personnel management*. Second edition. Reston, VA: Reston Publishing Company, 1981.

Dyer, W. G. *Team building: Issues and alternatives*. Reading, MA: Addison-Wesley, 1977.

Filley, A. C. Some normative issues in conflict management. *California Management Review*, 1978, *21* (2).

French, W. L., & Bell, C. H. *Organizational development: Behavioral science interventions for organization improvement*. Englewood Cliffs, NJ: Prentice-Hall, 1973.

Gordon, T. *Leader effectiveness training*. New York: Peter H. Wyden, 1977.

Higgins, J. M. *Human relations concepts and skills*. New York: Random House, 1982.

Huse, E. J. *Organization development and change*. Denver, CO: West Publishing Company, 1975.

Janis, I. L., & Mann, L. *Decision making: A psychological analysis of conflict, choice, and commitment*. New York: The Free Press, 1977.

Kane, J. S., & Bernardin, H. J. Behavioral observation scales and the evaluation of performance appraisal effectiveness. *Personnel Psychology*, 1982, *35*, 635-640.

Kaplan, H. I., & Sadock, B. J. *Modern synopsis of comprehensive textbook of psychiatry/III* (Third Edition). Baltimore: Williams & Wilkins, 1981.

Kearney, W. J. The value of behaviorally based performance appraisals. *Business Horizons*, June 1976, 75-83.

Kingstrom, P. O., & Bass, A. R. A critical analysis of studies comparing Behaviorally Anchored Rating Scales (BARS) and other rating formats. *Personnel Psychology*, 1981, *34*, 263-289.

Lawrence, P. R., & Lorsch, J. W. *Developing organizations: Diagnosis and action.* Reading, MA: Addison-Wesley, 1969.

Lefton, R. E., Buzzotta, V. R., Sherberg, M., & Karraker, D. L. *Effective motivation through performance appraisal.* New York: Wiley, 1977.

McGregor, D. *The human side of enterprise.* New York: McGraw-Hill, 1960.

Meyer, R. G. *The clinician's handbook: The psychopathology of adulthood and late adolescence.* Boston, MA: Allyn and Bacon, 1983.

Millon, T. *Disorders of personality: DSM-III, Axis II.* New York: Wiley-Interscience, 1981.

Millon, T., & Millon, R. *Abnormal behavior and personality: A biosocial learning approach.* Philadelphia: W. B. Saunders, 1974.

Pines, A. M., Aronson, E., & Kafry, D. *Burnout: From tedium to personal growth.* New York: The Free Press, 1981.

Rosinger, G., Myers, L. B., Levy, G. W., Loar, M., Mohrman, S. A., & Stock, J. R. Development of a behaviorally based performance appraisal system. *Personnel Psychology,* 1982, 35, 75-88.

Schein, E. H. *Process consultation: Its role in organization development.* Reading, MA: Addison-Wesley, 1969.

Schneier, C. E., & Beatty, R. W. Integrating behaviorally-based and effectiveness-based methods. *The Personnel Administrator,* July 1979a, 65-76.

Schneier, C. E., & Beatty, R. W. Developing Behaviorally-Anchored Rating Scales *(BARS). The Personnel Administrator,* August, 1979b.

Schneier, C. E., & Beatty, R. W. Combining BARS and MBO: Using an appraisal system to diagnose performance problems. *The Personnel Administrator,* Sept. 1979c, 51-60.

Schutz, W. C. *FIRO: A three dimensional theory of interpersonal behavior.* New York: Rinehart and Company, 1958.

Small, I. F., Small, J. G., Alig, V. B., & Moore, D. F. Passive-aggressive personality disorder: A search for a syndrome. *American Journal of Psychiatry,* 1970, 12 (6):7.

Tannenbaum, R., & Schmidt, W. H. How to choose a leadership pattern. *Harvard Business Review,* May-June 1973.

The Royal Bank of Canada: Monthly Letter. The act of listening. 1979, 60 (2).

Walter, V. Self motivated personal career planning: A breakthrough in human resource management. Part I. *Personnel Journal,* March, 1976a, 112-115, 136-137.

Walter, V. Self motivated personal career planning: A breakthrough in human resource management. Part II. *Personnel Journal,* April, 1976b, 162-167, 185-186.

Walton, R. E. *Interpersonal peacemaking: Confrontations and third-party consultation.* Reading, MA: Addison-Wesley, 1969.

8

The Educational Setting: A Cultural Milieu Fostering Passive-Aggressiveness

Richard Dean Parsons

"Johnny where is your homework?"
"I've asked you four times to take out your book!"
"Yes, you MAY be excused, I know you have to eat something for your diabetes."

Minor incidents—but major irritants to most teachers who have come face to face with the passive-aggressive child.

"I won't be able to make the meeting again"
"Gee, sorry I'm late again, but . . ."
"Gads, I forgot all about taking that baseline information you needed!"

Minor incidents—but major irritants to most administrators, or consultants working with the passive-aggressive teacher.

"Sorry, Mr. Johnson had to cancel his meeting with you."
"Next time I'll be sure to bring all of the data you requested."

"Yes, I know you have been working on this proposal for over a month, but I just wonder if we should do it—you know, is it worth it?"

Minor incidents—but major irritants to most consultants working with the passive-aggressive school administrator.

Each of these little scenarios is replayed daily within our educational institutions and each reflects the passive-aggressive response style manifested and fostered by that particular cultural milieu. Oppositional patterns of a passive character, while being antithetical to the defined, learning, experiencing, challenging, growth-producing environment of an educational system, are all too real manifestations of the apparent repressive forces operating within many educational systems today.

The current chapter will address the issue of passive-aggressiveness as it exhibits itself within the educational setting. In light of the extensive discussion of the various therapeutic views of passive-aggressiveness presented within the first section of the text, the current chapter will take a somewhat eclectic view of the diagnosis and assessment of passive-aggressiveness. However, far from being atheoretical, the chapter will outline a model which has been developed by this author and others (Parsons & Meyers, in press; Meyers, Parsons, & Martin, 1979) for assessing and intervening as a consultant to an educational system.

ORGANIZATIONAL MANIFESTATIONS

In order to understand the myriad of symptom manifestations, one must have a generalized sense of the definition of passive-aggressiveness. According to the American Psychiatric Association's (1980) *Diagnosis and Statistical Manual of Mental Disorders* (DSM-III), the diagnosis of passive-aggressive personality requires that there be resistance to demands for adequate performance in both occupational and social functioning, with the resistance being expressed indirectly rather than directly.

Passive-aggressiveness as a diagnostic category refers to a character disorder which prevents the individual from maintaining an effective, flexible relationship with others. Such individuals perceive themselves to be abused by those in control and thus view authority figures as unjust and tyrannical. Having a low sense of self-esteem and an inordinate fear of retaliation, the person is unable to directly express anger and aggressive feelings toward authority. Consequently, he or she relies on passive procedures which provide a "safe," somewhat "hidden"

avenue for ventilation. Anger and hostility find expression in stubborn-ness, procrastination, dawdling, intentional inefficiencies, and "forget-fulness." The key distinction between this personality disorder and the transient passive coping style exhibited by many people is that these individuals *habitually* resent and oppose demands to increase or maintain a given level of function, persisting in their pattern of behavior across settings even when a more adaptive functioning is clearly possible.

While a number of additional parameters have been outlined for the differential diagnosis of the passive-aggressive personality disorder, the intent here is not to posit the pathology of the students, teachers, and administrators within education. Rather, the syndrome is employed as a framework to understand typical forms of resistance demonstrated within the school environment and to demonstrate the unique role played by the system in the creation and maintenance of this condition.

In order to fully appreciate and understand passive-aggression as ex-hibited within an educational setting, one must take an ecological view of this phenomenon. Such an ecological-systems orientation recognizes that the "problem" is clearly affected by the environmental conditions currently experienced. Thus it appears more appropriate to consider these "abnormal" reactions as reasonable ("normal") adaptations to ab-normal environmental circumstances, rather than manifestations of an abnormal person or "diseased" entity. Even though many professionals recognize the potential impact of the environment, they still frequently consider the *person*, rather than the environment, to be the disturbed element. Perhaps such a resistance to shifting perspective is based on the comfort one finds in holding to the "simple" notion of the person as problem, rather than attempting to confront the difficult and perhaps impossible task of identifying the causes within the complex structure of the environment. However, a consultant addressing passive-aggres-sion within the educational setting must be prepared to address this difficult task and to begin to assess and intervene within the entire educational system.

Passive-aggressive behavior is likely to be seen in everyone's response pattern at one time or another. As a transient mode such indirect expres-sion of anger might prove quite productive and even be socially toler-ated. However, the cultural milieu in which one operates might encourage such indirect expression as the primary or sole means of expression for negative feelings. In this case, transient behaviors might become relatively permanent distortions of the response style of indi-viduals within that setting and even generalize outside of that environ-ment. It has been this author's experience that the educational environment

often encourages and even reinforces, through secondary gains, the indirect, passive expression of such anger.

The nature of the educational system, its norms, goals, and roles encourage the exhibition of such behavioral patterns; thus, the historic reliance on the doctrine of "in loco parentis," the absolute authority of the "school marm," and the perceived dictorial power of the building principal or dean of students all stimulate the exhibition of passive-aggressiveness. Further, the demands placed on administrator, teacher, and student in this hierarchical, authoritarian system leave little room for direct expression of anger.

In analyzing the "system" of the school, one soon comes to realize that a number of individuals are involved as both etiological factors and targets for passive-aggressiveness. The generic symptom patterns previously described (i.e., stubbornness, dawdling, procrastination, forgetfulness) develop unique expressions for each of these targeted populations.

The child. The passive-aggressive child entering the school with what Sullivan (1953) has identified as the basic malevolent attitude (i.e., a feeling that he is in the midst of enemies and that any exhibition of tenderness to others will ultimately result in his pain) is sensitized to all manifestations of "injustice" and responds in such a way so as to insure a minimum of kindness is exhibited. Being angry with the injustice and the perceived overly dominating and controlling authority figures in his life, the child finds every opportunity to express anger and frustration. Even the most trivial demands from within the classroom stimulate and elicit aggressive concerns. However, as is typical with passive-aggressiveness, the student fears retaliation from the unjust authority and thus redirects this anger to passive expression. The energy required for subduing the intense feelings and the internal conflict drains the child's resources and thus the process proves detrimental to the teaching-learning relationship.

As Rabkin (1965) has noted, the educational process involves two basic elements: 1) the imparting of wisdom, and 2) the nuturance of a receptive, critical attitude and inquiring mind. Both require the active participation of teacher and pupil. Obviously passive-aggressive behavior will play havoc with the teacher-pupil relationship, thus disrupting the process. The redirection of energy and resources to defend against aggressive urges often precludes adequate attention to subject matter, especially that with aggressive overtones, such as violence-filled novels assigned for English, dissection required for biology, the study of wars in history,

or the discussion of channeling nuclear energy in physics (Blanchard, 1946; Jarvis, 1958; Liss, 1941; Sperry, Staver, & Mann, 1952). Further, even under conditions of minimal "violence," the passive-aggressive child is a prime candidate for poor achievement.

Weiner (1970) noted that the vast majority of achievement problems in adolescents who are not intellectually or socioculturally handicapped could be adequately understood in terms of maladaptive patterns of family interaction, which included:

a) a significant amount of underlying hostility, usually toward parents, that could not be directly expressed;
b) concerns about rivalry with parents and siblings generating marked fears of failure or success; and
c) a preference for passive-aggressive modes of coping with difficult situations (pp. 265-277).

Thus, underachievers concerned with the problems of hostility and rivalry earn low or declining grades by a passive-aggressive mode of coping with the school situation. They studiously and selectively apply inactivity to their academic tasks; they study less, complete assignments less promptly, and reserve their energies for extracurricular activities (Frankel, 1960; Wilson & Morrow, 1962). And, even if they should absorb knowledge relevant to their school subjects, passive-aggressive under-achievers will utilize inactivity techniques to ensure that their knowledge does not elevate their grades. They remain silent during class discussion, affecting disinterest or stupidity, "forget" to copy down or turn in assignments or examinations, "overlook" a page or section, or somehow misinterpret the instructions on a test so as to disqualify many of their answers.

In addition to venting their anger via underachievement, passive-aggressive students often target the teacher, as authority, for a barrage of subtle, yet intensely annoying behaviors. Symptoms ranging from going to the bathroom frequently to always lagging behind, forgetting homework, asking real yet overly inane and repetitive questions, "not understanding and needing help," and needing assistance to find the page or button a coat—all place excessive demands for teacher attention —attention which the teacher finds difficult and supplies begrudgingly. The unending demands, the lack of productivity, and the absence of payoff for the teacher most often result in the teacher's own expression of frustration, helplessness, anger and guilt. Such expression feeds back

into the child's perception of the oppressive injustice of such authority and thus the vicious cycle is stimulated to continue.

The teacher. The oppositional and passive-aggressive child does grow up; in fact, he or she often grows up to become the adult responsible for the education of such a child. As with any professional group, teachers experience frustrations, anger, disappointment, anxiety, and a variety of stressors. The constant esteem-shattering effect of being at the beck and call of 30, 40, or more children each day, as well as the often unnecessary red tape and unending administrative demands, often underlie the experienced frustration and hostility of an educator.

In a milieu where mixed messages are often the norm, frustration is likely to abound. Messages such as "teach, grow, be creative . . . but keep order," "adapt to meet the individual needs of your students . . . even though you have 40 in the class," and "care, extend, and humanize for yours is a noble profession . . . so what if you are underpaid," create conditions in which teachers may begin to resent the oppressive authority defining this position while lacking the assertiveness or self-confidence to directly confront such forces.

In addition to these sources of frustration and anger, educators experience a number of role conflicts which are unique to the profession and not only exacerbate the professional frustration but also subvert attempts to directly ventilate the experienced anger and frustration. As professionals defined as having the authority over and responsibility for the children in their charge, educators often find themselves in inter-role conflict as this one professional role—of omnipotent, all-knowing master of the classroom—comes face to face with the realities of graduate student status or the vulnerability of having the supervisor, principal, or department chairperson take liberty with their class to "evaluate" them and their teaching style. The clash of these roles often creates a special tug-of-war in which one's sense of control and autonomy is tested.

Viewing these sources of frustration from within the framework of the norms and role expectations of the teaching profession provides insight into the basis for the need for passive expression. Teachers, though frustrated and angry, are expected, because of the nature of their position, not to express anger or frustration. Rather, they are told that as educators they must be the "models" for appropriate behavior, that on their shoulders rests the development of the youth of tomorrow, and that they are "professionals" and as such should be above such things.

Considering the environmental demands and constraints, it is understandable that teachers often attempt to control their environments through passive manipulation of the significant others in that setting (i.e., students, peers, administrators). The in-class use of excessive sarcasm, confrontational questioning, and embarrassing evaluative comments on student performances; the assignment of inordinate homework; the use of rigid marking standards; and "pop" testing—all may reflect passive expression of teacher anger. With peers and administrators, the passive-aggressive teacher is most likely to prove stubborn, obstructional, and intentionally inefficient, especially in terms of committee assignments and task-product deadlines. Finding fault with committee suggestions, using pessimism and cynicism as evaluative modes, missing or being late for appointments, and "forgetting" to prepare for previously arranged meetings may also signal the existence of the passive-aggressive teachers.

Such passive manipulation and exhibition of anger, when viewed from a systems perspective, might be termed "adaptive antagonistic activities." According to Argyris (1970), such reactions often reflect the negative impact of a highly repressive, hierarchical, authoritative organizational structure. As such, it is the author's feeling that consultants attempting to diagnose and intervene with passive-aggressiveness within the educational environment must be skilled not only in individual psychometrics and psychotherapy but also in system analysis and organizational development procedures.

SYSTEMS ANALYSIS AS DIAGNOSTIC APPROACH

The model of consultation developed by this author along with others (Parsons & Meyers, in press; Meyers, Parsons, & Martin, 1979) clearly emphasizes a broad-based orientation for the analysis and intervention of mental health problems in the schools. Instead of assuming that the problem lies within the client and beginning with individual assessment, this approach leads one to assume that the environment (i.e., the system) has a major role to play in the etiology, remediation, and prevention of the passive-aggressive behavior. Such an assumption directs assessment efforts to the analysis of the operative interpersonal and system forces and leads to the use of intervention strategies which not only remediate (reduce or modify the passive-aggressiveness) but also provide the foundation for achieving primary prevention via system modification.

In assessing passive-aggressiveness in the school setting, it is useful to view the educational system as a viable entity, composed of units or components that are actively interrelated and interdependent and that

operate in a particular way to produce the current passive-aggressiveness. As such, the assessment requires the identification of the principal individuals involved, along with the system's structures and processes. The goal of such analysis becomes the identification of each component's contribution to the development of hostility within the system and the repression of direct expression.

Members of the System

In assessing the system, one needs to consider the unique nature of the members (i.e., student, teacher, administrator) involved. From this perspective, one develops clinical profiles of the system members, pointing to their unique values, skills, and orientation, and assesses how these come to bear on the current passive-aggressive functioning and climate of the organization.

In focusing one's attention *directly* on the student/teacher/administrator as client, traditional individual interviews, focused observational strategies, and psychometric testing techniques may be employed to gather significant diagnostic data. However, given the current author's emphasis on extrapersonal factors, it is suggested that the diagnostic procedures also focus on the significant others in the environment. This second, *indirect* approach to diagnosis identifies the significant other (i.e., the teacher when the student is exhibiting passive-aggressiveness, or the administrator when the teacher is the client) as the target for assessment and intervention. The goal is to assess the behavior, attitudes and/or feelings of the significant other as they bear on the client's passive-aggressiveness and then intervene as appropriate. Such an approach is similar to Caplan's (1970) consultee-centered case consultation. Some of the goals for intervention might include: to increase the "other's" knowledge of self and the client; to develop the other's management skill(s) in handling the passive-aggressive client; to promote self-confidence (thus reducing need to be overly defensive or repressive); and to encourage professional distance in order to stimulate an objective view of the client and the work situation. While the primary focus is the significant other, it is assumed that this assessment and intervention with the significant other will result in changes for the client as well.

The System-Structure and Processes

As noted earlier, the position taken here is that passive-aggressiveness within the educational setting is most effectively conceived as an extrapersonal, ecological problem; thus, prime consideration is given to the

elements within the system leading to the creation and maintenance of this syndrome. The focus of this *systems* level assessment is to ultimately improve the organizational functioning of the system as a whole, thus indirectly reducing the experienced frustration and hostility and the repressive forces inhibiting direct expression of feelings. Such modification of the system's structure and processes should result in improved mental health functioning of the students, teachers, and administrators currently in the organization and prevent future manifestation of such passive-aggressiveness.

One of the clearest examples of such systems level consultation occurs when the consultant moves the school away from an autocratic, task-oriented nonparticipatory model of governance and operation toward one in which a more positive view of human nature is held and from which an organizational-managerial style promoting self-reliance, responsibility, and involvement at all levels of decision-making can evolve. Such an increase in the members' ability to participate at all levels of system functioning not only reduces potential frustration but also encourages direct expression of feelings by all involved.

Because of its breadth of focus as well as its potential to serve both as a remedial and preventive service, consultation at a systems level is seen as the most desirable form of consultation within the school setting. In carrying out such consultation, this author has found the Community Oriented Programs Environment Scale (Moos, 1974) to be a valuable diagnostic tool. This scale provides data on ten separate factors, including 1) involvement, 2) support, 3) spontaneity, 4) autonomy, 5) practical orientation, 6) personal problem orientation, 7) anger and aggression, 8) order and organization, 9) program clarity and 10) staff control. Each of these specific subscales, which have been defined by Moos (1974), has special significance for the analysis of the passive-aggressive milieu:

1) Involvement: Measurement of how active members are in the day-to-day functioning of their program;
2) Support: The extent to which members are encouraged to be and actually are helpful and supportive toward one another;
3) Spontaneity: The extent to which the program encourages members to act openly and to express their feelings openly;
4) Autonomy: How self-sufficient and independent members are encouraged to be in making decisions about their personal affairs (what they wear, where they go) and in their relationship with the organization;
5) Practical orientation: The extent to which the member's environment

orients him toward preparing himself for release from the program. Such things as training for new kinds of jobs, looking to the future, and setting and working toward goals are considered within this dimension;

6) Personal problem orientation: The extent to which members are encouraged to be concerned with personal problems and feelings and to seek to understand them;

7) Anger and aggression: The extent to which a member is allowed and encouraged to argue with members and staff, to become openly angry and to display other aggressive behavior;

8) Order and organization: The importance of order and organization in the program in terms of members (how they look); staff (what they do to encourage order); and the house itself (how well is it kept).

9) Program clarity: The extent to which the members know what to expect in the day-to-day routine of their program and the explicitness of the program rules and procedures.

10) Staff control: The extent to which the staff use measures to keep members under necessary controls (e.g., in the formulation of rules, the scheduling of activities and the relationship between members and staff).

It has been this author's experience that the scales are valuable for utilization with administrators, faculty, and, with modifications, students in the classroom. In addition to the growing body of research supporting its interpretation, the value of this instrument rests in the ability to tie the specific assessment to intervention strategies. Thus, in those situations in which the classroom or school organization might be profiled on the scale as low in autonomy, involvement and spontaneity and high on order and organization, organizational development procedures aiming at humanizing the school environment (e.g., increase faculty and student representation on decision-making bodies, provide students with freedom to structure the order of learning tasks, etc.) are clearly prescribed.

CONSULTANT STRATEGIES AND INTERVENTION SKILLS

Many varied intervention strategies exist for remediation and prevention of passive-aggressiveness within an educational setting (e.g., assertiveness training, organizational development, communication training, individual psychotherapy, group process, etc.). Each of these strategies

attempts to 1) increase the clients' awareness of the current nature of their passive-aggressive response style and the contribution of the system to this passive-aggressiveness; 2) identify the factors maintaining the current status; and 3) facilitate development of the capacity and resources to identify and establish alternative positions in both the individual and the system. Using a systems framework, this author has identified two generic approaches to the intervention of passive-aggressiveness in an educational setting, i.e., reducing the "need" for passive-aggressiveness and increasing one's sense of autonomy and control.

Reducing the "Need" for Passive-Aggressiveness

The first step in this intervention model is to provide the system and its members with feedback about the assessment data gathered, in order to help them understand their system. Increased awareness often leads to questions regarding "why" and "what to do." It has been this author's experience that the "why" can often be answered simply by noting that passive-aggressiveness "works." Regarding "what to do," a two-pronged approach seems appropriate. One must begin to 1) identify more effective alternatives (i.e., strategies that "work" better) and then 2) implement such alternatives into the system. Following this line of reasoning, the primary intervention questions to be addressed are:
1) What are the generic skills needed to reduce the need for or value of passive-aggressiveness?
2) When a specific skill is learned or competence is developed, will it result in improved adjustment?
3) When skills or competencies are developed or when emotional adjustment improves, will these changes be maintained within this system?

An individual student or teacher exhibiting passive-aggressive modes of behavior might need extensive counseling or in-depth psychotherapy. However, the interventions of choice are those aimed at increasing the competency and adaptive capacity of all the members of the system, particularly in the area of assertiveness and communication skills, and thus concurrently reducing the need for such passive-aggressive responding.

A workshop format allows the consultant to intervene with several members of the system at one time. For example, Parsons, Stone, and Feuerstein (1977) employed a workshop format to teach faculty cognitive

restructuring and rational-emotive principles as a means of reducing anger and frustration. Similarly, a workshop format can be used to develop faculty assertive skills or classroom management competence, thereby reducing the value or need for continued use of passive manipulative techniques.

Modification of the curriculum to increase social adaptive skills has proven to be an effective mode of intervention with passive-aggressive students. Spivack and Shure (1974), for example, have used curriculum to increase: 1) students' interpersonal problem-solving skills; 2) their sensitivity to and perception of others' feelings; 3) their awareness of the casual effect of their own behavior; and 4) the perception of alternative strategies for solving problems.

Such competency training and skill development will provide both faculty and students with a varied repertoire of efficient responses to the unique strains of education, thus reducing the value of passive-aggressive modes of response.

Increasing Autonomy and Control Within the System

A second group of interventions focuses on increasing one's autonomy and control. This form of intervention begins with the plans generated during the feedback session. These interventions must reflect a collaborative effort, with both the consultant and the staff members contributing ideas and reaching consensus about the final plan. This is a crucial stage in the intervention in passive-aggressive systems, since the consultant wants to be certain the target populations are actively involved, so that the plans will be owned by those who need most to experience the power and sense of worth which accompanies such intervention planning.

Because the focus is on maximizing the autonomy and sense of control, the consultant needs to serve as a facilitator rather than a leader, aiming not to resolve, but to maximize the actual productivity of the group. Further, the consultant needs to insure that the interventions developed are reflective of the data gathered during the diagnostic phase. The focus at this level of intervention is on identifying areas in which increased student and teacher control and autonomy are both needed and possible.

Often increasing autonomy requires minimal adaptation of the existing system. For example, simply moving away from a lock-step curriculum design, in which each child in the class is required to perform the same chain of academic tasks in the same sequence (e.g., 9:00 a.m.—math; 9:30 a.m.—phonics, etc.), to a work-station model, in which students

are provided modest freedom to choose (i.e., 9:00 a.m.—phonics or silent reading or spelling; 9:30 a.m.—math skills or concepts or ?), provides students with an increased sense of autonomy. Similarly, holding class meetings, in which student feedback, suggestions, and recommendations are solicited and incorporated into classroom policy and plans, fosters a sense of control within the students.

A similar tactic may be effective with faculty, in that allowing faculty members to select their own committee assignment, room assignment, lunch period, or extracurricular activity responsibility often provides them with increased autonomy and reduces the sense of frustration which lies at the core of the passive-aggressive behavior.

Sometimes, however, changes within the existing system's organizational structure and processes are required. Of all forms of intervention, the one with the broadest and most long-term impact is that which helps the system redefine and restructure itself, so as to promote autonomy, shared responsibility, and collaboration in decision-making at all levels (i.e., classroom, faculty, board, etc.). Such system modification promotes direct expression of emotions and the mutual, respectful treatment of all; it thus serves both a remedial function by reducing the need for passive-aggressiveness and a preventive function by removing the ecological factors active in its creation. One clearly articulated model for such a humanization of the educational environment is presented by Schmuck and Schmuck (1974).

It should be cautioned, however, that while such structural and process-oriented changes are ultimately the most desirable, they are extremely difficult to accomplish, since organizations are inherently resistant to change. Change, therefore, should not be expected to occur all at once. In fact this author has found that it is not advisable to attempt to orchestrate the entire process; rather, it is more productive to develop a group of staff members who will take responsiblity for developing detailed plans for structural changes and devise recommended approaches for implementing these changes. The composition of this "ad hoc" work group, in terms of the relevant staff and administrative personnel, is crucial to the success or failure of the group. Group innovators, supporters, participants, and formal and informal leaders from all levels of the organization should be included to provide for the generalized owning of the final plan and a reduction of any fear of turf intrusion.

A final point should be considered. When intervention plans have been developed, the consultant, in an attempt to further foster control and autonomy in the system and its members, needs to pull back and leave the responsibility for implementation with the staff. Nevertheless,

the consultant should continue to provide support and serve as a facilitating resource. Thus, allowing system control does not mean abdication of responsibility by the consultant. Rather, the consultant needs to identify at least one person in the system who will take responsibility for coordinating the intervention plans. Then, when the consultant comes back for a follow-up, it is clear who should have overseen the implementation of each plan. This provides the system with a means of accountability which will help to insure success. It is not expected that each intervention should be working smoothly at the time of the follow-up. However, with the built-in system of accountability, the process of revising and improving the plans which have not worked will be more efficient and more indigenous to that system.

CASE ILLUSTRATION

While serving as a consultant to a community mental health setting, the author experienced a clear example of the system-wide impact of passive-aggressiveness, along with the nature and specific system factors contributing to the creation and maintenance of this syndrome. The mental health center was responsible for providing direct (i.e., psychotherapy) and indirect (consultative) service to a rural catchment region. In addition to serving the residents of the community, it provided direct and consultative services to a local health center and five elementary schools. One of the schools to which the center provided service (both direct and indirect) was very enthusiastic and eager to contract for services and began referring a large number of students for what the school staff identified as: "negative attitude," "destruction of property" (i.e., marking desks and bathrooms), and "learning difficulties due to inattentiveness and failure to complete assignments." Because of the volume of requests for service and the similarity of the referrals, the consultant scheduled a conference with the principal and referring staff. The agenda for the meeting was twofold: 1) to begin to assess the general milieu of the school, and 2) to identify the broadest, most indirect form of intervention (i.e. system, teacher, etc.) plausible.

Assessment

Unstructured Observation. Using the rationale previously described, the assessment moved from general (unstructured observation) to focused (survey) strategies for data collection. Walking into the school, this author was immediately "impressed" by what appeared to be a *highly*

structured, orderly school. In addition to being clean (absent of the graffiti which was so typical for the community) and neat (no papers or trash, desks straight), the school was markedly quiet. Through the closed classroom doors, students could be seen sitting quietly in ordered rows of desks doing their work or attending to the teacher. Entering the school prior to the lunch period provided an opportunity to experience the classroom by classroom procedure (which was standardized regardless of grade level) used to move the children to the lunchroom. Starting with the first grades the children would stand row by row and file out in single line, without talking, following the assigned upperclass monitor to the lunchroom. On those occasions when a child laughed or spoke out, a reprimand was in order; if this behavior continued exclusion from the line and a trip to the principal seemed to follow. The atmosphere of the school appeared rigid, overly oppressive, and characteristically authoritarian.

Interviewing the Members. Moving to a more focused level of data collection, this author began to informally chat with the teachers (individually and in small groups at lunch). Through this interviewing, he soon came to realize that the faculty perceived that the majority of the children referred as troublemakers were "intentionally" trying to make them (the teachers) look bad and as such needed to be punished before they themselves got into trouble. Further, there was almost complete agreement that the priority for the school administration was the maintenance of order within the school (system structure analysis). Such order was actively "policed" by unannounced visitations of the principal and department chairpersons to the teachers' classrooms. The staff expressed concern that the students' disrespect would reflect on their "professional" competency and result in poor performance evaluations (system processes). Most of the discussion regarding the nature of the school and the "problem children" was guised in innuendo, sarcasm, and "black humor," with little direct expression of anger and frustration. Further, when directly confronted about their own feelings, the faculty became extremely defensive, providing rationalization for the need for such an orientation, and then returned to the indirect forms of ventilation.

Following the model of service delivery previously outlined, assessment was directed at the systemic factors (i.e., teachers and administration) involved rather than the intrapsychic variables operative within the children referred. It was hypothesized, therefore, that the manifested

reaction of the children was tied to the overly repressive, authoritarian style of the faculty. Consequently, an appointment with the principal was scheduled to gather additional data reflecting faculty profiles and preferred teaching styles. This interview, however, provided a basis for reconsidering the initial hypothesized role of the teacher as the "prime" etiological factor. It appeared that the focus needed to be broader, so as to include not only the role of the teachers and administrator but also the impact of the system's structure and processes on the development of the passive-aggressive behavior.

Dr. H., the building principal for over 15 years, was quick to outline his theory of education and to note that in essence teaching was a subversive activity. Further, Dr. H. noted that the faculty members were very similar to the children in that they were more interested in school holidays, summers off, and the avoidance of "hard" work than in education. Thus, he needed to "run herd on" them in order to "get the job done."

Dr. H. painted a picture of his own managerial style and organizational focus which was founded on the assumption that people are inherently lazy and will not work unless forced to do so. His orientation also assumed that people are incapable of working on their own towards a goal and so must be coerced to perform, often by threat of reprisal. Following from such a set of operational assumptions about the nature of the worker his managerial style placed emphasis on control and authority and task performance through force and negative coercion. Given the apparent "dehumanized" view which the principal held toward the management of teachers, a second series of hypotheses emerged as guides to this consultation diagnosis and intervention.

It now appeared reasonable to assume that the initially observed overly authoritarian, repressive teacher style was an extension of the norm modeled by the principal, as well as a reaction to the experience of being managed within such an atmosphere. Therefore, in an attempt to begin to narrow the diagnostic hypotheses, data were gathered about faculty absenteeism, turnover, alienation, and manifestation of apathy. The data collected suggested that the passive-aggressive behaviors exhibited by the students, that is, their resistance, negativism, obstructionism, etc., were also exhibited by the staff. Missing meetings, coming late, failing to complete reports on time because of being overly involved with "other teaching responsibilities," and excessive absenteeism were but a few of the symptoms commonly exhibited by the faculty.

The data collected suggested the existence of what Argyris (1970)

termed "adaptive antagonistic activities" and thus supported the hypothesized existence of a hierarchial, authoritarian, repressive system conducive to passive ventilation of anger and frustration. It was concluded that the students' passive-aggressive behaviors were a direct result of the repressive forces experienced within the classroom, which were both an immediate result of the sense of frustration and oppression experienced by the teachers and the ultimate consequence of the school's highly oppressive structure and processes.

Focusing the Assessment Through Survey. In order to more clearly delineate the sources of this adaptive antagonism, the Community Oriented Programs Environment Scale (Moos, 1974) was administered to the staff. The results overwhelmingly demonstrated the staff's perception of the system as providing little or no opportunity to independently make decisions or to become actively involved in the operation and maintenance of the system. The staff members perceived their role to be defined as one of minimal involvement, with priority given to order, organization, and control to the almost complete exclusion of creativity and spontaneity.

While the history of the school (previously a completely unruly, unproductive setting) and the current interaction with the external forces of the environment (a transitional environment with much racial tension) supported the rational need for control and order within the building, the manner in which such order was achieved (at the expense of the individual sense of autonomy and esteem) proved ultimately destructive to the organization, its staff, and its student clientele.

Intervention

Having come to the realization that the most productive interventions would be at the system level (as opposed to the teacher or student level), the staff at the mental health center contracted to engage in organizational development consultation. The first goal was to increase the administration and staff awareness of the current state of the school (i.e., organization with one-way communication, autocratic decision-making, and low levels of trust). Secondly, the intent was to provide the administration and staff with alternative models of functioning and facilitate the development and adaption of such organizational strategies into the existing system. A number of specific interventions were initiated to develop the staff's level of professional competence and increase their sense of autonomy and control within the school.

Increasing Staff Competence. As a first step in the development of staff competence and adaptive capacity, steps were taken to increase the availability of non-evaluative, objective data to the faculty regarding system operations, student performance, and their own teaching style. Such information and data provided a basis from which they could independently evaluate current levels of functioning and make modifications as needed. This provided them with both increased decision-making competence and autonomy to function. One specific example of such data provision was the supplying of departmental budget expenditures on an ongoing basis. This information allowed the members of each department to establish priorities for purchases and begin to consider long-range planning as a developmental strategy. Engaging in such planning enabled them to influence the nature and direction of the institutions; thus, again, a sense of professional competence was enhanced.

Increasing Autonomy and Control. A second group of strategies aimed at identifying and maximizing the special talents of the staff within the given structure. For example, while the school had as part of its organizational structure a committee on community relations, such a committee had never been formulated. Rather Dr. H. served as the contact person with all community groups. A brief survey of faculty interests and resources helped to identify four faculty members who wanted to become involved in developing summer activities in the community and creating programs aimed at reducing the high rate of vandalism. This survey also identified a number of other interest groups among the faculty, which were later established as "ad hoc committees" (for example, committees on curriculum evaluation, computer acquisition, and library development). Since these committees could be developed and operated within the existing system structure, they were implemented rather readily. In addition, each provided an avenue for faculty input into the system and thus helped to foster a sense of autonomy and control.

Even with the modifications noted, the basic operating assumptions of the organization were less than totally humanizing and continued to support the destructive "we-they" uncooperative orientation in the school. The "do only what I must" frame of mind—be it from students or faculty—was reflective of and reactive to the highly dictatorial, authoritarian system of management. Complete redesign of the organizational structure was needed. Such a process is not easily achieved! Policy committees, grievance boards, student representation, and dis-

tribution of power were but a few of the issues which needed to be addressed. To facilitate the consideration of the need and process for humanizing the school, an inservice program was developed around a presentation and discussion of the model of education presented by Schmuck and Schmuck (1974) in their text *A Humanistic Psychology of Education*. The brief inservice program not only was well received by the faculty members but also stimulated them to present a plan of action for Dr. H.'s consideration. Encouraged by the positive impact of the changes previously noted and the success of "ad hoc" groups, Dr. H. acquiesced to the faculty's recommendation for the development of a long-range planning committee whose task would be to consider appropriate means of modifying both the curriculum and organizational structures in order to facilitate the development of a more humanizing environment.

The Trickle Down Effect. The consultation model employed (Meyers, Parsons, & Martin, 1979) suggests that changes at the institutional level will have both immediate and long-term effects across the various levels of the system. In this case it was noted that, in addition to creating in the system a more facilitative, productive environment, discussions about the value of autonomy, self-control, and esteem-building as applied to the productivity of faculty members soon evolved into discussions of student and classroom productivity. Further, the generic approaches employed at the system level (i.e., increasing competence and autonomy) soon appeared in modified form in the classrooms. Desks were rearranged from straight rows, with all attention and communication directed toward the teacher, to small work group arrangements in which much communication and learning occurred among peers. In addition, many of the faculty members moved from lecture and teacher-directed activities to the use of work situations, where each student could pace his or her own productivity and make decisions about which activity to pursue at any one time. Such modifications increased the students' competence in self-governance and provided them with the opportunity to employ autonomy and control in their own program development. Consequently, filtering down of system interventions was evident in the creation of positive learning environments and the alleviation of previously experienced frustration and need for indirect expression. Eventually, there was a reduction of referrals for treatment of passive-aggressive children.

REFERENCES

American Psychiatric Association. *Diagnostic and statistical manual of mental disorders.* Third Edition. Washington, D.C., 1980.

Argyris, C. *Intervention theory and method.* Reading, MA: Addison-Wesley, 1970.

Blanchard, P. Psychoanalytic contributions to the problems of reading disabilities. *Psychoanalytic Study of the Child,* 1946, *2,* 163-187.

Caplan, G. *Theory and practice of mental health consultation.* New York: Basic Books, 1970.

Frankel, E. A. A comparative study of achieving and underachieving high school boys of high intellectual ability. *Journal of Educational Research,* 1960, *53,* 172-180.

Jarvis, V. Clinical observations on the visual problem in reading disability. *Psychoanalytic Study of the Child,* 1958, *13,* 451-470.

Liss, E. Learning difficulties? Unresolved anxiety and resultant learning patterns. *American Journal of Orthopsychiatry.* 1941, *11,* 520-524.

Moos, R. H. *The social climate scales: An overview.* Palo Alto: Consulting Psychologists Press, Inc., 1974.

Meyers, J., Parsons, R. D., & Martin, R. *Mental health consultation in the schools.* San Francisco: Jossey-Bass, 1979.

Parsons, R., Stone, S., & Feuerstein, P. Teacher-in-service training: A tool for maximizing counselor effectiveness. *The Guidance Clinic,* March 1977, 13-16.

Parsons, R. D., & Meyers, J. *Consultation skills: Training, Development and assessment.* San Francisco: Jossey-Bass, in press.

Rabkin, L. Y. Passive-aggressiveness and learning. *Exceptional Children,* 1965, *32,* 1-3.

Schmuck, R. A., & Schmuck, P. A. *A humanistic psychology of education.* Palo Alto, CA: National Press Books, 1974.

Sperry, B. M., Staver, N., & Mann, H. E. Destructive fantasies in certain learning difficulties. *American Journal of Orthopsychiatry,* 1952, *22,* 356-365.

Spivack, G., & Shure, M. B. *Social Adjustment of Young Children.* San Francisco: Jossey-Bass, 1974.

Sullivan, H. S. *The interpersonal theory of psychiatry.* New York: Norton, 1953.

Weiner, I. B. *Psychological disturbance in adolescence.* New York: Wiley, 1970.

Wilson, R. C., & Morrow, W. R. School and career adjustment of bright high-achieving and under-achieving high school boys. *Journal of Genetic Psychology,* 1962, *101,* 91-103.

9

The Medical System: A Complex Arena for the Exhibition of Passive-Aggressiveness

Harold R. Musiker
and Robert G. Norton

Medical systems provide an extraordinarily rich and complex theater in which to observe the interplay of passive-aggressive behavior. Medical systems can encompass the entire health system in the country, or the system in a given geographic area, all the hospitals in the community, a hospital with a variety of levels of complexity, subsystems within a hospital or health care unit on down to such interacting dyads as administrator-physician, nurse-physician, nurse-patient, and physician-patient.

As is the case with most professional services which impinge on the public at large, there are a host of bureaucratic interactions, perhaps more than in any other profession, to be found in medical systems. At a national level we have organizations such as the American Hospital Association. There are various cooperative arrangements between medical schools and hospitals to determine, for example, national ranking and placement of interns and residents. There are regional medical as-

sociations, as well as national associations of nurses, social workers, physical therapists, radiologists, radiological technicians, laboratory technicians, etc. In addition to these mutual interest associations, we have the Surgeon General of the United States, the Public Health Service, the Food and Drug Administration, the National Institutes of Health, State Health Departments, and a multitude of other training, educational, and standard setting organizations.

The authors of this chapter have worked in a variety of hospitals, private practice and other medical settings of various size and complexity. In so doing they have acquired a range of observations and experiences from which they draw illustrations. Interactions involving passive-aggressive behavior may be observed between major institutions, between the institutions and their subsystems, between individuals in relationship to one another or to these fairly large systems, etc. Because many of these institutions bear some degree of authoritarian relationship to some other, passive-aggressive behavior is perhaps the only socially practical or possible way of showing resistance. The various role definitions and special needs of these components and the range of possible interaction options make confrontation or open conflict either unfruitful or inappropriate; hence passive-aggressive behavior is often a fairly useful, if not very efficient, way of expressing disagreement or a negative attitude.

Over the past hundred years the medical system in this country has evolved not through any conscious deliberate plan, but through a combination of scientific, professional, and political action. The first medical schools were founded in this country a little over 200 years ago. These followed medical schools in Europe by several years. The training of physicians was largely based upon an apprentice system with little scientific base. There was really no other way to teach what little was useful to the physician. Medical treatment consisted of a very primitive pharmacopoeia and the ubiquitous purging and bleeding, which often did more harm than good. Hospitals, as we know them now, simply did not exist. They were "pest houses" or hospices for the care of the dying. They existed largely for the care of the homeless and those who lacked social support systems in the form of family to take care of them when they were ill. They were primitive and at best offered very limited care and precious little cure. There was little by way of a scientific base to what physicians did. The first beginnings of scientific medicine came with Pasteur's work, clarifying the origin of much disease. With this and Lister's antiseptic techniques, hospitals began to become places where patients could expect at least some kind of rational treatment.

The combination of antiseptic technique, the discovery of x-rays and the use of anesthesia allowed patients to be surgically treated. Out of these advances of medical science and technique came the rise of the modern hospital, largely towards the end of the 19th century.

We shall spend a good deal of time discussing the so-called general hospital because it is the most ubiquitous and probably the most complex of the medical settings within which passive-aggressive behavior takes place. Patients today for the most part receive medical care in a general hospital or in the doctor's office rather than at home, which was the more typical place of treatment at the turn of the century. Some hospitals have become so complex that it is perhaps better to describe them as medical centers. They have inpatient, outpatient, day hospital, long-term care, short-term care, intensive and general care units. Many of them are also surrounded with clinics, private physicians offices and staff physician offices, etc.

THE GENERAL HOSPITAL

It may be worthwhile to spend a little time looking in detail at the structure and nature of the general hospital. It has been said that there are two organizations that are essentially unmanageable, at least in the sense of the classic pyramidal flow of authority and responsibility from apex down to base. One is the large university, the other the general hospital. In both cases there is an administrative and professional structure bringing expertise to bear on an audience. In the hospital setting that is, of course, the patient. The practitioner in both settings, professor or physician, has guild, personal, and professional interests which relate sometimes only tangentially to the larger organization and to the ultimate consumer of the practitioner's services, the patient. Sometimes, in the most complex of hospitals, the large medical school teaching hospital, there are further competing loyalties and subloyalties. In any case, the hospital patient who is the ultimate consumer has very little to say directly about the nature or the kind of services delivered and is usually a passive recipient of those services. Decisions as to what services are to be offered, regardless of cost, are made for the patient by the admitting physician and the strictures and structures of the hospital. The free forces of the market normally do not influence such institutions as hospitals, at least, in their day-to-day operation. Because of the complex interaction between administrator, physician, and the numerous subspecialties found on the medical, nursing, administrative staff, and tech-

nical staff of a large hospital, it is difficult to find simple organizational structure. It is our premise that the application of standard organizational design results in an organization which encourages the use of passive-aggressive behavior in normal everyday interactions within the hospital.

The Hospital Administrator

The professional hospital administrator is a rather novel development in general hospitals. Up to the 1940s most hospital administrators, at least those in senior positions, were physicians or nurses. Today most hospitals are managed by professional administrators with specific training in the field of hospital and/or business management. Support departments such as housekeeping, buildings and grounds, food service, etc., are all managed by nonphysician personnel with little or no education in the clinical patient care process. With the rise of the clinical subspecialties, we began to have nonmedical and clinically trained personnel running such departments as respiratory therapy, physical therapy, various laboratories and other services which impinge directly on patient care and which are heavily involved therein. These services may be "ordered" or requested by the patient's physician, hence allowing the personnel to interact indirectly with the physician and directly with the patient.

The administrators of the hospital, particularly of the upper two or three levels of echelon, are high enough on the managerial ladder to set policy, review budgets, and in general become involved in interaction with medical staff and/or hospital-based physicians insofar as they control financial resources and resources of space, personnel, and capital equipment. Increasingly, there is often a subtle but still real conflict between these personnel and the physician as to the goals and general direction that the hospital will take.

Hospital Organization

As has been noted earlier, hospitals are among the most complex organizations in our society. Relationships between and among individuals within the hospital organization are complex and are often complicated by the difficulty in applying routine, and contemporary organizational structure to the hospital environment. It is our premise that the application of standard organizational design results in an organization which encourages the use of passive-aggressive behavior in

order to deal with normal everyday interaction in the hospital. Let us examine this premise through a review and discussion of hospital organization.

There are approximately 7,000 hospitals in the United States today. Of these 7,000 hospitals, the majority are organized as nonprofit, private, and public (tax-supported) institutions. The remainder of the institutions fall into predominantly two categories: 1) those hospitals with religious affiliations, which are managed and controlled by religious orders; and 2) those institutions which are managed by for-profit corporations with profits accruing to stockholders. The number of for-profit corporations has increased rapidly in the past few years. The hospital organization which we will examine is a private not-for-profit hospital. However, the theory is applicable to other types of hospitals as well.

The typical organization of a hospital is shown in Figure 1. The figure shows a standard organizational pyramid with individual employees defined in groups led by group leaders responsible to higher level managers ultimately responsible to a chief executive officer and a board of trustees. In a classical industrial organization, power and authority flow from the top of the organization, and relationships between individuals, as defined by the chart, are relatively simpler and more straightforward than they are in a hospital organization. We will examine the organization by dividing it into four "zones" according to level on the organizational chart, looking at relationships between individuals in each of these zones, and seeing how organizational design encourages passive-aggressive behavior.

Zone 1. The typical private, not-for-profit hospital is ultimately governed by a group of individuals or members of the corporation from whom the hospital's ultimate legal existence flows. These so-called corporators are typically prominent members of a community and are, in law, the actual ultimate decision-makers of the organization. Ironically, however, these corporators typically meet but once a year and their sole function at that time is to elect a board of directors to be more actively involved in the operation of the institution for the common good of the community. Traditionally, there is little, if any, formal contact between members of the board of trustees and members of the corporation regarding matters of hospital operations. The board is solely responsible for operation of the hospital. The corporators can be thought of as stockholders in the typical industrial organization.

The board of directors of the typical community hospital is composed of influential members of the community which the hospital serves. The

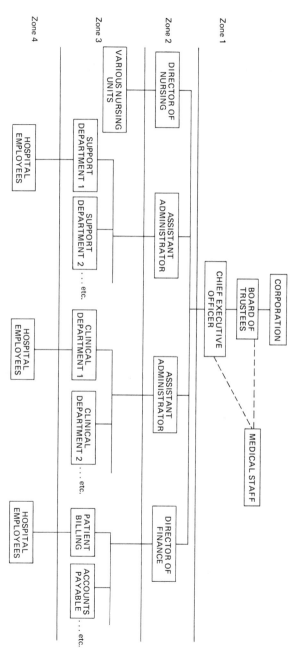

Figure 1. Typical Hospital Organization Chart

board members are typically not familiar with the internal workings of a hospital or with principles of hospital management. Certainly one would not expect them to be conversant with clinical principles related to care of patients within the organization. In order to discharge their responsibility for overall management of the hospital organization, the board of trustees appoints a chief executive officer. Organizational relationships which the authors believe breed passive-aggressive behavior begin at this level. The vast, but understandable, lack of awareness on the part of board members of the activities of the hospital and ultimately the activities involved in patient care presents the first opportunity for passive-aggressive behavior. A board must make decisions regarding the overall direction and/or programs of a hospital or policy decisions regarding practices of the institution, which may be difficult for the organization to carry out. The chief executive officer, however, derives his authority and responsibility from this board and, therefore, an outward show of disapproval with the activities of the board would be unfavorably viewed by its members. Obviously, the least controversial way of dealing with decisions made by that board and dealing with the activities occurring in zone 1 of the chart would be for the chief executive officer of the institution to passively accept what has been decided and either minimally carry out the directions he or she receives or, more likely, subvert the decisions reached by the board of directors and manage the organization as he/she sees fit. We do not mean to imply that this is a common occurrence. The point, however, is that the organizational structure of hospitals lends itself more easily to the encouragement of passive-aggressive behavior as a way of dealing with organizational problems. This is true at the upper levels of the organization, i.e., between the board of directors and the chief executive officer, as well as subsequent levels.

Zone 2. Relationships in zone 2 of the typical hospital organization, that being the relationship between the chief executive officer and assistant officers of the institution, be they assistant administrators or, in corporate titling, vice presidents, are probably most comparable to relationships in ordinary industrial organizations and present the least encouragement of passive-aggressive behavior. Typically, the chief executive officer of a hospital started as a junior-level officer in a hospital organization and has risen through the organization to the chief executive slot. His or her relationship with the assistant administrators in the hospital is direct, so that here the line of authority and responsibility

is much more clearly established than in other parts of the organization. The assistant administrators recognize lines of authority more in the traditional sense due to the fact that their training, background, and understanding are most similar to training and background of the person with whom they are relating in the organization. When relationships exist between the different professional categories of the organization, the opportunity for passive-aggressive behavior becomes more pronounced.

Zone 3. The relationships between department heads in the hospital and assistant administrators encourage passive-aggressive behavior. In fact, the interactions which occur on this level of the organization will most likely foster this behavior. Relationships between department heads in the hospital and members of the administrative staff vary depending on the type of department involved. In a classical sense, lines of authority and responsibility clearly run from the assistant administrators to the department heads involved. In some departments, for example, materials management, purchasing, data processing, business office, etc., these relationships are relatively clear, and harmonious relationships usually exist between the individuals.

Relationships between the assistant administrative staff and clinical department heads may be less clearly defined and may encourage passive-aggressive behavior. Most of the clinical departments in a hospital are managed by an individual whose original background and training were in the clinical discipline offered by that department. For example, the director of respiratory therapy is most typically a respiratory therapist who has, through good performance, risen in the organization and is now functioning in a management position in the department. Such individuals typically have years of background and experience in providing clinical care to patients. Most have professional credentials which symbolize their background, training, and performance in their respective professions. Here we have loyalties to a profession with its own reward systems which may be independent of or in conflict with the needs of the hospital organization.

Department heads have a dual role in the hospital: 1) to provide the best possible patient care services through the resources available, and 2) to manage the activities of the department in a responsible way from a business point of view. Although it would be more advantageous if they were, these two functions are not always in concert. In many situations, the professional leading the department may wish to provide

a new service to patients, to alter a procedure in the interest of caring for patients, or to make other modifications of a clinical nature. These modifications may not always be the wisest from a management point of view. For example, it may not be in the best interests of the institution from a broad perspective to provide a particular procedure in a clinical department which will be of value to a very limited number of patients and may be extremely costly.

As professionals trained to provide services to patients, managers of these departments are clearly placed in situations of conflict. Many times their relationships with the administrative staff will influence them to lean in the direction of making the most advantageous decision from a management point of view. However, in this situation passive-aggressive behavior from a department head is extremely likely. No one likes to confront a superior regarding an issue of conflict in a direct fashion. For this reason, much indirect, passive-aggressive expression of conflict occurs in these relationships. There is procrastination regarding accomplishment of certain management objectives, as well as situations of selective obedience to certain policies and procedures. There are even situations where policies and procedures are ignored totally by those closest to decisions regarding patient care processes.

The encouragement of passive-aggressive behavior on this level of the organization is probably most prevalent in large organizations. The greater the organizational distance between administrative staff members and the actual end product of the hospital, i.e., provision of patient care, the more likely we are to find passive-aggressive behavior on this level of the organization.

Zone 4. Similar organizationally induced passive-aggressive behavior occurs on this level of the organization. Relationships between individual professionals providing care to patients and their departmental heads can become strained when the individual caregiver is placed in the position of trying to decide between the best interests of his or her patients and the best interests of the organization as a whole. Staff members will often do what they believe is individually the correct thing for the patient, in spite of organizational policies and procedures which might dictate differently.

Again, in this zone, reactions to conflict between individual caregivers and the departmental managers are more likely to be passive-aggressive than confrontational. When issues of the right decision vs. the wrong decision are complex, passive-aggressive behavior is more likely to occur. For this reason, as well as the doubt which surrounds many individual

decisions regarding patient care, passive-aggressive behavior is often seen in this level of the organization.

Two areas of the hospital organization deserve special attention because of the likelihood of passive-aggressive behavior within these sections of the hospital. These two areas are in medical staff relationships and organizational posture and in the role of the nursing department.

The Physician. Physicians are trained in a tradition which goes back thousands of years to the priest physicians of ancient Egypt and other physicians of the pre-scientific area. The attribution of life and death power which physicians are given by the general public because of their training gives them feelings of omnipotence and some degree of impatience with those not trained in their own science and skills. While dependent for support upon the general public and often quite fond of their patients, there is a feeling that they know what is best. In their office, they control the office staff and make sole determination as to appropriate evaluation and treatment. This autocratic tendency tends to be in conflict with the needs of other systems within the general hospital.

This interaction becomes especially relevant when the physician interacts with the nurse in whose hands the day-to-day care of the patient is left. The physician "orders" the procedures and treatment he wishes the patient to receive. The administration of these procedures is handled largely by the nurse, the pharmacist, the x-ray department, the laboratories, and, in teaching hospitals, by junior physicians, interns, and residents. The physician expects that orders will be carried out in a direct and timely fashion. The other departments and persons with whom he interacts, having their own ego needs and feeling pressure to deal with the needs of many patients, may sometimes delay or obstruct carrying out "orders."

A physician who wishes priority treatment for his patient often encounters passive resistance from the other subsystems within the hospital. His intermediary, the nurse or the ward secretary who arranges for these other procedures via the phone, may also show resistance to these orders if the physician is considered unpopular or arbitrary. If the intermediary in the ordering process, i.e., the ward clerk, is not convinced of the genuine emergent nature of the orders, passive-aggressive behavior is likely. Physicians also complain about how slow service is, how hard it is to get information from various segments of the hospital, or about carlessness of the nurses in performing some functions for the patient.

Sometimes the wishes of the physician who is a member of the medical staff in private practice and the needs of the hospital for training residents and physicians conflict. There may be competition for scarce beds or other hospital resources. A physician, despite his not wishing so, may be assigned an intern to work with him. Because of the need to provide teaching opportunities to the house officers, the physician himself may be in a "one down" situation via-à-vis the chief of his service, who is often a member of the medical school faculty and who exercises review and judgmental control over physicians on the staff. In a hospital affiliated with a medical school, that person is often a fulltime employee of the hospital and/or medical school, and there may be genuine differences of opinion between him and the private physicians as to the way a service should be administered and managed, how many beds allocated to physicians, the availability of operating rooms, the obligation of the private practitioner to give free time to clinics and teaching services, etc.

There are multiple loyalties tugging a physician between his being a respected member of the community, his need to perform a certain amount of charitable care and/or teaching work, and the very real financial rewards of an intensive private practice. Just as the private practitioner has multiple pulls on him, so does the physician functioning as a member of the teaching faculty in a hospital. Pressures are upon this individual to obtain grants, to conduct research so as to maintain his position on the faculty and enhance it, to attract research fellows and generate publications and papers, to teach, as well as to supplement his income. Conflicts between and among medical school faculty for space, budget money, and grants are no less intense than the kind of political infighting that may go on in any large industrial organization. Here again, direct confrontation is neither approved nor generally effective and it is necessary to make end runs around obstacles rather than confronting them head on, ignoring some pressures and passively resisting others.

In recent years the physician has been faced with a modest rise in consumerism and opposition even in the most sacrosanct area of practice—the doctor-patient relationship. Patients increasingly question physicians. There has been a tremendous rise in the number of malpractice suits brought, reflecting this active resistance on the part of the patient.

Maternity hospitals specializing in obstetrical services have radically changed their attitudes toward breastfeeding, rooming in, and natural prepared childbirth over the last two decades, from indifference and outright hostility to compliance—even to the extent of creating what are now called "birthing suites." Much of the motivation for these changes

has come from women who are anxious to reclaim from the medical profession some degree of control over the childbirth process.

Physicians, however critical they may be in private about these movements, find themselves contrained to give, at the most, passive resistance to them. Interestingly enough, a recent dilemma that has made the headlines in this area affects nurses more than physicians, particularly in the area of abortions. Physicians are apparently willing to go along with pressures on the part of women to have abortions in the second trimester. It is the nurses who must assist in the delivery process who balk at abortions which produce recognizable fetuses. They feel ambivalent about terminating a pregnancy, since this is something they personally value. They spend much of their time fighting to extend and preserve the lives of infants at risk who are only slightly older and larger than many of the fetuses whose lives are being terminated. Their resistance comes out in passive-aggressive manner.

The Nurse. The prototypical nurse of 30 or 40 years ago was a woman trained in a hospital-affiliated school of nursing, a three-year course which led to a diploma and the awarding of an R.N. degree. Typically, the woman came from the lower middle class, was an upwardly mobile individual, and was often among the first members of her family to go into a profession (her brother may have gone on to college). In schools run by some religious orders she was trained to stand up when a physician walked into the room. In general, the nurse moved into what is structurally and in a sense legally a subordinate role to the physician. Physicians were almost exclusively white males. The few female physicians almost invariably went into pediatrics or some "laboratory" aspect of medicine such as radiology, pathology, etc.

Even today, when 30% of slots in medical schools are filled by females, the overwhelming majority of nurses are still female and still must act in a subordinate role. In general, the hospital physician throughout the country is still largely male, and the nurse female. Their roles, therefore, mirror some of the superior-subordinate roles which our male-dominated society has structured, offering women only passive-aggressive ways of objecting to the authoritarian and controlling male. Two concurrent movements—the rise of women's liberation and the increasing professionalism of the nurse—have sometimes led to role conflicts between older nurses and the new wave, and more expressly between nurses and physicians who feel themselves somewhat challenged by such new creatures as the nurse practitioner and the nurse clinical specialist, who are seen as encroaching on the physician's traditional turf.

Increasingly nurses are trained outside hospital-based schools of nurs-

ing in junior college and baccalaureate programs. Just as there has been pressure for school teachers and others in traditionally female positions to upgrade qualifications, making the masters degree the journeyman's degree for the mature teacher, so, too, there is pressure on nurses who wish to become career nurses to obtain not only the baccalaureate but also advanced degrees in one area or another. The rise of professionalism among nurses, coupled with the women's movement, has lead to a new spirit of questioning and challenging, which permeates even the legally and socially sanctioned hierarchy with the physician at the top of the pyramid. Again, by virtue of traditional roles and legal responsibility, often the only way the nurse can challenge established procedures is through passive-aggressive behavior.

Consider for a moment the situation in which nurses are placed in hospitals. They are responsible for nursing care for their own individual patients, especially in today's primary nursing or professional nursing practices. While responsible for the nursing care of their patients, they are also responsible for carrying out the orders of physicians in the care of these patients. In addition to the conflict potential resulting from this somewhat loosely defined relationship, nursing also finds itself in many organizations in a role of coordinator of the services of other departments. They are responsible, for instance, for making arrangements for services for their patients with other hospital departments. When those other hospital departments cannot perform the services as requested or required, it is often nursing which must intervene on the part of the patient and place the necessary pressure to make the ancillary services responsible. We have, therefore, placed the nurse, in the classical hospital organization, in the interesting position of having to respond to an individual, i.e., a member of the medical staff, who has no formal relationship to that nurse that can be shown on an organizational chart or in the classical administrative sense. The nurse is also responsible for coordinating the care provided by other health care professionals. We have given nursing no or little authority to carry out this task. These two relationships, both with medical staff and with other health care professionals, by their very nature, encourage individuals to use passive-aggressive approaches to problems. Conflict resolution in the absence of clear lines of authority and responsibility is difficult at best, and to avoid conflicts which one cannot resolve, given the unclear nature of lines of authority, one is more likely to use passive-aggressive procedures.

The Patient. Patients are becoming more sophisticated about medical matters, although recognizing their dependency within the doctor's of-

fice and within the hospital setting. When a patient enters a hospital, he/she surrenders a great deal of autonomy. The right to decide when to wake, when to sleep, what foods to eat, when to eat, what clothes to wear, whether one can spend one's time in bed or out of bed and even where one may move his bowels are determined by "orders" written by the doctor and interpreted and carried out by the nurse. The patient is encouraged to become a passive vessel on which the physician, the nurse, and the other clinical workers in the hospital work their magic. Studies by medical sociologists indicate that patients are fearful of "rocking the boat." Even though there have been changes, e.g., the development of patients "bill of rights," patients are still often fearful of expressing their own needs and challenging "the system." One of the fears is that they will then become known as a difficult or obstreperous person and that the nurse in her passive-aggressive way will be slow to respond to a call, or that the nurse and/or doctor will ignore pain or more serious symptomatology and not be there for the patient when a true emergency occurs. Interviews with patients indicate that they are usually fairly positive in their praise of the quality of medical and nursing care that they get. They tend to see their physician and nurse as hardworking, dedicated, and even overworked, which is certainly true part of the time, but only part of the time. They do not wish to be seen as difficult patients.

The same is to some extent true, although to a lesser degree, for the patient seen in private practice. The patient is in no position, either by virtue of ignorance or fear, to challenge the authority of the physician. The techniques that the patient is then free to use are pretty much passive-aggressive ones—coming late, forgetting to pay bills, not taking medications, not following "orders." Conversely, the nurse or doctor facing a difficult patient may use passive-aggressive means to avoid the patient or to be slow to respond to the patient's need. Patients who are upsetting or embarrassing to medical staff are treated with passive-aggressive behavior. Patients who are dying often receive a lower frequency of interaction with physicians and other hospital staff.

Passive-Aggressive Interaction Between Physician and the Hospital

One of the ways in which physicians demonstrate passive-aggressive behavior is their reluctance to complete discharge summaries on patients. Because it is a tedious and onerous task, they often delay this rather significant procedure. Hospitals use aversive techniques to obtain compliance. The procedure utilized is to deny the physician admission of new patients until he has "cleaned up his act" by completing discharge

summaries on patients who have already been discharged. Physicians also use passive-aggressive behavior by not answering their page, by having secretaries screen calls, by not attending meetings and conferences. Again, the procedures available to authorities or to patients for changing physicians' behavior in such situations tend to be aversive.

Patient-Physician Passive-Aggressive Behavior

One of the issues involved with patients is difficulty or reluctance to follow through on prescribed treatment regimens. Patients "forget to take their pills," go off their diets, etc. Obtaining adherence to prescribed regimens is a major problem for physicians. One suggestion that seems to work well with pill-taking is to link the pill to a positive event, thus, to get the patient to take pills with meals, coffee breaks, etc. This is especially effective if spouses or significant others in the patient's life can be also involved. The literature on compliance suggest a higher rate of success when contingencies can be modified or controlled by significant others so as to enhance compliance. This is true not only for pill-taking but also for adering to weight reduction diets, etc.

One promising approach to prevent passive-aggressive resistance on the part of the patient is to bring the patient into the treatment program as a cooperating partner. When the patient views the physician as a teacher/coach rather than a priest/magician, he/she is more apt to feel that he/she has a personal stake in the treatment process. Therefore it is less likely that he/she will resist or passive-aggressively deny what is going on in the pathology or in the treatment.

A POTENTIAL SOLUTION: INTERVENTION

Given the nature of hospital organizations and their influence on passive-aggressive behavior, what can we do to minimize interactions which encourage this behavior? Many people believe one way to do this is to break up the traditional hierarchy of a hospital into more manageable units more closely focused around the process of caring for patients in the hospital. This can be done through the establishment of what has been called the matrix organization. This type of organization attempts to divide the organization into groups by program responsibility, so that, for instance, a group of individuals providing care to patients in a division of the hospital might be organized with a joint reporting relationship to their individual departments and to the leader of the program of which they are a part.

For example, a team of professionals might be assembled to provide care to surgical patients. The team may consist of physicians, nurses, respiratory therapists, physical therapists, other health care professionals, as well as the ancillary support staff necessary. These individuals would function as a team and the director of the program to which they are assigned would have responsibility for making decisions about the use of resources in that program.

Individuals in the departments would also have responsibility for reporting professional activities of their various professions back to the main department. A respiratory therapist, for instance, assigned to a surgical intensive care group would have responsibility for general supervision of her professional activities assumed by the individual leader of the surgical intensive care group. Specific responsibility for the activities of the individual in the profession would relate to the respiratory therapy department. This type of organization attempts to bring the lines of authority and responsibility into a clearer focus, organized directly around the patient rather than around the entity of the hospital as a whole. Its proponents indicate that it encourages closer cooperation and collaboration among the individual caregivers and encourages direct conflict resolution on the level of the patient care activities, rather than funneling conflict up through the large organization for resolution on a higher level. The matrix organization is shown in Figure 2.

Examples of Passive-Aggressive Behavior

Two illustrations follow which support the general premise that passive-aggressive behavior is encouraged by the type of organization prevalent in hospitals.

The first example involves space conflicts within the hospital organization. The control of space is a major issue in most hospitals today. There is never enough space for various needs of departments within the hospital, and the space is generally never as centrally located as people would like to see it. Ownership of space in a hospital is an indication of status, power, and authority. Therefore, conflict frequently results around the use of space in a hospital organization. When this occurs, intervention by an administrative officer of the hospital is usually required.

A recent experience of one of the authors involved office space on a patient care unit within a community hospital. This space was used as a consultation office for a clinical dietitian assigned to a group of patient care stations. The space was used for charting diets in consultation with

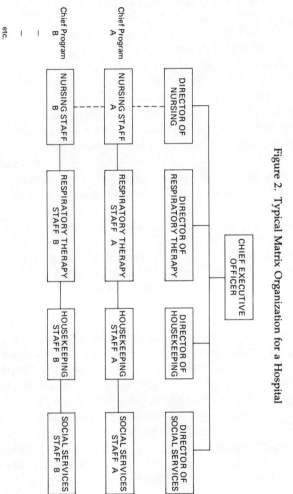

Figure 2. Typical Matrix Organization for a Hospital

physician staff members and consultation with other health care professionals regarding dietary issues.

The nursing staff of the patient care unit identified a need for general
use space for consultation and for use by families of patients on this
unit. The unit was devoted to seriously ill patients, many of whom were
newly diagnosed cancer patients, and the need for a family room for a
quiet time and grieving was substantiated. When it was determined that
the use of the space occupied by the dietary department for this family
room was appropriate, the dietary department was given alternate space
in another location removed from the patient care units.

Obviously, it is difficult for one to be outwardly and actively opposed
to providing an appropriate opportunity for family counseling and family
grieving. The reaction of the dietary management staff was predictably
concerned and, since they recognized the need for this family space,
outwardly cooperative. The first reaction was that they would move *but*
that the alternative space proposed was too drafty and modifications
would have to be made to the heating system. These modifications,
although rather substantial, were performed by the hospital's maintenance department, and approximately one month later, the space was
ready to be occupied. At that time, the management of the dietary
department indicated that the space was now acceptable but that the
furniture which was in the previous area would not fit well into the new
space and that, therefore, they would have to order new furniture before
they could make the move. The new furniture was ordered, resulting
in another six-week delay in the move. At that time, the manager of the
dietary department indicated that things looked pretty good, but that
the telephones in the new office would have to be connected to the main
dietary department telephones so they could be answered by clerical
personnel. This was not true in the previous location.

These three "OK but" reactions were followed by two more of less
consequence until finally an order was issued by the administrative
officer involved to literally go up over a weekend and move the dietary
personnel belongings from the space on the patient care unit to the new
location. All through the incident, the manager of the dietary department
expressed support for the decision; however, she resisted at every turn
through the raising of different obstacles. This type of passive-aggressive
behavior frequently occurs in hospital organizations in which a decision
is made for the good of the organization but does not receive uniform
support and so is resisted in a subversive fashion by hospital personnel.

The second example occurred at a more fundamental and lower level
of reaction to hospital policies. An ambulatory service for children with

developmental and other disabilities was provided through a university hospital with funds received through a combination of federal and state grants. As a result of federal budget cuts and restrictions in state funding, the financial viability of this operation became extremely questionable.

To deal with this problem, administrative staff members and members of the professional and management staff of the clinic developed a mechanism for charging patients of this clinic modest fees for services rendered at the clinic. A proposed fee structure was developed and patient volume estimated to assure a financially viable operation in the future. A system was organized to collect information regarding patient encounters so that bills could be sent to third-party insurers and in some limited cases to patients themselves. The system was organized based on volume projections which had been estimated through review of volume in the preceding 12-month period.

Once the charging system was instituted, hospital officials began to notice a decline in the number of patients being officially processed through the center. Further investigation revealed that members of the professional staff in the center were seeing patients and not booking them through the official system so as to avoid their having to pay the bills. This occurred in spite of the fact that the overwhelming majority of the bills would be reimbursed by third parties and not result in any direct payment by the parents of the individuals receiving the service.

SUMMARY

Passive-aggressive behavior occurs in medical care systems as it does in other systems where there is an opportunity for adversary relationships, where there is an opportunity for hierarchical relationships, or in any relationship where people feel threatened and are not free to act. In medical systems we note that these occur between physicians and nurses, physicians and patients, nurses and patients, senior and junior physicians, and within the administrative structure of large hospitals between superiors and subordinates and/or between departments.

Reorganizations of systems to take advantage of natural groupings and other changes in the administration or in the structure can possibly alleviate passive-aggressive behavior. Attempts to share value systems and to understand "opposing" viewpoints and utilization of behavior modification procedures or the ultimate threats of aversive consequences are also potential ways of ameliorating, preventing, or reducing passive aggressive behavior.

10

Passive-Aggressiveness Within the Religious Setting

Robert J. Wicks

Organized religion* typically is an "ideal" environment for the development and nurturance of passive-aggressiveness. The constant smiles of the Hare Krishna sect followers are really only mild caricatures of the sweet veneers that many Christians believe they must wear if they are to consider themselves true followers of the Gospel.

Worshipers, those in ministry, and the social unit within which they operate (i.e., church, religious community, Christian school) are often dynamically loyal to a style which praises control, suppression, repression, denial of anger, and avoidance of conflict. As one might expect, the results of such a psychological philosophy of living can easily lead to personal devastation, an apathetic community, or "religious" causes that are based on a legalism or extremism, serving to unconsciously deliver hostility instead of the "Good News" of the Gospel.

When anger is not recognized and channeled constructively in a religious person or community, a lack of growth and/or an increase in personal/communal pathology is the expected outcome. Illustrations of this, unfortunately, are easy to uncover. The following are four obvious ones:

- The accommodating minister who gets along with *everyone* in the parish but develops an ulcer, hypertension, and/or problems with alcoholism or obesity in the process.
- The nice—but insular and stagnant—Christian church or school that is so fearful of anger being experienced in its midst that it discourages and denies conflict in any form.
- The Catholic female religious who does everything by the letter of the law and devotes much of her energy to keep from breaking it herself and to ensuring others don't venture out of its bounds as well.
- The Christian activist (e.g., for peace, anti-abortion) who acts with such a vengeance that his/her message defeats the purported Christian one he/she claims to be delivering to others by witnessing the truth.

The fact that illustrations of Christians who are not in touch with their anger, much less aware of their ability and need to use it constructively, are abundant can be traced to the traditional misunderstandings that Christians have had with regard to anger.

CHRISTIAN CONFUSION ABOUT ANGER

Perfection as a goal can be inspirational. Yet, when it has as one of its tenets the elimination of anger as an emotion, it is a threatening, misguided norm for Christians to follow. Taking *New Testament* injunctions out of context is probably one of the key determinants of confusion or distortion which leads Christians to want to avoid anger at all costs.

Jesus' admonition to "turn the other cheek" and Paul the Apostle's encouragement to "put off the old nature" have long been consciously and indirectly employed as supports for the need to subdue one's anger. However, to interpret Christ and Paul in this way is to assume that loving one's neighbor and reviewing/renewing one's life in Christ is tantamount to denying one's own God-given human nature—which includes emotions such as anger. Christians seeking such perfection may also make light of, or deny, Christ's own displays of anger at the injustices he saw.

As Fox (1972), a Catholic theologian, points out in his very popular book on American spirituality, such an outlook can lead to the removal of justified anger from the center of the Christian's prayer life, which in turn can make life in faith a compartmentalized, artificial one.

Piety and social intransigence go to church regularly hand in hand. In this way, love of neighbor is confused with "being nice" (anger, one's very capacity for moral outrage, is a sin) and questions of

justice are conveniently considered outside the realm of one's prayer life. In contrast, we have seen that the only real "answer" to prayer is a changed person on the one hand and a changed people, that is a changed world or culture, on the other (Fox, 1972, pp. 100, 101).

Augsburger, who is in the Pastoral Care Department at Associated Mennonite Biblical Seminaries in Elkhart, Indiana, and the author of *Anger and Assertiveness in Pastoral Care* (1979), also points to the confusion Christian leaders in particular may have when distinguishing between inappropriate "niceness" on the one hand and being a good pastor to those whom he/she is trying to serve on the other. The results of such "niceness" can be quite negative.
In his words,

> Chronic niceness in a pastor tends to elicit comparable niceness in others, with the result that the negative feelings are not readily shared and resentments accumulate. . . .
> Habitual niceness inhibits the free expression of natural responses. It prohibits easy discussion of differences, making it hard to initiate frank interchange. Participants are kept on guard by the fear that their relationship could not survive a spontaneous hassle if one should erupt.
> Professional niceness maintains distance between persons. . . . Irritations are handled with a "soft touch" and the more intimate levels of trust and risk go unexplored. . . .
> Perpetual niceness creates patterns of denial in relationships, and the pastor's denying style can help set the tone for a whole community's "united front" method of suppressing conflict . . . (p. 8).

From the above comments by both a Catholic and a Protestant theologian, the problems with passive-aggressiveness among religious individuals are obviously coming to light and being discussed at last. Moreover, such recognition that anger is a part of full religious living, as well as something that is part of the natural order, means that it can't be as easily dismissed as something inherently "secular" or irrelevant for the believing Christian, as it was in the past.
Even in the case of "passive-aggressiveness," the issue of misplaced and poorly dealt with anger in religious groups is coming to light, as can be seen in the following quote from *Inside Christian Community* (Hammett & Sofield, 1981):

Passive-aggressive persons are extremely difficult to deal with because conflict never surfaces and they are unwilling to cooperate. They manage to maintain a rather serene picture of themselves as well-controlled, proper, nonviolent human beings. But they are not the peaceful or loving personalities they pretend to be. When they are confronted with the disruptive nature of their style, they do not easily give it up. Often they remain remote and inaccessible to healthy relationships. If any relationship begins to build, the passive-aggressive person quietly withdraws, leaving hurt behind. *Unfortunately, this personality is common in religious communities* (italics supplied, p. 75).

Consequently, no longer is the bittersweet veneer of passive-aggressiveness seen as the religious ideal to be followed and modeled. Christian writers and lecturers are now openly condemning such pseudo-love of neighbor.

Because of changing attitudes, mental health consultants and private practitioners can now deal with anger-related problems in religious organizations and individuals without undue concern that their interventions will be generally dismissed on theological grounds. In fact, pastoral theologians from the larger Christian denominations are now supporting appropriate assertiveness as a way to deal with anger constructively (Augsburger, 1979; Burwick, 1981; Mickey & Gamble, 1978).

Theories about passive-aggressiveness and indirect expression of anger, as well as concomitant methods of intervention based on these therapeutic modalities, have already been discussed in detail in this volume. Knowledge of this material is obviously a first step in preparing for analysis, diagnosis, and strategy for intervention with the religious individual or organization having a problem with understanding and handling the emotion of anger. In addition, views of how the psychological consultant operates have been presented elsewhere (Platt & Wicks, 1979). However, prior to an intervention in the religious setting, it might be helpful for the independent practitioner or consultant to review some additional, more culture-specific factors in organized religion and a related paradigm for intervention.

TRAINING THE TRAINERS: IMPROVING MINISTERIAL ASSERTIVENESS

Being "religious" or wanting to reach out is naturally not a guarantee that one's results will be positive in a helping relationship. Still, as the demise of the era of self-interest and self-help books finally arrives, in

its place there is hope that persons in a position to help (i.e., those in ministry) will be open to books and mental health consultations—in the form of lectures, group workshops, and individual therapy—so they can find out how they might better reach out to others (Wicks, 1982). As part of this educative process, one of the goals for the mental health professional who writes or works with religious organizations is to alert this group to the presence of and methods of dealing with passive-aggressiveness in their congregations, peers, superiors—and *themselves*. By doing this, anger can be seen and dealt with holistically rather than in a negative "pseudo-Christian" light so they, as well as those with whom they interact and those they lead, can be more alive and truly Christian.

To accomplish this, consultants and therapists will naturally employ standard intervention methodologies, determined by their own theoretical bias and practice experience. To facilitate such a consultative process, the remainder of this paper will provide illustrations of, and methods of dealing with, passive-aggressiveness and problems in owning one's anger in religious settings. The following topics will be considered:

1) *Recognition* of non-Christian ways of thinking and dealing with others in terms of passive-aggressiveness.
2) Including reference to "passive-aggressiveness" in the "consciousness examen" (Aschenbrenner, 1972) or *introspective process* (Wicks, 1983) Christians are urged to undertake on a daily basis.
3) Developing *strategies for personal and communal assertiveness* which are in line with Christian ideals.

By focusing on the need to become more adept at sensing indirect anger, by knowing better how to analyze it, and by increasing Christians' practical methods of handling it in themselves and others, mental health consultants can then provide the Christian or Christian communities with whom they work an opportunity to become more alive and effective within the faith they profess.

Recognition

Appreciating when and how passive-aggressiveness is present is the logical place to start in presenting an overview of this style of indirectly dealing with anger. In the Christian setting—though naturally by no means restricted to it—there are a number of "classic ways" in which

persons demonstrate passive-aggressiveness. In working with Christian leaders (e.g., superiors, parish leaders), noting such illustrative ways anger seeps out can be a helpful beginning. *Corrective instruction, memos, and training others to avoid anger* might be good examples to begin with here. Naturally, there are many more illustrations, but this should serve to open up the topic.

Preachers, local superiors, and "prophetic colleagues" who wish to "help" their fellow seminarians, ministers, etc. stay on the right path can use opportunities for corrective *instruction* as times for corrective *destruction*. Illustrations of this are not as few as one would hope. If the consultant mentions several as part of a consultative presentation, the religious group being assisted may be helped to start to identify with the point being made. As can be seen in the illustrations, rank or position in the community has no bearing on the opportunity for or presence of passive-aggressiveness.

- A priest who becomes angry at dinner hosts who try to force him to drink more than two alcoholic beverages may not deal directly with his anger at them; instead, he may make it a general issue "for the good of the whole parish" and preach on this type of situation on Sunday.
- A minister who has difficulty living with his associate pastor may spend a good deal of time each day telling her what faults she has—naturally, this is all for her own good so she doesn't continue making the same mistakes.
- A seminarian who drops hints for his roommate to be more orderly, based on the assumption that there is some value to doing this indirectly rather than discussing his annoyance more directly, may be quietly trying to drive the other person up the wall (without apparently being un-Christlike . . . heaven forbid!)

Writing *memos* is also a popular way to be passive-aggressive or indirectly angry at another person; the technique is well used because it allows us to send the barb from a distance. Consequently, in a religious community such written communications are frequently employed to safely censure someone else. A superior may write a note to a member of the community to inform him or her of problems that have come to her/his attention via another religious sister/brother in the community. A community member may take similar steps. In response to a verbal request to undertake some undesirable task, he/she may respond vaguely or critically in writing to the request rather than dealing with the potential disagreement directly with the superior.

Another familiar memo technique is to leave a message posted regarding something that has produced anger. The memo usually has three elements: 1) justification of one's own stand (as being correct and "Christian"); 2) reference to the injury being caused by other(s) who are vaguely recognizable from the information given; and 3) "pseudo-forgiveness" of the person(s) who did it (so he/she/they shouldn't retaliate by being angry). The following is an example of a note that might well be seen on a convent refrigerator:

Thursday, February 12th
Signing out the car is something which I feel I have a responsibility to do; consequently, I try to do this well in advance so as not to cause anyone any inconvenience. Yesterday, I wanted to borrow the car for my usual weekly visit to help my parents and the car was gone. It had been signed out at the last moment to deliver some goods. Though this possibly could have waited, and though I understand that it was a worthwhile trip and I recognize I must also compromise, I do ask that we try to set up these journeys in advance in the future so we don't cause unnecessary hardship to each other.

Thank you.

Too often the problem of passive-aggressiveness also continues because Christians *train one another to avoid anger*. Meetings are ideal places for this to occur. If the dynamics are not understood, then healthy persons who are trying to be aware of and constructively deal with anger can be co-opted into seeing their own process, rather than a distorted religious one, as inappropriate.

Example 1

Father Smith: Jim you really seemed to be upset at our parish council meeting.
Jim: Yes. The way Bill and Mary were trying to close out options other than their own in dealing with the youth group infuriated me. I wanted to let them know, so we could openly deal with it.
Father Smith: This is a Christian group Jim. We all have differences, but anger isn't going to help; you ought to think about controlling it a bit better. We can always drop hints to them when we see them alone.

Rather than encouraging Jim to learn how to channel his anger openly

in a way that would not be destructive to others, he is encouraging him to suppress it. Only resentment and hidden agendas will result from this action. Also, if it is dealt with as he suggests, the community will never deal with their fears of conflict. Thus, they will never achieve the intimacy needed to become a cohesive group—or in religious terms, a "faith community."

Example 2

Missionaries may be expected to spread the word of Christ anywhere the church sends them. However, although they are obedient to the call of Christ through the church, they are human beings with feelings. And one of these emotions, which is neither good nor bad, is anger. Anger can be an appropriate reflection of frustration, conflict, and fear of the unknown. In the following example, the house superior is trying to undo the young religious sister's distorted view of anger and her belief that everything that's not tied to outward expressions of love should be buried.

Sister Joan: Eileen, your assignment to Africa instead of the central American region of Latin America must have been quite a shock.
Sister Eileen Therese: It's God's will.
Sister Joan: God's will or not, you must have really been upset.
Sister Eileen Therese: When I took the vows I knew I wouldn't get my way all the time.
Sister Joan: We all know that, but you have been studying the culture and listening to those Spanish tapes for a year.
Sister Eileen Therese: There's no point talking about it; the decision has been made. I wish those who got the central American assignment all the luck and blessings they need.

The underlying theme here is that to be angry is wrong. The belief is that the anger somehow is a reflection of disobedience, weakness, and hostility toward those who got the assignment she wanted. The strength of the training she received early in religious life is hindering rather than helping her to own her anger and deal with it effectively.

This owning of anger is essential not only to promote honest interpersonal relations among Christians but also to help them focus clearly on the validity of being angry at injustices and disgusted with what is wrong with society today. Anger is not only a personal human emotion but also sometimes a sign of our intense concern for others. To quote Fox (1972) again in his book addressed to fellow Christians:

We must develop our capacity for outrage and adult anger, it appears, from purifying our love. For the relation of love and anger are inextricable. Anger is as sure a signal of love as smoke is of fire. Where one's capacity to become outraged at injustices is smothered and barely smolders, so does one's capacity for loving justice. It follows then that the development of the prophet in each of us waits for the development of the mystic in each of us. With growth in our powers to love life will advance our urge to share it and wrestle with its enemies. Adult anger is not buckshot anger, exploding in every direction at slight provocations. It is finely aimed and honed anger rising from a care for the beloved, not from an overly sensitive or hot-headed reaction to inconveniences. One's care for life fully lived can surely hone one's capacity for anger so that it finds a productive and creative channel in which to accomplish its work (p. 139).

So, in understanding problems the religious have in appreciating anger as a part of being fully Christian, mental health professionals can now join with theologians in dealing with this difficulty. Not only is anger a natural emotion which alerts people to the frustration of their own realistic and unrealistic needs, but it also points out when others are touching sensitive areas in their own psychological makeup or are committing community injustices which are personally unacceptable. Anger, then, can be a diagnostic tool to help people to learn about themselves, their defenses, their limits, and their beliefs, *but* such diagnosis cannot take place if anger is seen as forbidding and buried before it can be viewed and analyzed for what it is.

"Examen of Consciousness" and "Christian Introspection"

Whether in prayer, moments of meditation and contemplation, or in periods of introspection, Christians have long been expected and disciplined to take stock of their lives on a daily basis. In Roman Catholic circles, those in ministry have been usually educated to make a daily examen of consciousness. Though this practice has been on the wane, there has been recent interest in it and urging to continue the practice (Aschenbrenner, 1972).

More recently, there have been a number of books on self-examination and personal awareness for Christians. Of them, one of the recent ones (Wicks, 1983) strongly suggests that the religious take the time to view their personalities introspectively with an eye to how God might be influencing their lives. The goal is to help people see how their person-

ality facilitates their ministry and when they "trip over it" (i.e., become overly defensive) in their effort to reach out to others.

Wicks (1983) includes a section on anger. With respect to passive-aggressiveness, the utilization of the process this book describes (Christian Introspection) or the consciousness examen—which is more traditional to Catholics—offers an opportunity to see the vitality of anger and the destructiveness that comes with trying to deny anger "for the greater glory of God."

Any self-examination process has a place to review motivations for behavior and how and why certain emotions and thoughts arise. If this part of the process is taken seriously, then passive-aggressiveness and self-righteousness which are destructive to the whole community can be curbed. The following illustration of a professor in a Christian college involved in a noon review of his morning demonstrates how a person can refocus a problem with anger if he owns and channels it correctly.

> Phil really made me angry today. He wants me to drop everything and pay attention to his project. I have a lot to do that is more important than working with him. Maybe I have taken my time, but he sure didn't try to help me when I needed some assistance on the Faculty Affairs Committee. I don't think his values are in line with those of the school. I'm not just angry at him as a person, but what he stands for; he's paranoid; he's always looking out for himself and worried that someone is getting ahead of him. He even went to the chairperson when he didn't see my name on the roster to teach as many courses as he is teaching. That backstabber. He couldn't come to me; I'm glad I found out about it, so I could recognize him for what he really is.
>
> The question is, though, whether he is a worm or not, why am I giving him so much power? Why am I getting so angry? Whether he is right or wrong, what button is all of this pushing? Worm or not, why am I making myself so angry at him? A lot of people have done worse things to me. Why am I getting so bent out of shape? A lot of greater injustices are present in the world—what is it that I'm so sensitive about?
>
> It's obvious that I am putting his work on the back burner. He says I'm dragging my feet and I'm making righteous excuses, but they *are* excuses. I could have helped him out. If he didn't help me out, why didn't I let him know I was angry more directly? If he did go to the chairperson, why didn't I tell him about it; tell him I felt threatened?

Maybe that's it. I feel threatened. It's one dose of him and several doses of me feeling insecure. But I still feel that I don't agree with his philosophy, but I don't feel as angry. But why am I threatened? What button is he pushing? Let's see . . . I know I don't want to be viewed badly by others—I've had that problem for years. But why is he getting to me on that? Ha. I'm afraid people will like him and not me. Also, he always challenges me. I can't throw my charm and bull past him because he feels so competitive.

Well, the relationship isn't going to be great, but I can deal with things directly and if he is paranoid about what I might be doing to undercut him, I don't have to play the game and stall him, be angry when he catches me, and keep the vicious circle moving. I don't have to like everybody; I don't have to like him. Yet, I really would like to stop giving him so much power and maybe I can do that by trying to deal with the sensitive areas in me he is somehow aware of and is exploiting.

The above stream of consciousness in the introspective process is dealing directly with owning anger and seeing why the person's perception of another person's actions and comments is increasing it. The professor is not beating himself for feeling angry, just questioning himself as to why he feels so upset. The person is not saying, "I should be nicer to Phil." Instead he is trying to determine why he is being passive-aggressive and full of anger in response to Phil. The person is not denying that there are true reasons for his anger; this is important because certain injustices in society deserve anger. However, neither is he trying to hide behind his anger against the injustices he feels the other person is guilty of in this instance.

Obviously, not everyone is going to be able to undergo and achieve the above preliminary results in an initial introspective period. Yet, in working with religious individuals there is a need to alert them to the presence of anger as a vital force which helps in understanding oneself, others, and society's transgressions against healthy living.

To help achieve a better recognition of anger and indirect expressions of it (including passive-aggressiveness), as well as motivations the religious have with respect to uncovering and dealing with anger, some basic questions might be included in the daily examen or introspective process. Several types of them might include:

What did I get angry at today? (*Not*, what made me angry?)
With whom did I get angry today? (*Not*, who made me angry?)

In addition to the apparent reason for my being angry or annoyed, what might be other reasons in me that would be responsible for the anger being so great?

How did I deal with my anger or annoyance? Did I try to conceal it? Did I deny it or play it down? Did I feel like covering it in a pseudo Christian cover ("Don't get me wrong, I don't dislike him, just what he is doing to the institution and himself." "I really feel he is misguided; he's really not a bad person.")?

How did I spontaneously allow my anger to rise and come to the surface today without worrying that it would cause other people to dislike me?

Was I able to review my anger and try to constructively deal with disagreements, with the understanding that communications won't solve everything, but that opening up a discussion about our differences is certainly a start? Or did I just try to scare people with my anger?

Did I present my anger to the source of it, or did I put the anger on someone else or make believe I wasn't angry?

The above questions are but samples of the kinds consultants and practitioners can assist the client(s) to use in an effort to uncover, own, appreciate, and deal with the anger that comes up as a part of life. When religious individuals normally use time for examination of self, these periods provide a natural opportunity to help make them more sensitive to both the love and anger in themselves, so they do not develop into packaged Christians who deny real spontaneity of emotions as part of respecting life both in themselves and others.

Modeling Assertiveness: Combining the understanding of anger with the practice of ministered assertiveness

Once the individual Christian and the religious community stop seeing the emotion of anger as being either good or bad and recognize it as a sign of their own personal vitality, they will be able to distinguish between *experiencing* the emotion of anger on the one hand and the way anger is dealt with or *expressed* on the other. With such an awareness they can begin to work on employing their anger constructively, instead of trying to eliminate it through suppression, denial, avoidance, or passivity. In addition, they can also avoid the opposite extreme of confusing assertiveness with aggression and believing that they should prevent being stamped on themselves by stamping on others first or in return.

To aid religious persons in expressing anger assertively, especially in individual counseling or therapy, mental health professionals need to help them examine the situations where anger occurs. By looking at the motivations, thoughts, feelings, and fears involved in different encounters, the therapist or counselor improves understanding and sets the groundwork for assertiveness.

For purposes of consultation with religious communities, where a lecture and/or workshop format is used, case illustrations and alternate possible responses can be presented as a way to facilitate discussion and review of personal styles of dealing with situations which often involve passive-aggressiveness and/or other indirect methods of dealing with anger.

Ministerial assertiveness is grounded on a belief that effective Christians can and should understand what makes them angry, be able to translate it into a specific issue, find the courage to recognize and remove unfinished business in their personality so the conflict area can be put into realistic perspective, and be able to communicate their concerns to others in a manner which doesn't unduly raise defensiveness. It is also based on an appreciation that sometimes people are angry with others because their needs or expectations are unrealistic. When they are realistic, ministerial assertiveness calls for an openness—an openness which doesn't justify being aggressive so they drive others away, which doesn't glorify a passivity or prevent a free, real interchange, but which allows angers to be dealt with as they arise, not when they blow up after a long period of being buried in a sea of "niceness."

FINAL COMMENTS

In essence, mental health consultants should feel free to vigorously intervene in religious settings to uncover and help Christians deal with passive-aggressive and indirect forms of expressing anger. Too often the private practitioner and consultant are put off by the religious in their efforts to help them affirm the right to feel and express anger in a constructive manner. As has been noted, the religious would often see anger as a "sinful tendency" and would cite quotes like the following one from Ramsey (1950) to support their claim:

> The first assertion Christian ethics makes about man is that he was created for personal existence within the image of God, and that Jesus Christ most perfectly reveals this image. The second assertion is that man is sinful. So fundamental is this doctrine in

Christian thought that it cannot be overlooked. Indeed, many theologians regard it as basic equally with the first for any full understanding of man in the light of God. This has been the view not only of the more "pessimistic" thinkers; it was the view also of John Wesley, whose emphasis upon "going on to perfection" is well known (p. 284).

In giving lectures, workshops, group sessions and individual consultations, the assertive mental health professional does not have to directly disagree with this concept of sinfulness. He/she might do well to see such a philosophy of sinfulness in the same context as the tendency toward repetition compulsion or continuing an inappropriate response repertoire that has been reinforced in the past. The difference which should be cited is that *this tendency toward sinfulness (or, in psychological jargon, to repeat inappropriate behavior) is not reflected in experiencing anger or trying to deal with it creatively and constructively, but lies rather in the tendency to let it out in a shotgun fashion* (Fox, 1972) *or suppress it in such a fashion to have it come out in an undetected disturbed fashion.* If there is a desire in the religious person to be virtuous (or psychologically healthy), then it should lie in the courage to face him/herself and own up to his/her own anger and deal with it for the purpose of growth—personal and communal.

Another "religious" defense to embracing anger is under the rubic of "sacrifice." Sacrifice has often been the watchword of Christian and other religious communities. This sacrifice can be misdirected when Christians supposedly sacrifice anger, only to have it come out and afflict others in a pseudo-Christian, sugary fashion. The real sacrifice for Christians, mental health professionals should note, is in facing up to their own needs, both realistic and unrealistic, and being honest and caring (religious charity) in trying to face their real feelings and negotiate openly with others about them.

The key, then, is to utilize religious persons' concern with sin and their natural tendency toward self-evaluation in light of the Gospel (Aschenbrenner, 1972; Wicks, 1983), by redirecting the focus from an unrealistic, dehumanizing desire to eliminate all angry emotions to appropriate assertiveness. In this way, they can live fully without being a slave either to anger or to inappropriate controlling mechanisms which compartmentalize anger out of awareness but not out of existence. Mental health professionals can then help religious communities raise the necessary anger against societal injustices and help religious leaders to breathe new life into some of their "nice," but possibly dead, institu-

tions, which are now spending all of their energy avoiding growthful conflict.

REFERENCES

Aschenbrenner, G. Consciousness examen. *Review for Religious*, 1972, *31*, 14-21.
Augsburger, D. *Anger and assertiveness in pastoral care*. Philadelphia: Fortress, 1979.
Burwick, R. *Anger: Defusing the bomb*. Wheaton, IL: Tyndale, 1981.
Fox, M. *On becoming a musical mystical bear*. New York: Paulist, 1972.
Hammett, R., & Sofield, L. *Inside Christian community*. New York: LeJacq, 1981.
Mickey, P., & Gamble, G. *Pastoral assertiveness: A new model for pastoral care*. Nashville: Abingdon, 1978.
Platt, J., & Wicks, R. (Eds.). *The psychological consultant*. New York: Grune & Stratton, 1979.
Ramsey, P. *Basic Christian ethics*. New York: Scribner's, 1950, p. 284.
Wicks, R. *Helping others*. New York: Gardner Press, 1982.
Wicks, R. *Christian introspection: Self-ministry through self-understanding*. New York: Crossroad, 1983.

*For the purposes of this paper, "organized religion" will refer to established Christian denominations (i.e., Roman Catholic, Presbyterian, Methodist, Baptist, etc.)

Epilogue

The preceding chapters have offered a multi-dimensional perspective on passive-aggressiveness—both the individual syndrome and the organizational experience. The first section of the text presented varied analyses of the clinical profile, etiology, and psychotherapeutic processes representing the major therapeutic orientations. The theories selected were chosen for their diversity, rather than their inclusiveness. The hope was to provide a broad perspective on passive-aggressiveness, highlighting insight and underlying dynamics, as well as behavior and interactional factors, in order to expand our own theoretical spectrums.

Section II provides the practitioner with guidance regarding the salient issues surrounding the assessment and intervention of passive-aggressiveness within a system or institutional framework. Although each consultant has his own theoretical paradigm (e.g., behavioral, psychodynamic, existential) and consultative form (e.g., mental health, organizational development, process consultation), the manifestation of passive-aggressiveness within an organization presents unique demands and requirements of the practicing consultant and as such is the point of focus for each of the contributions to Section II. The settings selected were not meant to be inclusive; rather they are representative and di-

verse, demonstrating the complexity of passive-aggressiveness in organizations.

CONVERGING/DIVERGING ON PASSIVE-AGGRESSION

Passive-Aggression—A Clinical Entity?

The implication that passive-aggressiveness entails a covert or indirect expression of anger or dissatisfaction appears to be a point on which each of the theoretical perspectives agree. However, the degree to which this "indirect expression" reflects a pervasive, relatively permanent *character trait* is clearly open to debate.

The existence of an entity of relative permanence or pervasiveness is most clearly supported by those proponents of an intrapsychic conflict orientation. However, Stricker (Chapter 1), while providing the strongest theoretical argument for such a "trait" focus, hints at some concern even within the psychodynamic ranks regarding this question of trait, by noting that a number of psychodynamic theoreticians present passive-aggressiveness as a defense or isolated response, rather than a trait. The cognitive and behavioral orientations, as might be expected, challenge such typology and choose to direct their attention to the unassertive response style (Chapter 2) and the cognitive schemas (Chapter 4) which "operationally" define passive-aggressiveness.

The question of trait becomes even more clouded by the apparent interactional perspectives supplied by Bonds-White (Chapter 3), Kaslow (Chapter 6), and the contributors to Section II. These authors, while suggesting the role of personality predisposition, choose to highlight the ecology, milieu, or setting in which the individual operates as the variable of importance in understanding this "entity" called passive-aggressiveness. Such a perspective supports the notion that passive-aggressiveness is less a personality trait than a situationally adaptive response pattern. Finally, the ultimate statement against a syndrome/trait approach to passive-aggressiveness is presented by the existential-experiential perspective. Mahrer (Chapter 5) desgnates not only passive-aggressiveness but the entire issue of "syndrome" and "etiology" to the realm of the meaningless. The issue of whether or not passive-aggressiveness is a relatively permanent and pervasive personality trait is clearly open to question and needs further research.

A Question of Etiology

Throughout the presentations in Section I, early childhood experience—in the form of possible contamination of one's ego state (Chapter 3), the frustration of unresolved dependency needs (Chapter 1), or the development of an unassertive response style or cognitive schema (Chapters 2 and 5, respectively)—seems to be a point of common etiological concern. In addition, environment is seen as important by each of the contributors, as either a precipitating or eliciting factor. The importance given to environment ranges from its being viewed as a condition which, while not necessary, can augment passive-aggressiveness and facilitiate its manifestation (Chapter 1, 3) to its being seen as a necessary yet nonsufficient condition for passive-aggressiveness (Chapter 6).

The contributors to Section II appear to concur that sociocultural milieu plays an essential role in the development and maintenance of passive aggressiveness. The highly repressive, bureaucratic environments of the hospital (Chapter 9) or school (Chapter 8), as well as the strict authoritarian leadership and repressive codes of behavior often found in business (Chapter 7) and religious (Chapter 10) settings, are clearly viewed as the essential factors in the development and maintenance of passive-aggressiveness within those organizations. Thus while predisposing factors are considered, environmental demands are seen as clearly influential in the etiology of the individual "syndrome," "style," or "attitude."

Therapeutic Strategies

While it is not at all surprising that each of the strategies discussed reflects the particular theoretical paradigm presented, it is noteworthy that both personal and extrapersonal interventions are presented across theories. Each contributor points to the need 1) to assist the individual in becoming aware of his/her anger and hostility, and 2) to provide more effective and efficient means of expression. Further, in most cases contributors stress the importance of intervening at an extrapersonal level. Thus, for example, various systems presented (e.g., Kaslow's family therapy, Bush's organizational development system, Parsons' educational model) all highlight the need for renorming and modifying the structure of the system in order to reduce the need for passive-aggressive

behavior. Further, even the most "intrapsychic" orientations (e.g., psychodynamic, TA) posit the importance of environmental interventions—either to reduce the suppressive parental attitude (Chapter 1) or to cross the passive-aggressive "games" (Chapter 3).

The theoretical presentations offered in Section I serve to undergird the clearly ecological approaches taken and expanded upon in Section II. Clearly, when it comes to passive-aggressiveness, a simple medical model will not suffice. Issues of internal dynamics, behavioral response style, ecological factors, etc., all need to be considered when developing an intervention plan.

THE FUTURE

Passive-aggressiveness is neither a simple nor singularly identified entity, nor can it be neatly summarized in one finely wrapped package of "manifestation-etiology-intervention." Clearly, we as practitioners have been "soft" in our approach and understanding of passive-aggression, assuming general understanding of and agreement about this phenomenon. Our experience in editing this volume has increased our appreciation and awareness of the importance of not taking such a simplistic view of human functioning. Moreover, this effort has highlighted the real value and importance of applied and theoretical research.

The contributors have brought both theoretical and clinical acumen to their discussion of passive-aggressiveness. What is needed is for their theories and constructs to be empirically tested, so that a validated "model" of passive-aggression might be outlined. Similarly, while each of the contributors describes in great detail his/her theoretical intervention plans, the effectiveness of these intervention plans and strategies has yet to be tested.

This text demonstrates convergence and divergence among the varied theoretical perspectives around one clinical disorder—passive-aggressiveness. We need to remove our theoretical blinders in order to dialogue across perspectives and by so doing sharpen our understanding of human functioning. It is our hope that the multi-theoretical perspective presented here may faciliate such dialogue.

REFERENCE

American Psychiatric Association. *Diagnostic and statistical manual of mental disorders.* Third Edition. Washington, D.C., 1980.

Index

Abortions, 205
Adaptive antagonistic activities, 180, 190
Adolescents
  achievement problems in, 178
  acting-out by, 149-50
  passive-aggressiveness in, 136
  predisposing factors of passive-
    aggressive personality in, 147
  in transactional analysis, 53
Adult ego state (in transactional analysis),
  44, 47-49, 56, 59, 61-65, 67
Aggression
  assertion and, 78
  in definition of passive-aggressiveness,
    136
  direct, 94
  in interpersonal relationships, 93
Aggressive personality , 6
Agitation, 51, 59
Alig, V.B., 8
Allport, Gordon, 138
American Psychiatric Association, 6-7,
  135, 163, 175
Anal personality, 9
Anger, 11, 12, 27, 230
  in cognitive-behavioral approach, 75-79,
    83-84, 93

expressed by children, 177
  in religious settings, 213-26
Antecedent stimulus variables, 32
Anxiety
  in cognitive-behavioral approach, 73-74
  operant conditioning and, 29
Approval addiction, 92
Argyris, C., 180, 189-90
Assertion
  aggression and, 78
  in interpersonal relationships, 93
  in religious settings, 216-25
  workshops in, in educational
    environments, 185
Assertion training programs, 95, 169
Attention-centered bodily
  experiencing (in existential-experiential
    psychotherapy), 108-10, 112, 117-19
Attributions (in transactional analysis), 46
Augsburger, G., 215
Authoritarianism
  in case history of school, 187-92
  in medical systems, 195
Authority, 16, 27
  in case histories, 19, 22-23, 117
  organization of, in hospitals, 198-202,
    206

233